ALMOST

A L M O S T

12 ELECTRIC MONTHS CHASING A
SILICON VALLEY DREAM

by Hap Klopp *&* Brian Tarcy

RESILIENT PRESS

TABLE OF CONTENTS

INTRODUCTION

"The world is shifting to an innovation economy and nobody does innovation better than America. Nobody does it better. No one has better colleges. Nobody has better universities. Nobody has a greater diversity of talent and ingenuity. No one's workers or entrepreneurs are more driven or more daring. The things that have always been our strengths match up perfectly with the demands of the moment."
— PRESIDENT BARACK OBAMA, December 6th, 2011

WHAT IS SILICON VALLEY REALLY LIKE? America's greatest hope for innovation is in Silicon Valley. This geographic magnet of talent and money is where the action is, and so to take a swing here is unlike taking one anywhere else. Imagine the joy of creation and the dream of reward.

What is Silicon Valley really like?

There are well-known stories of gigantic successes, but Silicon Valley is actually full of many more failures. In fact, the true "secret sauce" of Silicon Valley culture is that it does not shun failure. It embraces it.

So what is that like? What happens on this sliver of land on the West Coast where large intellects with even larger egos chase gigantic ambitions, and then things go wrong? What is that like? That's what Silicon Valley is really like. It is vibrant and chaotic. It always feels like a big thing is about to happen, but it usually does not happen. It almost happens.

Almost…the word hurts the soul. So much effort falling into oblivion. And it keeps happening again and again, this amazing effort. Why? What is it in Silicon Valley that makes it okay, and in some ways essential, to swing for the fences?

While companies outside of Silicon Valley generally view failure as a career-ending disgrace and the people involved are shunned, Silicon Valley companies prize the experience gained and believe in the positive benefits of "failing forward."

Silicon Valley's difference is that it expects failure and it embraces failure. Whereas "greed is good" to Wall Street, failure is good to Silicon Valley. "Nice try, learn from it, now go get 'em again" is the prevailing attitude. Proof of this can be seen in the portfolios of most Silicon Valley venture capitalists. A common VC portfolio is based on the hope that three of ten investments will be home runs, three will be write-offs, and the remaining four will be mediocre and have to be sold off or somehow disposed of prior to the closing of the 7–10 year fund. What is left from those that weren't home runs (the failures) is a huge number of experienced and skilled employees who can be re-purposed for the next great entrepreneurial effort.

In Silicon Valley, it is understood that experience is what you get when you don't get what you want. It is an atmosphere where people are allowed to fail. In Silicon Valley, those who have failed are very attractive prospects for the next venture. This makes the culture self-perpetuating, as high- powered, risk-oriented entrepreneurs are encouraged to dream big dreams that sometimes do, in fact, come true. Particularly when given a second chance. When people experience failure and can actually figure out what went wrong, they have an incredible foundation for future decision-making.

So what is Silicon Valley really like? Well, Steve Jobs was kicked out of Apple.

But after Jobs was ousted from Apple, he created Pixar, and then he eventually rejoined and energized Apple to reach unimagined heights.

Pixar and Apple became two quintessential examples of Silicon Valley successes coming out of the ashes of personal failure.

Failure is a great teacher. Unfortunately, it kills many of its pupils while destroying their own net worth. And in startups, it often wipes out the investments of friends and family as collateral damage. A heavy price to almost make it. And even for all that learning, the reality of "almost" is that it haunts you in the middle of the night. And in communities less aware than Silicon Valley, it creates a permanent, indelible scar on an entrepreneur's record. But near San Francisco—and increasingly in like-minded cities around the country—that scar means something else. It has value.

An October 2012 conference on failure called Failcon, in San Francisco, attracted more than 750 people interested in learning lessons from failure. It is a hot topic, with reason. These lessons mean something, and learning from the mistakes of others is cheaper than learning from your own mistakes.

Every story is so personal, so indelibly inked onto the souls of those who experienced it. It hurts, but it toughens the spine. In fact, the list of failures who went on to succeed goes far beyond the legend of Steve Jobs. Marc Andreessen experienced early failure, then went on to found Netscape. Max Levchin, who was CEO of Slide, the social apps maker, was too slow to compete and went out of business, only to rebound and create Paypal, which sold to eBay for $1.5 billion. Frank Quattrone bounced back from a clash with the SEC and federal authorities while he was with Credit Suisse to found his own company, Qatalyst Group, which now advises companies such as Yahoo and Google. And the list goes on and on.

There really is something to the idea that failure is the best teacher.

Failure also makes for a great narrative, full of heroes and villains, and lots of greed. Throw in a few High Noon-style corporate showdowns, screaming emails, and flying food thrown by an angry employee, and you begin to viscerally understand what Silicon Valley is really like—the high energy, and the high anxiety.

That's why this story is much larger than the tale of one company's chaotic, failed attempt to build a big, important business that "changed the world." Through the prism of 12 electrifying months inside Ardica Technologies, an entrepreneurial fact about Silicon Valley emerges: Failure is more common than wild success, and it teaches truer lessons about business, about life, and about innovation.

So what is it really like to work in a grind-it-out startup when one of the best technology companies in the world shows interest in what you are doing?

Call them Big Silicon. They were the perfect partner—one of those elite Silicon Valley technology companies that many of our team would have loved to work for if they weren't working for us. Well known in Silicon Valley and, in fact, the entire world, Big Silicon was growing rapidly. It had repeatedly launched blockbuster innovative, premium products, plus it had a ton of cash in the bank which could be used for product development and acquisitions.

Imagine how the lure of fast cash can derail the hard work of building a business. Now imagine working for a company that was told its innovation didn't meet the sky-high standards of Silicon Valley.

Big Silicon was interested, maybe even very interested, but in the end they passed

Almost.

Imagine working for a company that had a shot at creating a worldwide brand as fast as anyone ever had, if it hadn't gotten derailed by the mirage of overnight riches via a sale to the fabulously successful Silicon Valley company, Big Silicon. Now imagine the hard work of brand building disintegrating because of a faulty product and a dysfunctional management team.

Almost hurts.

This story of 12 crucial months in Ardica Technologies sunburst existence would be a metaphor if it were not real. With compelling lead characters straight out of America's culture wars—the hard-nosed naval officer and the Berkeley guy—this, at first glance, is a great parable about focus. A great American brand in an emerging area of need could have been built, should have been built, and almost was built, but two competing paths led to a split that derailed what had once looked like a sure-fire dream. Focus or perish. Keep the main thing the main thing. Failure teaches these hard lessons.

This story of Ardica Technologies also provides a real-world case study answer to the perennial business question: Do you sell what you can build, or do you build what you can sell?

With a supporting cast featuring young Stanford geniuses and entrepreneurial marketers, this real life metaphor had some real life lessons to teach about building a business:

- Invention without commercialization creates a stillborn company
- When you run out of money, you make bad decisions
- Multiple cultures cannot exist in one company
- "Get rich quick" is not a strategy
- Failing to plan is planning to fail

When a group of people work so hard and come so close—when it almost happens—that's when the agonizing truth of almost hurts the most. But that is also when you learn the most. This knowledge gained by failure is actually the secret sauce driving great innovation forward. For the Silicon Valley innovator, along with the sting of failure comes the true prize of wisdom, resilience, and an emboldened desire to get it right the next time. That's what Silicon Valley is really like.

THE PLAYERS

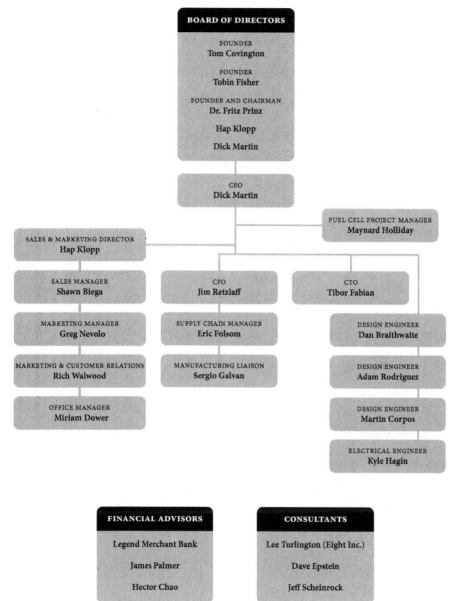

BOARD OF DIRECTORS

FOUNDER
Tom Covington

FOUNDER
Tobin Fisher

FOUNDER AND CHAIRMAN
Dr. Fritz Prinz

Hap Klopp

Dick Martin

CEO
Dick Martin

FUEL CELL PROJECT MANAGER
Maynard Holliday

SALES & MARKETING DIRECTOR
Hap Klopp

SALES MANAGER
Shawn Biega

CFO
Jim Retzlaff

CTO
Tibor Fabian

MARKETING MANAGER
Greg Nevolo

SUPPLY CHAIN MANAGER
Eric Folsom

DESIGN ENGINEER
Dan Braithwaite

MARKETING & CUSTOMER RELATIONS
Rich Walwood

MANUFACTURING LIAISON
Sergio Galvan

DESIGN ENGINEER
Adam Rodriguez

OFFICE MANAGER
Miriam Dower

DESIGN ENGINEER
Martin Corpos

ELECTRICAL ENGINEER
Kyle Hagin

FINANCIAL ADVISORS

Legend Merchant Bank

James Palmer

Hector Chao

CONSULTANTS

Lee Turlington (Eight Inc.)

Dave Epstein

Jeff Scheinrock

PRANKS AS PROLOGUE

ONE DAY WHILE LOOKING OUT at San Francisco Bay from a fourth-floor window in the American Industrial Center, engineer Adam Rodriguez tossed one of Ardica Technologies' Moshi battery-based power systems to the ground to see if the Moshi could withstand the damage. It did. When another engineer went to retrieve the Moshi, he was bombarded with water balloons.

"Oh no, they haven't grown up," said Miriam Dower, Ardica's office manager and marketing coordinator.

The laughter that followed the water balloons seemed to echo from a nearby place—a former California horse farm that was converted in 1891 into Stanford University. Ardica Technologies—like Yahoo, Google, Hewlett Packard, and The North Face—were incubated at Leland Stanford's old ranch. The founders of Ardica, former Stanford students, brought a joyous fraternity-like culture into the company.

It should, therefore, not surprise you that the company's traditions included pranking employees on their birthday. When CEO Dick Martin's birthday came up, every employee dressed the way Dick dressed every day, with a black Izod shirt and off white chinos. Each of the young engineers carried an overflowing briefcase, just like the CEO, who was more than twice their age. There is a photograph of several employees all standing next to Dick looking like his clones. Halfway through the day, after seeing all the employees dressed this way, Dick, oblivious, turned to one engineer, Martin Corpos, and told him that he thought Corpos was dressed "rather sharp."

Pranks weren't just for birthdays either. The engineers at Ardica Technologies liked to play with fire, literally. Setting a flame to follow a precise line of ethyl alcohol to startle a fellow engineer was considered a riot.

"The most memorable prank? Well, outside of our CEO, I have the biggest propensity for falling asleep at my desk," said Martin Corpos. "We were working and I was sound asleep when the guys laid down a ring of ethyl alcohol around my desk and then lit one end while a ring of fire surrounded my desk. It's a crazy feeling to wake up that hot."

LET'S CHANGE THE WORLD

June 2009

THERE WAS A YELLOW SIGN, meant in jest (I hoped), that was on the wall near Adam Rodriguez's desk, which was on the North Side—on the left as you entered the door to Ardica Technologies. The North Side was where the engineers worked. I worked on the South Side, the business side.

My name is Hap Klopp. Among other things, I was on the Board of Directors and I was the marketing director for Ardica. I liked to think of myself more as a witness to greatness, a cheerleader for the young entrepreneurs who were building this visionary company that was attempting to market green, lightweight, miniaturized, and portable power. I was simply helping guide this five-year-old startup to finally become an overnight sensation. We were accelerating by my proven motto: "fail forward," or as our CEO Dick Martin liked to say, "fail fast forward."

Anyway, the sign said:

"In case of intense fire, RUN!!"

The word "fire" was circled in red marker. When I saw it, I knew there was no imminent fire. It was just a part of the culture, like the 25-foot-long bar that was also on the North Side. Funny things happened over there, such as the Intern Olympics. "We take a half day and torture the interns," said Miriam.

Torture, she admitted, was a bit strong, but interns were asked to compete in silly camaraderie-building events such as the pole hug. This old four-story factory in the early industrial area of San Francisco's waterfront known as Dogpatch is supported by three-foot-wide round white columns that look like giant golf tees and seem designed to host the pole hug contest. You wrapped yourself around the column with both arms and both legs and held on for as long as you could.

Meanwhile, over here on the South Side, was Jim Retzlaff, our new CFO. He understood when he was hired for the position—which we advertised on Craigslist—that his job included the unwritten stipulation that he would have to face an intense fire without running and then hang off a column for an unknown period of time.

"By definition, a startup is messy," said Jim. "You are under sourced—particularly in staffing and money. I am not surprised by these issues."

When we hired Jim in January 2009, his first task was to clarify what we already knew. "I did an audit and I learned that the company could have declared bankruptcy," Jim recalled.

The audit, done line by line on weekends with CEO Dick Martin by his side, showed trouble with the books. The numbers were wrong and he even found factual errors—names entered in the books as investors that didn't match cancelled checks. It took some time, but he straightened things out so we at least knew where we stood. That was January.

While Jim was digging, he discovered other things as well. "This was an R&D company, you know. They treated it like a frat house. You saw the bar. They spent money like it was free," he said. "And the health care plan was not the Cadillac plan. It was the gold-plated Rolls Royce plan."

Jim thought the perks belied the fact that the company had never sold anything, and so he was trying to provide something new at Ardica—oversight. Until recently, the team of mostly Stanford geniuses were too busy for oversight.

We were Ardica, and our geniuses were inventing a new kind of green power source. In fact, we were at the crossroads of three big trends:

- increasing consumer mobility
- exploding demand for portable electronic devices needing light-weight, long lasting power
- expanding sustainability and environmental movements

In June 2009, our engineers were racing against time in an effort to revolutionize how we all thought about power, deliver our first products that were integrated into clothing and, more importantly, to satisfy "the big client."

Those were exciting times at Ardica. They were also scary times. We were attempting to create green, lightweight, miniaturized, and portable power. We would provide more power than batteries with less weight and almost no pollution. When you brought our green power with you, it would increase mobility while decoupling you from the electrical grid.

"Right now, one of the biggest issues is accounts payable," said Jim. "I am responsible for keeping everybody happy and us out of collection," he said. "I'm selling faith in the company and faith in our ability to pay bills."

His attention to detail, his dedication, his smarts, and his tenacity were all appealing, but what really set him apart was his grasp of the big picture. "I truly believe in the company. That's why I'm successful [in selling faith]. I am open and honest. This goes with my ability to sleep at night. I am an investor in this company above and beyond my stock options. I knew the company was looking for investors…I've got a lot of skin in the game. I'm a big believer."

He looked a little like a cross between William H. Macy and Conan O'Brien. He had a blond pompadour and some restrained Fargo mannerisms that came from his upbringing. "Both my parents were born in North Dakota and I was born in Minnesota. I stayed there until I was seven and then we moved to Oregon."

Jim's grandfather was an entrepreneur who ran a large chain of drugstores. Jim's father was a surgeon. "There was no doubt that I was going to be a surgeon," he said. "But then reality presented itself."

The reality of school led him instead to study both psychology and accounting at the University of Oregon and Southern Oregon State University. "I am well-rounded. I use both my left and right brain," he said.

He was 48. He first worked for KPMG, one of the Big Four accounting firms. And then he took a job with Levi Strauss & Co. as an internal auditor. It gave him some insight into the clothing manufacturing business. His next move was into startups: "[A] string of startup high-tech companies, none of which made it." He then worked in the mortgage industry for five years "until it started going down the crapper," he said in that straight-shooting Midwestern way of his. In July 2008, he was laid off from the mortgage company but had accumulated enough assets to be able to be picky looking for a job.

In November, he responded to our Craigslist ad. We were immediately interested. So was he. "They were doing something unique with the whole advanced fuel thing. There were whispers of (acquisition interest from one of Silicon Valley's most successful consumer goods companies, a worldwide brand that, for the sake of this book, we'll just call, Big Silicon.) but they were never specifically laid out. I knew they were working with the military. And the heated garments were very cool. I knew right away that this was something I could be proud of."

Plus, he added, he was impressed by the leaders of the company, Dick and me.

Jim said my presence helped him believe in the company. "Why would the founder of The North Face waste his time with some lame-ass company?" he asked rhetorically.

So he joined up. From his previous job at the mortgage company to Ardica, "I took a 25% pay cut, I am working twice as hard and I am twice as happy. I feel like I am doing something so much more important."

He was helping keep it afloat with a world-class juggling act, although he admitted that "a lot of this is blocking and tackling." Basic stuff. For instance, payroll came around every two weeks and there were vendors looking for money and engineers looking to buy stuff from vendors.

6

There have been investments. "Dick's personal funds helped," said Jim. Dick invested in the company, as did others in the "friends and family" category.

Referencing the time before he arrived when the company cut salaries to minimum wage, Jim pointed out, "The company has a complicated, convoluted history."

But even knowing all this, Jim was happy to be there.

He alternately described his role as that of "gatekeeper" and "an up-tight white guy" trying to keep control of the very limited funds. But, he said, "The engineers constantly need to buy things. The reality is that whatever it is they need, they actually need. They need a certain piece of equipment for their research. And so everything they are doing is an investment that will reap a return."

On the other hand, he said, "We have to be very careful about what we spend money on. We can't just buy every cool gadget." He paused and then explained. "I have to pay enough to the vendors so that they keep shipping stuff to us."

It was that balance that Jim had to strike as we waited for more money to come in.

2

TIBOR FABIAN, our Chief Technical Officer and one of the co-founders, put it best. "Working for a startup, I compare it to a ski jump, like in the Olympics. Imagine starting down the ski jump at night with the lights turned off in the landing zone and then hoping the lights will come on before you land," he said. Tibor was a Stanford Electrical Engineering PhD.

When I first heard Tibor's ski jump metaphor, I laughed. As an entrepreneur who has launched and helped launch many companies, I know how true it is. And then, as inspiration for this book, I re-read Tracy Kidder's Pulitzer Prize-winning book, *The Soul of a New Machine*, about the launch of a new computer in 1980. And I discovered, at the end of Chapter 1, a similar metaphor, cited by a consultant to Kidder, about skiing and recovery from near disaster. The similarity is not just in metaphor. What is truly striking is the similarity of the nascent computer business in 1980 and the fuel cell business of now. "New" and the creation of "new" remains interesting, and, yes, it has a soul.

It's true that "genius" is not a word one should throw around lightly. But in the case of Ardica's engineers—Tibor Fabian from Slovakia; Adam Rodriguez, the surfer dude; Dan Braithwaite, the kid from LA; Martin Corpos, a Stanford engineer who minored in archeology; and heck, maybe even Brian Payer, the intern from Cleveland who wanted to invent a type of electronic paper you can erase and print on again—the label sure seemed accurate. There were more geniuses at Ardica than any new business could possibly expect to have, including two who were accepted for astronaut training and a few entrepreneurs who had launched a slew of successful businesses. We were a small lineup of the best and the brightest and most energetic and, well, craziest, because ours truly was a leap of faith.It was something more than that as well. Our CEO, Dick Martin—with the most impressive resume of anyone you've most likely ever met—succinctly described our quest like this: "It's a good thing. It's a noble project. To change the way people work and live—to me, that's great science."

We were Ardica and we were out to change the world.

It is no exaggeration to say that Ardica was trying to create a new paradigm—green power on the go, untethered from the grid.

You say you want a revolution? Let me introduce Dan Braithwaite. "A lot of this hasn't been done before," said Dan, a design engineer and one of the original group who formed Ardica. "We're making it up as we go," he said, as if it were random and easy.

They were, in fact, making it up as they went, but there was nothing random or easy about their approach.

Dan, who is Chinese-American, had a crew cut and he was thin, with a perpetual-motion personality. At 5'10", he played recreational basketball, but his real competitiveness came out in business when someone said something couldn't be done. At 28, he was the guy to deal with the big client's big project. Yes, Dan was lead engineer on the F-43 project.

What is the F-43 project? Well, in June 2009, as I wrote this, we were all sworn to secrecy, so my clichéd answer would have been "if I told you I'd have to kill you." But the real answer was that F-43 was a fuel cell project, driven by clean energy, for a partnership with one of the most successful companies in Silicon Valley, Big Silicon.

Yes, the big client. At that moment, negotiations were ongoing. It was tense and exciting. They were on the verge of making some big decisions, and we were trying to guide them. For instance, would our product say, as we preferred, "Ardica-enabled" on the side, thus making us a household brand? Or would it be a product put out only under the brand name of Big Silicon? Tens of millions of dollars valuation for Ardica rode on such a decision.

And although that might be a very exciting part of the Ardica story, it was not the only part. Not by any means. We were on the cusp of many different technologies: a battery-based system, a hybrid system of battery and fuel cell, and the F-43 fuel cell system for Big Silicon.

The F-43 project, certainly, was a key launching pad. And that's why this book was being written. There are rare moments in the world's history when something revolutionary comes along. I didn't even know for sure where we were going yet but recognized that it was important. And I was excited enough to write about it and share the ups and downs of the next 12 months as we raced against time, competition, and the idea that what we were attempting was impossible.

Like most of the Ardica team, I am a Stanford graduate. But unlike their engineering focus, my background is business, specifically entrepreneurial business. After getting my Stanford MBA, I founded The North Face— arguably the preeminent global apparel, outdoor, and mountaineering brand—and I was CEO for more than 20 years. Since then I have acted as consultant to literally hundreds of startups, spoken at entrepreneurial conferences, written a couple of business books, and mentored many prospective founders. I am a serial entrepreneur.

Whereas the Ardica team had more degrees than a thermometer— engineering degrees like EE, ME, CE, PhDs, Masters, and double PhDs—I have an MBA and a ton of real world experience. The other difference between me and most other members of the team is age— about 30 years.

Of course not everyone was under 30 at Ardica, just most of the engineering staff. But age was not important except to maybe tell the tale of some engineering prodigies. The only age that was important was "brand new," which is what we were creating.

We were making battery-based power systems that could be incorporated into clothing. This system, called the Moshi, could keep you warm all day with on-demand heat, while at the same time charging your iPod 20 times or your iPhone 10 times. The system could be removed from your clothing and inserted into your backpack or briefcase to provide you mobile power, both inside and independent from clothing. We were also developing a hybrid system of battery and fuel cell that would reduce a soldier's load of batteries from 30 pounds to 10 pounds. But, what was even more exciting was the last thing we were working on.

3

W E DARED TO IMAGINE a new world in which a wind farm in West Texas would be used to power a new kind of high-density, completely clean hydrogen fuel that is as portable as a battery but lasted much longer, had higher output for the weight, and left behind no pollution. "We're going into the energy business," said CEO Dick Martin. "Energy is a big thing in the world today. We're going to capture the energy of the wind and convert it into green fuel. This will change the way people do things. It will give more mobility with environmentally good products."

We were Ardica and we wanted you to become Ardica-enabled. This was more than just marketing copy. We really were, as our CEO said, pursuing something noble. We were also, as CTO Tibor Fabian said, hoping the lights came on at the "startup landing pad." And we were also in the midst of articulating our identity by making sure we got to create it ourselves. It was all happening at once.

The name Ardica was invented in much the same way that the name of the rock band Foghat was invented. According to Tibor, Tom and Tobin [Tom Covington and Tobin Fisher, two of the founders, who had moved on to the Board of Directors and were no longer involved in the daily running of the company] were playing Scrabble one afternoon. They drank a few cans of beer and came up with the name. "We wanted a name that was unique and doesn't mean anything, with the idea that we should give it the meaning."

And while the Scrabble-created Foghat's biggest hit was a song called "Slow Ride," Ardica itself had been a slow process of research and development. "Until this month, we had never sold anything to the consumer," said Miriam. "It's been five years."

But that was about to change. We were currently developing our first products for the outdoor and hunting markets with our partners, Mountain Hardwear and Sitka, respectively. We were siting a factory and inventing a new fuel while simultaneously revolutionizing the outdoor industry. And, maybe most importantly, attempting to lighten the load that soldiers need to carry into battle. We were Ardica, and the time had come to change the world for the better. All of our projects had this potential.

I have always believed that the best way to motivate people is to find motivated people. Everyone at Ardica was motivated to do great things, which was why I first joined the Board of Directors when the company was very new.

I was enticed to join the Board after speaking at a 2004 entrepreneurial conference at Stanford. On this particular occasion, two of the founders, Tom and Tobin, approached me and told me about their new fuel cell venture called "Ardica." These young men then asked me in the kind of language that I love, if I would like to help them make and market clean energy and, in doing so, change the world and help save the planet. I said yes. Of course I said yes.

I agreed to join the Board because nothing energizes me more than young, smart people with big dreams. They told me they were creating a business that worked on fuel cells, clean tech, environmentally friendly products that would decouple consumers from the electrical grid while facilitating the desire for expanded mobility. They were creating on-the-go power. Perfect! So I thought. They used the word "products." I heard them. I am sure of it.

In fact, the plan was to start by putting power systems into clothing.

The idea was to create heat on demand and also to be able to run or charge all of the electronic devices that modern consumers own—phones, iPods, MP3 players, GPS devices, lights, etc. They told me that the launch point was outdoor clothing, which is an industry that I know well. They thought I could help. I knew I could. Plus, this sounded like fun.

Initially, my involvement was limited to Board-like work, and helping raise money for research and development and helping them make connections in the outdoor world. I say "Board-like" because there were no real Board meetings and I never officially received any papers that confirmed I was on the Board. There were periodic executive level meetings, but at the time I was fully involved in Canterbury of New Zealand, one of the world's leading rugby companies. I was busy but I believed in the technology of Ardica and how it fit into my business philosophy.

I call the philosophy "turning the arrow back." The simple explanation is taking a new technology and applying it to an existing product, creating what appears to be an entirely new industry. I'd done it before when I was with The North Face, when we applied ripstop nylon, developed during the Vietnam War for parachutes, and used it in jackets, tent tops, and sleeping bags. I'd seen Nike do the same thing by applying what they called "air technology" to $50 running shoes and making them, with some great Michael Jordan branding, $170 shoes. And I knew here at Ardica we could take our new technology and apply it to many existing products.

The theory has worked in a lot of fields besides sports and apparel, and it has always existed. Transistors, for instance, were applied to radios in the 1950s, making radios portable and changing the nature of entertainment forever.

At a company called d3o, where I was Chairman, we were selling a material that is flexible but on impact becomes instantly rigid, then immediately flexible again—perfect protective clothing for sports, military, and casual wear. At Canterbury of New Zealand, where I had invested, we introduced Ion-X, a material that embedded negative ions in the fabric, which then interacted with the positive ions in the wearer's bloodstream, increasing blood flow and oxygenation. The opportunity I saw at Ardica was bigger.

Whenever I speak to aspiring entrepreneurs, people always ask me, "Where do I get the idea?" Well, this is where.

Turning the arrow back refers to the fact that all businesses start off with lots of creativity, lots of product differentiation, lots of margin, and lots of fun—but few make much profit because they sell so little. So, the business managers push for larger and larger volume. The problem is, once they get this volume, the company's creativity, differentiation, and margins give way to supply chain efficiency, constant lowering of costs, and homogenization. Here is where I see the opportunity. Because, if you can apply some unique technology, you can reinsert the entrepreneurial benefits (high margins, big product differentiation, creativity) and leverage the existing high volume of sales. The combination can be staggering. Sometimes it creates whole new businesses; almost always it brings lots of profit.

In Ardica's case, our portable, miniaturized power systems (fuel cell and battery) could be applied to clothing and all sorts of consumer electronics. It could make clothing into mobile power stations. And given Ardica's revolutionary patents, we could bottle and distribute clean energy at a time when everyone craved such a thing. This was "turning back the arrow" big time and an unparalleled business opportunity.

In the executive meetings, I discovered that they did a fabulous job of creating new ideas and garnering patents around miniaturized power systems and fuel cells. They even continued to use the word "products." The only problem was they were only doing research and one-of-a- kind prototypes and they had never finalized a single product or sold anything. So, all the cash flow was one way—out the door. The outside, non-management Board Members never did really delve into the details. Maybe because there never were any formal Board meetings, maybe because they didn't get any financials or regular reports. Whatever the cause, the founders of the company who were also Board members acted fairly independently and proactively and seemed to be constantly raising money—or maybe more aptly described, they were constantly scrambling to find money to meet payroll.

Lack of capital forced people to focus on what they were doing, which was combining brilliant engineers from numerous disciplines and working well together. They came up with patents and products that large companies with five times the budget couldn't match. Ardica was a great think tank.

But with no sales, the cash kept dwindling. Strategy gave way to survival. Marketing and branding went on the back burner. Or, more accurately, on no burner. The $3 million of cash they raised ran out. It more than ran out—they began spending other people's money (OPM) in supplier credit and personal credit cards. They tried going back to their first round of investors but found those people had no more to invest.

By January of 2008, it became obvious that changes were needed. More management was needed, and an infusion of cash was desperately needed. The company owed more than $1 million and creditors were swarming. The IRS was also on the company for back taxes. Ardica was, in fact, on life support, and way past using money from friends and family.

The brand name and logo were not registered, and the company didn't have a phone system or even a listing in the phone book. It didn't have a seller's permit nor did it have any of the required certifications associated with shipping and providing electrical power. Lawyers and creditors were making trouble.

But lawyers and creditors could not see what I realized, which is that this fantastic group of people at Ardica were smart, motivated, and they had a great dream. They had developed some incredible knowledge, and they had some very important patents. Ardica was for real. By this point, they had spent years working together developing patents, prototypes, teamwork, and camaraderie. They had sacrificed together, they had grown together, and they just needed to develop their plan into a real business.

At was at this point that Dick Martin was asked to become CEO.

Dick approached me and said he would take the job if I would expand my work to oversee sales, marketing, and branding, areas he did not feel comfortable handling.

We each had our comfort zones, but I felt sure that I would be comfortable working with Dick. Although he had a military background and I definitely did not, it seemed we both understood how to get things done.

Late one Friday afternoon, he returned from Bank of America with a story about how he used his karate training to kick the bank door, making an explosive sound. He wanted the bank to open up and allow him to make a deposit. Checks were being written against the deposit, and although the bank was officially closed, he refused to take no for an answer. When the manager and the security guard came to the door, they let him in to make the deposit. It was amazing. I'd never heard of a bank altering its hours for anyone before. Dick's spontaneity and taking the matter into his own hands (or, more accurately, feet) seemed very creative. We both got a big laugh when he said, "The bank manager will know who I am now."

And although I wasn't the kind to literally kick in doors, I had tasked myself with something akin to that. At that point, Ardica had not had one sale. Yes, a perfect opportunity! After all, when you've never sold anything, even one sale would show tremendous sales growth.

"The turning point," said Dan Braithwaite, "was getting the sales and marketing guys here." Dan was right in one way. Our sales and marketing team was the best in the business. But all we really did was make the obvious clear to the team. As Dan pointed out, "We needed something we could sell right away."

I AN BRAITHWAITE WAS THERE for Ardica's incubation at Stanford. In college, Dan, who grew up in Los Angeles, "tried all sort of majors including political science and urban studies" before finding his calling in engineering. He became interested in fuel cells and started working in Dr. Fritz Prinz's Rapid Prototyping Laboratory and eventually developed a fuel-cell-powered scooter that he showed in a booth at the Graduate School of Business's "Cool Products Expo."

About this time Tom and Tobin approached Dr. Prinz about a business idea they had to produce a hydrogen generator. "That didn't work out," said Dr. Prinz. "I suggested another technology using printed circuit board technology for making fuel cells." This idea came out of his Rapid Prototyping Laboratory, and any idea that comes out of there remains of interest to him.

Dr. Prinz, Chairman of the Board of Ardica, was involved in other startups as well, all by former students. In the case of Ardica, he introduced Tom and Tobin first to Tibor and then to Dan. "I know the students, I know their interests and I know their capabilities. I linked their interests and capabilities to an opportunity. That's what professors at Stanford do."

In the fall of 2003, Tom Covington and Tobin Fisher met in a class called "Formatting of New Ventures" and immediately gravitated to each other. Tobin was studying for his Masters in product design and Tom was studying for his Masters in mechanical engineering. There were 60 people in the class and they split into groups of four to, as a class assignment, form a new venture. "I thought Tobin was a very interesting dude," said Tom. "We hit it off very well." Tom, the original Ardica CEO, recalled the original plan in the class was to work on a hydrogen generator because a cousin of one of the other members of his group had theoretically developed the technology.

Tobin, the original Ardica President, said their class teammate, a Chinese-American who changed his name to David, introduced them to his cousin, who had changed his name to "Flaming." Later, when the cousin went into business, "he started a company called 'Flaming Hydrogen on Demand.'" Tobin laughed telling this story of something less than marketing genius.

They took that idea to Dr. Prinz. "It turned out the hydrogen generation technology was crap," said Tom. But Dr. Prinz steered them in a different direction.

The initial discussion, according to Tobin, lasted about 15 minutes. Dr. Prinz, according to Tobin, said, "Starting a company is a lot of work. You sure you are up to it?"

"And that was it. He cut right to the chase. He was right about the work, of course."

Dr. Prinz told them about Dan's scooter and thought that there might be some kind of business in the idea. The scooter, said Dr. Prinz, "was pretty cool. Dan impressed me when he built the scooter. He worked day and night. He hardly got any sleep at all, but he did it."

Soon it became more than a class project. Tom and Tobin and the others from the class, along with Dan, began meeting "in random rooms on campus," recalled Dan. "These were once-a-week meetings, and by the spring the meetings had become more serious." At the time Tibor, from Slovakia by way of the Vienna University of Technology, did not have a green card to work in the United States. But he became involved too.

"Dan and Tibor are extremely creative engineers," said Dr. Prinz.

"Smart and creative is a good combination. They are good in both domains—creative and analytical." Tom and Tobin were also very creative engineers, said Dr. Prinz, but they didn't have the same analytical ability as Dan and Tibor. All in all, though, it appeared to be a good startup team and Dr. Prinz offered guidance.

The idea they were working on evolved. They were thinking of a way to deliver hydrogen on a small scale. "Pretty soon they came up with a pretty cool idea," said Dr. Prinz. The idea was for a unique pump mechanism that allows for the mixing of water and sodium borohydride. "I was impressed," said Dr. Prinz.

According to Tom, the first thing the group considered was a fuel cell application for laptop computers. But that idea was deemed unfeasible at the time because of issues with the heat that came from fuel cells. "The heat issue was a killer," he said. But the idea never went away from his mind. The big goal, he said, was to work with a world class visionary company, someone like Big Silicon.

Instead and in the meantime, they built a prototype to power big video news cameras. People on campus found out about the plan and Tobin encouraged anyone who wanted to be part of the team to come to work. "Those who showed up were part of the team," he said.

Although the fuel cell for video cameras did not become a product because the market wasn't large enough, they were encouraged enough to keep meeting after they all graduated. "We showed it to some investors," remembered Tibor. They found believers.

At the time, Tobin was considering a couple of other entrepreneurial possibilities: a device to help Parkinson's patients walk and a mountain board that simulated a snowboard, but he decided fuel cells were the way to go. Tobin said the group then considered a huge number of possibilities, including power tools, electric trolling motors for fishing boats, and others. "The problem was going head-to-head with lithium-ion batteries," he said. Lithium-ion batteries had an established distribution chain and were much lower in price than any first-generation fuel cell could be. And that's when they began thinking about heated clothing.

Wearable technology was a burgeoning market and the customers were open to trying new things. It seemed a perfect fit.

At the time, Dan was entering his PhD program figuring he'd pull double duty. It was a grind, but it was fun and interesting. "We started meeting at people's houses," recalled Dan. "We'd rotate meetings so we wouldn't piss our roommates off."

When they finally sat down to play their name-the-company Scrabble game, they had already gone through a bunch of names. According to Tobin, "One of the names we considered was 'Teino,' but we found that it sounds very similar to the word for 'stupid' in Japanese."

5

ON FEBRUARY 4TH, 2004, Ardica Technologies was incorporated. At the end of the summer, Dan dropped out of his PhD program and decided that a fuel cell business was the future. The young men from Stanford, with a prototype and a dream, raised some money from friends and family angel investors. They set out looking for a space and found one on the second floor of the building we were currently located in in San Francisco.

We had since moved to the fourth and top floor of the building that once contained the factory of the American Can Company, in an old industrial area of San Francisco known as Dogpatch, east of Potrero Hill in San Francisco's Central Waterfront District. The American Can Company is credited with inventing the beer can, and although it's unclear whether it happened at the huge San Francisco building that now serves as home to many startups, I liked to think that the beer can was invented somewhere between where Dan and Tibor sat.

"We liked the higher ceilings," said Dan of the decision to locate the business. "We thought it would inspire creativity."

And so with a place on the second floor of the old American Can Company factory leased out, the young entrepreneurs went about furnishing the place. "We went around the city picking up free stuff that was listed on Craigslist," said Dan.

"It was kind of romantic at the beginning," said Tibor. "It was a tight group of people with high dreams and a lot of energy."

Tibor was brought into the Ardica fold through his association with Dr. Prinz at Stanford. Tibor was at the Vienna University of Technology in the PhD program when he decided to come to America. The head of his department introduced him to Dr. Prinz—who is himself actually from Austria and taught in Vienna—and helped him transfer to Stanford. There, Tibor worked on a number of things, including a miniature helicopter, miniature gas turbines, and a miniature fuel cell.

And when he met Dan, Tom, and Tobin, Tibor bought right into the dream of a portable, miniaturized fuel cell business.

As I sat there in the Ardica offices a couple floors higher from where they first started, I couldn't help but be proud to have joined up with these entrepreneurs who were doing something both brand new and yet as ageless as business itself. They were daring to dream and then do something about it.

I could look out and see Pier 70, one of the largest ship repair yards on the West Coast. In addition, I could see a half-dozen or so abandoned warehouses. This spectacular part of the old city is home to a large historic enclave of industry based around the shipyard. The American Can Company built this tin can factory in 1915. Prior to that, this was a baseball field. There is a photograph of this old building that shows the factory with a plume of dark smoke rising above it. At the time I imagine it was meant to evoke an image of productivity.

But times had changed. On March 29th, 2000, the San Francisco Chronicle said of this area: "It has both dot-com outfits and the San Francisco headquarters of the Hells Angels." And our company of young engineers was located in the historic American Can Company building, which was now called The American Industrial Center. Our goal was to create a new image of productivity.

"I took a huge pay cut to come here," recalled Adam Rodriguez, the project manager of our Moshi Battery System. Adam, who was Dan's roommate at Stanford, had already taken a job at a consulting company when Dan and the others started Ardica. For a year and a half, Adam worked in Atlanta and lived in the Westin Hotel. But although the money was great and he was on a path to becoming a partner, Adam realized, "It wasn't really what I wanted to do with the rest of my life. Working for The Man."

Adam, from Rochester, Minnesota, was 28. He is bilingual, having learned to speak Danish before English while growing up in Minnesota, but what he really spoke was "California." He was the Midwest kid who came out here to college in California and became our resident surfer dude with floppy brown hair. He usually wore shorts. While he talked, he was icing the hand that he strained while kite surfing. He was, on the side, a sponsored athlete as a kite surfer. There were gymnastics rings hanging from the high ceiling of the engineering side of our offices. Those were for Adam, who used them to stretch and exercise.

He was enticed to do engineering design work with his old roommate and with Ardica. "It's kind of exciting," said Adam. "Every day is new and different. It's more vibrant."

The reason that Ardica was more vibrant than a big company was because of the entrepreneurial nature of the company. It was a risk. In June, as we were about to launch ourselves as a brand, there were circumstances we were trying to control that we really had no control over. There was a complete lack of retail outlets for the fuel. We did not have approval from airlines to carry the fuel. We needed safety certifications from the U.S. and from around the globe.

But it didn't matter what we didn't have. We were going for it. We were staffed with entrepreneurs and risk takers. We had a kite surfer, a motorcycle racer, extreme skiers, a stunt helicopter pilot, and more on our staff. We had people who had started companies such as Inmedius, The North Face, Beyond Coastal, and Zinka. We had the guy, Greg Nevolo, who oversaw and participated in aviation events for Red Bull. We all loved an adrenaline rush, and the biggest adrenaline rush of all was creativity.

Tibor could honestly say, "This is the only job I've ever had. I haven't seen anything better than this."

For three years, Tom and Tobin ran the company essentially as an R&D firm relying on the money of angel investors. "It was a strong, motivated group," recalled Tom. "Very capable." Ardica was entrepreneurial at its core, with big dreams. The company, on Tobin's suggestion, decided it would make fuel cell-powered heated jackets. This, in theory, was a great idea. Fuel cell basics told them that a byproduct of the hydrogen energy produced is in the form of heat, so why not harness that heat? In practice, it turned out, we had not yet (as of June 2009) perfected the fuel cell solution for consumers that we were designing. Our biggest hurdle was how to establish a ubiquitous distribution of the fuel so that the customers could get what fuel they wanted, when they wanted it, wherever they wanted it.

"The history of this company is that we always think we are about to go to market real soon," said Dan. "It's always right around the corner for us."

"Deadlines always inspired the team," said Tobin. The first deadline they set was to have a working prototype of the jacket in six weeks. And they met that deadline with an ugly quick prototype they named "Frankenstein."

"We didn't show that to investors. We did it to prove to ourselves we could make this work."

On the last night when they were close they debated at 1 am whether to go home and sleep and look with fresh eyes or whether to push on and meet their deadline. They pushed on, said Tobin. "We started this tradition of doing a tour of the Anchor Steam brewery on the day after a deadline. When you finish the tour you can drink as much as you want and so that was our celebration. We always scheduled a tour for the day after deadline so if we didn't make deadline we didn't go on the tour."

6

THE SECOND PROTOTYPE WAS SHOWN to an investment group, Chrysalix, from Canada. In November 2004, that group had invested a much- needed $350,000, but only after Tobin and Tom had performed some last-minute magic with crazy glue on their prototype. Tobin remembered needing to fix the prototype and biting the top off the crazy glue because there was no other way to get it open. He almost glued his mouth closed but instead he saved the prototype.

The coat design went through about a half-dozen product revisions in two years—each used to raise money from investors. The pressure was high. "It was routine for us as a team to be finishing up a prototype just as an investor was walking through the door," said Dan. All the while they were getting subtle guidance from their mentor, Dr. Prinz at Stanford, and from me as a businessman and brand builder. The problem was that as soon as they produced a design they had a hundred new ideas and immediately started working on those. I don't think they ever truly "finished" a product until Dick and I arrived.

In November 2005, an investment group named Firelake offered $2.4 million, "but we turned it down," said Tobin. "We thought the valuation was fairly low and we could do better." In retrospect, he said, that might have been a mistake.

The company pushed forward building prototypes. Once, in 2006, we were at an Outdoor Retailer trade show in Salt Lake City, Utah. I was helping out part-time at the show and Ardica was displaying the heated jackets. Dan was the hero that day.

In order to show how great of a product a heated jacket really was, "We decided to hold all of our meetings in a refrigerated space," recalled Dan. "We wanted it to be as cold as we could get so we rented a refrigerated truck and decorated it with ice sculptures. " The idea was to have customers try the jackets on in a true winter environment, which would normally be difficult in a Salt Lake City summer featuring 100-degree heat. "We brought ten jackets with us but they broke a lot. My job was to be the man behind the curtain fixing the jackets." For hours in the cold and not wearing one of the ten heated jackets, "I played Mr. Wizard," said Dan. It was an entrepreneurial adjustment on the fly, repairing malfunctioning jackets and impressing the customers all the while.

They were learning. They learned, for instance, the cardinal rule of entrepreneurship: it always takes twice as long and costs three times as much as you think. As the risks became obviously riskier, they began to understand this economic reality even as they were hiring people. Miriam, our office manager and marketing coordinator, was hired in July 2006. "When they offered me the job, our former CEO told me that there was a chance I would not get paid on a regular basis," she recalled.

That former CEO, Tom, said, "There was never enough breathing room to think about what you're doing and plan ahead. That's a painful way for a company to exist."

Still, Miriam took the job. She was a graduate of The American University of Paris who had spent a year as an executive assistant at the Carlisle Group when she saw an advertisement on Craigslist for Ardica. "I felt like I was joining really intelligent young people working on a really cool concept," she said. "To be part of a startup, you feel like you actually matter rather than just being employee number 5,000." And her job in those early days was a sort of jack-of-all-trades, including accounting and payroll. She did the books and learned quickly that "it was very difficult to raise funds at that point for a fuel cell company."

Tobin added, "We had difficulty developing the technology and we had difficulty raising money. Those two are inextricably linked."

And thus Tom's prophecy came true. It was part of the reason he went from CEO to former CEO. "Everything changed when we ran out of money," recalled Tibor. "There was a huge portion of 2007 where we all worked for minimum wage. Naturally, that creates pressure everywhere and it facilitated a change in management."

7

I**T IS NOT EASY TO SURVIVE** working for minimum wage, particularly in San Francisco. It is especially vexing if you are a Stanford-educated engineer who could easily be making a large salary working for any of the many variations of "The Man" that Adam Rodriguez once worked for. Still. "You agree to do it the first day your paycheck doesn't come," said Adam. "And then it keeps going. But you've got so much invested. If there's five of us and we all keep busting ass..." he said and then he paused. "You are working with five of your best friends. You don't want to be the one to let them down."

But as Adam said, they all considered the question, "When do you cut your losses? At some point, someone was going to crack."

Yet, Adam noted, there was simply too much invested. Despite all signs that a banker or a lawyer might point to, failure was not an option.

"It's almost something you couldn't understand," said Dan. He stopped and looked off into space as he talked. You could almost see him looking at what he remembered. "A lot of things went into us persevering when we ran out of money...We had a certain dedication, a commitment, and responsibility we felt to each other. Each of us felt a very strong sense of ownership. We had a responsibility to ourselves, our friends, and our families. And our family's friends. We had people who invested in us. Giving up was not an option. We never considered it. But we had episodes where we ran short on cash. We missed a few paychecks. We ran short at least two or three times waiting for our next investment. Eventually we got to the point where the company pretty significantly ran out of money."

Tom called this his and Tobin's "come-to-Jesus moment." There had been, according to Tom and others, tension at the company for a while. Mostly, it was due to money, but some of it was brought on by the founders, who fundamentally disagreed on the direction of the company as well as on leadership style. Tobin was convinced that the idea of heated apparel was the right direction while Tom was in favor of creating a fuel cell that could fit into the sleeve of a laptop computer.

"The difference of opinion," said Tobin, "started to tear at the company." Two good friends had drifted apart and the company suffered. "It was very emotional for both of us. It turned work into almost a battle. Ultimately something broke down. We certainly tried to talk. At some point Tom felt like he couldn't talk to me anymore and then I felt like I couldn't talk to him. It was a sad experience."

Tom found himself incredibly disappointed. After all, he'd been on the path to becoming an engineer his entire life and building a business was his dream. It was why he left his previous job as an engineer with the Honda Racing Team.

In fact, "The reason I left what most would consider the best engineering job in the world was to start a company." Starting a company to Tom trumped even working on race cars. "It was great, exciting stuff," said Tom of his Honda job. He added, "Everywhere we went in the world was a party."

But it wasn't enough. He dreamed of being an entrepreneur as well as an engineer. Actually, from the time he was a child, his path towards engineering seemed set, "made obvious by how I spent my spare time. I liked to make a lot of things and break a lot of things." It was a typical engineering path of childhood tinkering, only he took a side route in which he learned a bit about ethics, as well as politics.

"I managed to get myself expelled from high school two weeks before graduation," said Tom. He had designed, with some help of others, a remote-control stink bomb that went off in the chapel at his Episcopal High School in Houston, Texas. At the time, he was the starting attack guard on the team that went on to become state high school lacrosse champions. In fact, the championship game was the Sunday after his stink bomb went off. He played and the team won. The next day, on Monday, he was expelled. His co-conspirators received no punishment. And young Tom found the situation "very, very interesting. It made me more attuned to the strategic implications of decisions." In other words, it seemed perspective informed all decisions, and all decisions have consequences.

Tom studied for a year at Texas A&M and then transferred to Colorado State University, where he worked in an engine lab and then entered, with a team, a competition to build a small race car. He was the leader of his team and it was there that he discovered "a passion for the high-performance engine." He had a blast working on the car with a group of motivated friends and the next year they entered again. But the team expanded from 10 to 30 people and Tom discovered how difficult it was "trying to lead a group of not very motivated people." In turn, he recalled, he led "in a tyrannical way. We got the car finished but it was in the trailer on the way to Detroit."

Nevertheless, "Some guys from Honda Racing were floating around the competition and they ended up hiring me." It was his dream job until he began to realize he missed the camaraderie of the group that was his first motivated team and decided, "I want to start a company but I don't know how." So he chose Stanford, known for its entrepreneurship program. In his final days at Stanford and the early days when Ardica was not yet officially formed, Tom was actually offered a job at Ford and almost accepted. "I thought it could be okay. But I was cognizant of the fact that I would be walking away from the original reason I went to school—to start a company."

In other words, Tom (like everybody) was deeply emotionally invested in Ardica.

He was also armed with the political lessons from his smoke bomb incident and the leadership lessons from his brief tyrannical reign as the head of the race car team at Colorado State.

Tom remembered a discussion early on about who should be CEO. Tom, armed with an MBA, thought it was obvious but, he said, Tobin still pushed the discussion. Later he identified that early moment as a red flag he should have seen. Still, he said, early on they were able to discuss their differences logically. "I remember thinking at the time that if only my ex-girlfriend and I had been able to talk things through like Tobin and I, we'd still be together."

Tobin also remembered the early days fondly.

Like Tom, Tobin found his way to Stanford from a prestigious place— IDEO, one of the top design firms in the world. When Tobin entered the Joint Program of Design, taught by the art school and the engineering school at Stanford, he knew that "a lot of people go to that program and then go work at IDEO. I went the opposite way."

Tobin, the son of two professors, was born and raised outside of Philadelphia. His father, a professor of operations management at Wharton, was an entrepreneur and Tobin always envisioned himself starting a company. And he was curious about how things were put together, so curious that sometimes "I'd get what I called 'good junk' and throw it up in the air and see what pieces fell out."

When he was about 10, Tobin successfully made gunpowder and then he blew a foot-wide hole in the ground. He remembered worrying for a time that the FBI was going to come get him.

As an undergrad he went to Yale and received a degree in mechanical engineering. From there, he worked as a strategy consultant to a Big Three auto company, where he worked on developing a fuel cell strategy. Later, he went to IDEO where he helped design products for the toy industry and hospital industry, among others. And then, at 25 years old, he came to Stanford, and met Tom.

By the time things fell apart, they had worked together for years.

Eventually though, with money concerns eating at them, disagreements between the founders became wider. A lot of it had to do with two different versions of the vision (clothing or computers), and some of it had to do with management style. There were discussions and arguments, and at first the board was unaware of the scope of the problem between the two.

When they finally had their "come-to-Jesus" moment, the two agreed to bring in a replacement to run the company "but then the Board got wind and asked me to step aside," said Tom. Tobin took over as CEO for five months, and then he also left the day-to-day operations of Ardica. Tom remained on the board, as did Tobin.

8

D R. PRINZ REMAINED a big believer in Ardica. He knew the founders and the technology. He knew their dedication and their level of intelligence. He also understood reality and so when it became clear that Ardica was teetering, he had an idea.

"One of the key issues, in order to not get diluted too much, is to get government funding. The question is how do you get government funding?" said Dr. Prinz, who knew a lot about startups of this nature.

All along, he had been talking about Ardica to an old friend of his from when they were both professors at Carnegie Mellon, Dick Martin. Dr. Prinz suggested to the Board that Dick would be a good CEO. At this point, Dick was an obvious person to help and he had an interest as well.

"He had leadership experience and he came from the government originally," said Dr. Prinz.

And in an instant, the approach went from dreamy to practical. In an email, Dick summarized his background:

I've had a lot of experience and success in running complex projects where "failure is not an option." Here are a few of the experiences:

- *Commanding officer of the first F-18 Tomcat squadron - flew the first fleet F-14 from Grumman factory on Long Island to Miramar*

Naval Air Station in San Diego, and developed the logistics, training programs, and tactics that enabled the F-14 to dominate over adversary aircraft. Helped form the Top Gun school (the one that inspired the Tom Cruise movie).

- *Developed first on-line computer system to manage aircrew and maintenance personnel training and management of spare parts, and used UC Berkeley management school faculty to optimize operations of the new F-14 squadrons.*
- *Executive officer (number two in command) of the nuclear-powered aircraft carrier NIMITZ on its first two deployments - new class of ship with two reactor systems, each with 550MW.*
- *Commanding officer of the nuclear-powered aircraft carrier CARL VINSON (third NIMITZ class carrier) during construction, sea trials and first deployment to the Med and Indian Ocean - developed, with the help of DARPA and ONR, the first ethernet and workstation system for operating the ship and used it to deliver the ship from Newport News Shipbuilding company 30 days early and $200M under budget and to set operational records.*
- *Founding Deputy Director for the Artificial Intelligence Program at Microelectronics and Computer Technology Company (MCC), the first pre-competitive consortium of competing computer companies in the U.S., which was formed to counter Japan's Fifth Generation Computing initiative.*
- *A founding director of the Software Engineering Institute (SEI) at Carnegie Mellon (CMU) which was founded to develop software engineering capabilities from computer science and is an organization like Lincoln Lab at MIT founded to develop radar technology and JPL at Cal Tech founded to develop capabilities for space exploration.*
- *Movedtothe School of Computer Science at CMU and pioneered user-centered, evolutionary software system development (spiral development risk reduction) building to three software labs and about $5.0M annual funding from DARPA and the Services going through*

the promotions to the rank of non-tenured full professor.
- *Founder of a CMU spin off software company, Inmedius, which is now an international company with customers including Boeing and EADS*

Look up the word "gravitas" and you will see Dick Martin's resume. From 2007 to 2008, he slowly found his way into the company—first as an advisor, then an investor, then a board member and in January 2008, he became CEO.

"When I was in the navy, I lived in Newport, Rhode Island," said Dick. "The America's Cup race was there at the time. I had just come off of the Carl Vinson aircraft carrier and I got invited onto a yacht to watch the races. My wife said, 'Oh my God, look at this boat. It's so wonderful.' She didn't say she wanted a yacht like that but she sort of said I could have a yacht like that if I wanted. And I said, 'Do you know what this guy does to have this big yacht. He's a garbage man. He owns a garbage company.'"

"I like something with more of an intellectual challenge," said Dick. "I like no-mistake kind of things. I love to do things that the next person doesn't want to do. Some people would rather play golf every day. But I'd rather come to work and it's easy to come to work in this environment."

And that's why Dick Martin with his incredible resume joined up with the young engineers of Ardica. "These guys are the best of the best," said Dick. "Some of them have real potential to go on and be real leaders of industry."

I joined the day-to-day management of Ardica about the same time and I saw the exact same potential that Dick saw. I saw a team of bright, fun-loving, energetic young engineers with a fabulous idea. They had a world-changing vision, a world-class team, and a disruptive technology, one that overthrows the natural order of things and starts a whole new base of thinking that could be used in a variety of applications.

I also saw that marketing and branding hardly existed.

Dr. Prinz said having experienced leaders join the company was not unexpected. "Usually startups start out with students and then whoever gives them money usually steers them to experienced people. This is a very common pattern in Silicon Valley startups."

The leadership style change was profound, according to Miriam. "It was a complete adjustment for me," she said. "Dick is more of an old school micromanager."

But Adam said, "The management styles are quite similar. He's not looking over your shoulder." He added that the company allowed everyone to have a flexible schedule. "It's not about putting in the hours," said Adam. "It's about getting the work done."

Dick said, simply, that he believes in leadership by example. "You have to have respect for people and people have to have respect for you. People know that I've technically been through a lot of stuff...I show confidence that we can do it because we're doing it. I allow people to fail. If there's an environment of, 'Oh my God, something went wrong now I'm in trouble,' that's not good. I like to move into problem solving. You're not in trouble for screwing up. You're only in trouble if you don't tell me about it."

Well, Dick knew about the problems at Ardica. So the first thing he did as CEO was save the company.

He contracted with a lobbyist he knew, Zel Lipsen, who landed Ardica a military contract to develop a hybrid fuel cell and battery system. The idea was to lessen the load that a soldier carries into battle. The battery system a soldier currently needs to carry into battle is 30 pounds. With a fuel cell/battery hybrid, we can lessen that to 10 pounds. The battery has two purposes. First, it handles all energy surges associated with electrical startups. Secondly, it serves as a backup to make sure that a soldier's equipment doesn't fail and need to reboot. A reboot of a soldier's equipment—computer, GPS, etc.—due to all the heavy encryption can take 30 minutes, and that's too long in a firefight. So our inventions would really bring value to the military. Interestingly, the research behind this project led, in a roundabout way, to the aforementioned F-43 project.

9

THE FIRST THING I DID as marketing director was hire Shawn Biega as sales director. I met Shawn more than a decade earlier when I did some mentoring at his snowboard apparel company, Bombora. We hit it off immediately. Although I am a couple of decades older than him, we shared similar philosophies about life, about business, and about adventure. I had already offered him a job at my previous company, Canterbury, but at the time he had been building his latest company, Beyond Coastal suntan lotion. But when I approached him about Ardica, the timing was right and he joined up.

Shawn was a fantastic ally in building a great team. He had tremendous contacts and was a virtual lightning rod for excited athletes and business people. Shawn was also an entrepreneur who loved making money and he had managed businesses since he was a teenager. I knew he was the right person.

So what did Shawn do? He made a sale! On his way to his first trade show for Ardica he met the head of product design for Mountain Hardwear, the outdoor clothing manufacturer. The representative from Mountain Hardwear said his company was interested in our Ardica Fuel Cell Power System to heat their jackets. It was brilliant in design and conception, and it did more than heat jackets. The idea was more ambitious than that. It powered things. That's what it really did. And we made it able to power things by attaching another product we invented, called a Technology Connector, that, at that moment, was able to connect to 80% of all devices that attached to a USB cord—sort of a Swiss Army Knife of charger tips. The fuel cell system had enough power to heat the jacket for eight hours, or recharge a phone ten times, or charge an iPod/ MP3 player 20 times. Shawn, with the help of a well-known Kentuckian named Jack Daniels who facilitated the friendship, made the sale.

In 2008, with our new management team in place, we were suddenly on a roll. We had a contract to develop a hybrid fuel cell and battery system for the military and we had a legitimate customer in Mountain Hardwear for our in-development fuel cell system.

There was only one problem. The fuel cell solution for Mountain Hardwear was not ready yet. The price was too high and we had yet to convince *any* retailer to stock the fuel cartridges that were necessary to keep the fuel cell running.

There was a meeting at Moshi, a restaurant nearby. And so over sushi and beer one night in April 2008, Adam, Dan, Tibor and others figured out a new product to satisfy the customer in the short term while continuing to develop the fuel cells. It was mostly Adam's idea.

The question was posed, "How fast can you make it?" and Dan answered, "So fast it will make your head swim." He then proceeded to draw the idea for the Moshi Lithium-ion Battery System on a cocktail napkin. The original drawing got framed and was hung in one of our meeting rooms. The name came from the restaurant, which they got from how Japanese people answer the phone. "Moshi Moshi" means "hello," and seemed a great name for our first product.

That night the Ardica Fuel Cell Power System was converted to the Moshi Lithium-ion Battery System with the idea that next year it could be easily replaced in the same jacket by the fuel cell system, once that was completely ready. Two days later we had a working model. The Moshi was wearable, lightweight, flexible and it came with a microprocessor, designed by Ardica's electrical engineers, that added the aspect of intelligent controlled distribution and monitoring of power. This entrepreneurial moment exemplifies everything that is good about small business. Outdoor Life Magazine anointed the Moshi as one of the top 10 outdoor products of 2009.

Thus, it was overnight—literally—that Adam and his engineer comrades redesigned the fuel cell system into a battery system. The Moshi was originally and quickly conceived as a placeholder for the fuel cell system that was still in design. The goal was for the Moshi to seed the market with the Ardica name while the fuel cell was developed. But the Moshi itself, of course, was no mere placeholder. It was a lightweight, flexible, smart, power-on-the-go system that was unlike anything else on the market. Instinctively we knew that all we had to do was convince everyone else.

And so three days after the Moshi was designed to replace the fuel cell that Shawn had sold, Shawn went to the customer and explained that the fuel cell system wasn't ready yet, *but look what is.* The buyer from Mountain Hardwear looked at the Moshi Battery System. He looked at Shawn. He smiled at Shawn. "Way to make lemonade," he said.

10

I N SPRING 2008, Speck Design, a consulting company working for Big Silicon, was leaving messages on Tobin's cellphone. But Tobin didn't return the calls because he didn't work at the company anymore. Which was ironic, because according to Miriam, "Back in the day, Tom always wanted to work with Big Silicon on a fuel cell project." And then, seemingly out of the blue, someone working for them was actually calling us.

But at the time, no one knew and it was almost one of the great missed opportunities in business history if not for Maynard Holliday, who played a crucial role in guiding Big Silicon to us.

At the time, Maynard—who later became our Fuel Cell System Production Manager—was working at Speck Design when Big Silicon contacted Speck about exploring concepts in energy efficiency. Maynard had looked into this area himself and found a lot of people doing research in miniature fuel cells, but one company stood out—Ardica. "They had the highest energy density," recalled Maynard.

The holy grail with power sources is the energy density—how much power comes from how small an energy source. For most portable products, the smaller the size of the energy source (sometimes called the "form factor") the more desirable, assuming that the small package is sufficient to power whatever device it is attached to for an acceptable period of time.

Doing that is easier said than done, of course, as the many complaints about portable device battery life will attest.

Fuel cells had a greater energy density (power at a lighter weight) than either the standard NiCad batteries used by most consumers for toys, flashlights and such, or lithium-ion batteries, which have a longer runtime than NiCads and are rechargeable.

But fuel cells did not yet have a standard form factor, and they also required an independent fuel source that is separate from the physical structure of the unit. Different companies were working with different fuels with different properties, creating some confusion in the market. The biggest drawback was that the consumer wouldn't know where to find the fuel because there were no established retail channels for the distribution. If Big Silicon was involved, of course, all of that could change.

So Maynard tried to contact Ardica, the company with the highest energy density, but the only contact number listed on our outdated website was Tobin's old cell phone. Ardica did not actually have a phone number listed in the phone book. So Maynard called Tobin to tell him/ us that Big Silicon was very interested in working with Ardica. He kept unsuccessfully calling Tobin. Finally, when Speck (and, by extension, Big Silicon) was about to give up, Maynard looked further into who the principals in the company were, he discovered the common denominator for many involved in the company, Dr. Prinz.

Coincidentally, when Maynard was an undergraduate at Carnegie Mellon, Dr. Prinz was his professor. He had remained in touch, and when he did research on Ardica, he discovered Dr. Prinz was on the Board. When Maynard finally reached Dr. Prinz at Stanford and told him of the failed efforts to contact Tobin, Dr. Prinz informed Maynard of the Ardica management change and told him to contact Dick. "Dick got right back to me and said, 'Let's meet,'" said Maynard.

One day not long after, Maynard and a few others from a "consumer electronics firm" came into the Ardica offices. "We would always Google who was coming in," recalled Miriam. And there were often people coming in, but, she said, "this was different. We all got dressed up that day."

The opportunity to work with one of the world-class companies was obvious from the beginning. Though the specifics were hush-hush, enough information passed back and forth early on that, according to Maynard, "they [meaning us, Ardica] were pretty jazzed."

Big Silicon was also pretty jazzed because we had something better than anyone else around. We held the key to the future. This was the birth of the F-43 program for fuel cell development for Big Silicon.

Dan remembered being excited because "the potential possibilities are enormous." He also remembered one other thing: "the emphasis they put on the secrecy of their product development."

The concept of fuel cells, even miniaturized fuel cells, was not new. But what we were proposing *was* revolutionary, and it was supported by a number of first class patents. We were creating miniaturized, high-density energy from renewable fuel. We had developed, as Dr. Prinz stated, "a pretty cool idea." And we had amassed five hard-earned years of institutional knowledge.

Fuel cells and harnessed hydrogen as a concept had been around for 160 years. This was not a new idea. In 1839 in England, Sir William Grove proved it was possible to produce electricity from the reaction of hydrogen with oxygen. However, there had been hurdles in the last 160 years, and although fuel cells were then being proposed on lots of scales, none were being proposed with the energy density we produced. That's why Big Silicon was interested.

According to the book *The Hydrogen Economy* written by Jeremy Rifkin, "The foundation is already being laid for the hydrogen economy. In the next few years the computer and telecommunications revolution is going to fuse with the new hydrogen-energy revolution, making for a powerful mix that could fundamentally reconfigure human relationships in the 21st and 22nd centuries. Since hydrogen is found everywhere and is inexhaustible, every human being on Earth could be 'empowered,' making hydrogen energy the first truly democratic energy regime in history." This may be hyperbole but it was hyperbole that we all believed in. We were now all sipping the Kool-Aid.

The computer revolution fusing with the hydrogen-energy revolution, as described by Rifkin, would mean that Big Silicon consumer goods could be Ardica-enabled. But these things weren't going to happen overnight. Big Silicon insisted that the F-43 project had to be totally energy efficient (i.e. green), recalled Maynard. "So finding the wind farm in West Texas was absolutely key," he said.

The idea was simple and elegant. One of our investors was building a 40-acre wind farm in West Texas and we planned to capture that energy and essentially bottle it into individual hydrogen canisters for long-term energy storage and distribution. We would be making clean energy for on- the-go use. Instead of emitting .86 kilograms of CO_2 for every kilowatt of power you use (the amount of environmentally damaging CO_2 you put in the air from hooking up to a traditional power plant through an electrical wall plug), our energy would be clean. The only pollution we would create would be when we trucked raw materials for the fuel or when we trucked our fuel canisters to retail stores. Our calculations showed we would cut CO_2 emissions by 94%.

Michelangelo had it right when he said, "The greatest danger for most of us is not that our aim is too high and we miss it, but that our aim is too low and we achieve it." No one at Ardica was aiming low.

Distribution of our fuel and fuel cells would be a key to our success (and we were counting on Big Silicon to help solve that issue), but we were the first company to be able to say of miniaturization in such a high density: *We can do that. We have the technology.*

"We make hydrogen storage in a small, portable fashion," explained Tibor. The simple explanation of a fuel cell, said Tibor, is that "it is an energy-conversion device." Put simply, we planned to use our groundbreaking technology in order to harness the energy from the wind or the sun, or even geothermal, store it in portable hydrogen containers, and then distribute it.

We thought it was a noble goal to try to change the world. We also thought it was a noble goal to try to create a special company and make a lot of money. In June 2009, there were still issues, of course. Big issues. Money remained at the top of the list as we were in the process of fundraising. Dick said he was convinced Big Silicon would invest. He also said it was not certain.

Meanwhile we already had three sure customers—Mountain Hardwear, Sitka, and Redwing—for our Moshi battery system. Others, including Spyder for their Olympic ski clothing and Hugo Boss for their fashion line, were very interested and we had started developing prototypes. The opportunity was enormous.

And for a very select group of thought and opinion leaders that we called "Trendsetters," we were creating our own line of a few hundred jackets. We were also considering developing variations of the Moshi and calling it the modular Moshi, which could have variations of size, weight, and power and hook together Lego-style. Our military contract was in place and development moved forward toward our goal of dramatically lightening a soldier's load.

And our partner negotiations with Big Silicon, as well as our financing negotiations—being run by Dick with me as an advisor and "eminence grise"—were tense and inextricably woven in with our money issues. There were major technology issues. We were developing two different types of fuel for our fuel cell system, ones that had entirely different supply chains, entirely different manufacturing processes, and which required entirely different safety certifications that must be secured before we could begin selling. There were issues surrounding patents, and we still needed to set up a factory, that Dick argued should be in Montana, for our Moshi battery power system as well as setting up an operation in Texas for creating fuel and fuel canisters near the wind farm. The clock was ticking.

As I stated, these were scary times at Ardica. And it was clear to me, at this point in June, that we needed a strategy meeting.

W E HAD TOO MANY OPTIONS and still not enough money. In May 2009, I began gently pushing the issue in the hope that we couldhold a true strategy session run by group of consultants, some of whom I had known for decades. We needed their help and I knew they'd do a good job. We needed to focus, prioritize, and do it as one team.

Since Dick Martin was the CEO, I could only suggest such a meeting. To get it to happen took some effort. At one point, Dick wrote that he was "a little bit annoyed" that I even suggested such a meeting.

Dick and I were an interesting team. We both loved entrepreneurship and we were both eternal optimists. But we also had differences. He was a Naval Academy engineer and a professor of Computer Science at Carnegie Mellon. I was a Stanford MBA and a lifelong entrepreneur. He had spent decades in the military and government. I had spent decades in Berkeley, California.

Dick was a squat, square-shouldered, quiet-voiced man with bushy eyebrows and the reserved demeanor of a lifelong serviceman. His intelligence was clear from his biography, as was his grasp of and exposure to the bigger technology and engineering world that Ardica was entering.

In my career I had focused on building world-class branded consumer companies. Dick had built world-class technology and ran precise military teams in many areas. He also knew how to find government contracts. I could hardly find Washington, D.C. on a map.

Dick Martin, who flew combat missions in Vietnam, had taught air-to-air combat, also called dogfighting. He once participated in high-level days-long war games at a think tank where each person in the room played a different role, such as the President of the United States, the Secretary of State or, in Dick's case, the commander of a ship. The person playing the president had actually worked for a previous president. Of course, in real life, Dick had been an actual commander on a ship. And so with this and more as background, he was reticent at first to accept my suggestion that we needed a strategy meeting. He sent an email to me in late May that began, "Let's 'manage by fact'" and then he went on to smartly and succinctly list some undeniable facts.

Later, in an interview, his confidence from experience showed. "Almost everything I have done has been brand new, startup, can't fail—that kind of thing." And since he had never failed and since Ardica was another brand new, and a startup, it was obvious that Dick didn't think we would fail here. He summarized it this way: "This is new, game-changing kind of technolo- gy we have. It's a high-risk endeavor. I've been involved in high risk before."

He was born in Granville, Ohio near Columbus and dreamed from the time he was a child of being a pilot. At the time, a company called North American Aviation was making the F-86 Sabrejet and his scout-master worked there. One day the scouts got to fly with the scoutmaster in a Piper Cub airplane and Dick immediately knew for sure that this was what he wanted to do with his life. Plus, he said, "I was always good at math and science in high school. It was very natural."

Out of high school, he attended the Naval Academy and received a degree in general science. He also became a navy pilot. In a period spanning four years, he flew more than 100 combat missions over Vietnam and landed on an aircraft carrier more than 660 times. When Dick said he's been in high-risk, can't-fail endeavors, he meant it.

While he was in school, he was selected into the Burke Program, named for Admiral Arleigh Burke, a World War II navy hero. "They picked the top five graduates for academic and leadership potential." And at that, he was on dual course to be a pilot as well as a student. He did both. He went on fighter squadron tours, and when he wasn't flying he was studying. He went to the University of San Diego for mathematics and then into the PhD program for physics. While in graduate school, "I taught air combat maneuvering, dogfighting. I helped the guys out and it kept me up with my flying." And he started the Top Gun School, made famous by the Tom Cruise movie.

Dick's story is part of the story of America. "I was selected as an astronaut during graduate school. I went through astronaut screening and got selected. Alan Shepard called me." But Dick had to wait a year while he was finishing graduate school and during that year, on January 27th,1967, a flash fire engulfed a capsule used for testing for the first Apollo Saturn mission. Three astronauts were killed and NASA suspended future astronaut hires.

"They pulled me out of grad school just as I finished because they ran out of combat-rated pilots. So they took me back in (as a fighter pilot)." During that stint, he was promoted to be the number two commander of his squadron and "I got combat experience as the executive officer of a squadron." And then Dick became the skipper of the first F-14 tomcat squadron, a group he remembered as "the best of the best."

It's how he came to speak of our young engineers.

And he knew something about engineering. With his background—skipper of the first F-14 tomcat squadron, PhD studies in math, combat tours, selected for astronaut school, and first in his class in electrical engineering at the Naval Academy—important people saw his potential. "I got a call from Admiral Rickover of the nuclear power program. I became second in command of the Nimitz aircraft carrier for its first two deployments."

When the Nimitz was launched in 1972, the legendary Admiral

Hyman Rickover, known as "the father of the nuclear navy," turned to Dick Martin. "He picked up my record," said Dick. "I didn't seek that one out. It just kind of happened."

Three years later, he was commanding officer of the Carl Vinson (the third Nimitz class carrier) during construction, sea trials, and first deployment. Part of his work on this project was done at Carnegie Mellon University in Pittsburgh where he helped build the computer systems for the Carl Vinson. This was the ship that was delivered 30 days early and $200 million under budget. It was the kind of thing, like almost everything Dick had done in life, that caught people's attention.

When he was with the Carl Vinson, he landed in Newport, Rhode Island and served as a senior fellow in the Naval Operations Strategic Studies Group at the U.S. Naval War College. He studied, as a prelude to his early Ardica days, crisis management.

Dick proceeded to Carnegie Mellon University as a software engineer, where he essentially started the school of computer science. It was another startup for Dick and he succeeded. There is almost too much biography to summarize this quickly with Dick, but one of the most important connections, at least to Ardica and this book, happened at Carnegie Mellon where he met a man destined to become his friend, Dr. Fritz Prinz, who at the time ran a lab there.

Years later, after Dick had put in a couple of decades at CMU and helped start a couple of companies, Dr. Prinz approached Dick about the difficulties and opportunities with Ardica.

Dick saw the same thing that I saw and that we all saw: opportunity. But he saw it from his own perspective. "I'm a technologist and I have a strategic vision for where things go," he said. "I've got a vision of things and I can see how the future unfolds...I've got a vision of how to create things. I can look at something and think, 'I know how to make this happen.'"

Early on, he proved his ability to work in a crisis, raising quick money and getting government contracts. He was calm, directed, and a great, detail-focused leader. His calm nerve was exactly what you would expect from a pilot who flew more than 100 combat missions. Dick was very tactical in his approach to matters, which is why he was so great in a crisis.

On the other hand, my background as an entrepreneur had made my thinking very strategic in nature. After all, in my various entrepreneurial ventures the same issues cropped up again and again and I'd learned it is best to avoid the majority of crises instead of managing your way through them. Still, no matter how hard you try to avoid them, there will be some crises. There is always an 11th hour crisis. If you haven't had it, it's not the 11th hour yet.

12

D ICK AND I HAD DIFFERENT BACKGROUNDS and different management styles. Dick's military background had focused on top-down management, but he was quick to point out his diverse background. "Don't forget I was a professor for 20 years and then I ran a software company that was high tech." In each situation, he said, "The environment was different but how you deal with the people is not."

My style had always been participative management. I wanted to know others' opinions. And that's why I wanted a strategy meeting, to get all our minds together and figure out how to make best use of our over-extended financial and human resources. I knew that the best way to implement a strategy was to get "buy off" from the team on our direction. We'd been hiring new people, and the team had been growing. One year ago there were eight people at the company; now there were more than 20. But there had never been an indoctrination program or even an explanation of our goals. In fact, it had been trial by fire. And while the team had reacted remarkably well, growth meant we would be adding people, products, and customers and those could cause exponential disconnects, conflicts, and mistakes. There would be a multiplier effect if it were not harnessed properly.

More to the point, we needed an overall strategy. There were lots of issues that I saw:

- Product quality? How would we judge? What would our warranty be?
- Were we a fuel cell company long term? Did "power system" include fuel, heaters, controllers, clothing, etc.?
- Company strategy? Were we a manufacturing company or a licensing company? If Big Silicon wanted us to license only, what would be our strategy?
- Sales strategy? How would sales of three areas (military, commercial, Big Silicon) fit together? When would begin global sales, and what would be needed to support that?
- Financial strategy? Banking strategy? Exit strategies? Terms to customers?
- Environmental strategy? Compensation strategy?
- Intellectual property strategy? What would we cover and how did this tie to negotiations with Big Silicon?
- Negotiations with Big Silicon? What did they want, and what could they offer? Where was the win-win? And on and on...

It was a lot to consider. We simply had more to do than we had people. We had more to do than we had financial resources, and therefore we had people working on many things but not finishing any of them. We were becoming paralyzed by opportunities and we were on the verge of missing opportunities because we were not spending money on things we needed—such as the safety certifications for the sale and transport of our products.

Where to put our resources? This should be the focus of a strategy meeting. As CEO, Dick was deciding things unilaterally and then was forced to make quick decisions on how to spend what little we had when people from three different departments were begging for the same pot of money. Meanwhile, Jim was struggling to meet payroll.

It had become a short-term/long-term game in which we were often trading the vital for the urgent, and our strategy appeared to be the equivalent of 5-year-old children chasing a soccer ball. We were slowing down our response times and innovations while constantly chasing the urgent. We were expending way too much energy just surviving. It was time, I argued, to thrive.

Dick thought we were on a good path. Our differences began to surface, different visions and different styles. I felt we needed to be unified. I wanted everyone—not just Dick and me—but *everyone* on the same page. I wanted everyone involved in writing that page. All for one and one for all…it may be cliché, but it works.

Dick knew another way that works. The military way. He would argue that he had seen the world from many sides, but he also argued against the need for a strategy meeting.

Ours were different visions and styles. Neither was wrong. But it was time to figure out what we were, what we had and could get for resources, and what we could do. The financing we were expecting was dribbling in, but we still expected another $2.5 million soon. That's what Dick had told us. When it happened, he said, it would change our world. But we needed to be ready.

Finally, in late May, Dick agreed to have the consultants come in and see if they could help us define and articulate our strategy "in a minimally disruptive and costly way." While I wanted to include the entire company in one room together, Dick limited the first half of the meeting (four hours) to five top management people and then reluctantly agreed to include two others. The afternoon session would be split into two two-hour segments for the sales team and then the engineering team. The sales team and the engineering team would not be in the same room at the same time.

13

I T WAS A GRAY, windy San Francisco morning and we were gathered on the 19th floor of Dick's apartment building in the special events penthouse and party area trying to see the future. From there, we had sweeping vista views of the skyline and the Bay Bridge, but what we had all gathered to look at were Ardica's opportunities.

It was June 12th and the strategy meeting I had been pushing for was finally here. We needed to make some decisions and, in order to facilitate this meeting, I had invited some bright and well-connected consultants—Eight Inc.—to run this day-long event for the company.

I'd been involved in at least 40 strategic plans in my business career and I had a pretty good idea of what works best. Whether it was The North Face, Merrill Lynch, Royal Robbins, Prudential Bache, Canterbury, or others, the plan always included:

- Customer and market input
- Research and reading about industry, competition, and trends
- A clear, succinct business definition
- Clear, concise qualitative and quantitative goals
- Comprehensive strategies (not just product or financing)
- Commitment by the team to the plan
- Expert input on critical variables

We simply didn't have the time to develop a lot of this on our own and Eight Inc. brought expert advice in areas where we were involved, such as wearable technologies, branding, intellectual property, and strategy. In addition, and maybe most importantly, Eight actually had worked on a number of projects with Big Silicon. Eight's team brought perspective. Today, they brought four people. One of them was the gregarious and insightful Lee Turlington, who had worked with me as my head of apparel sales and marketing and product development when I ran The North Face. He subsequently went on to spend more than ten years as head of apparel product development and wearable technologies for Nike.

I first met Lee drinking beer when he was my employee at The North Face. "It was my first month in the company," recalled Lee by phone a short while after the strategy meeting. "Hap was planning a party for Buckminster Fuller to come visit The North Face. We were building a geodesic dome tent." We were a young company and Lee came in as a raw materials specialist but he was involved, as we all were, in everything. "It was a special place, those early days in Berkeley," said Lee.

My philosophy then, as now, was to involve as many people as possible and to respect every opinion. That's why in Lee's 16 years with The North Face, as my company grew Lee Turlington's career grew. He started as a raw materials specialist, which he described as "an entry-level position," and by the time he left he was vice president of sales and marketing. Lee was bright and he learned a lot of my theories. He also had gone on to other highly successful consumer goods companies and got a very valuable, broader perspective. His outsider's view along with his partners from Eight Inc., I was sure, would bring us some help in creating our Ardica vision.

Lee, who now lived in Portland, Oregon, grew up in Clinton, North Carolina, a place he described as a typical small town. As a boy, he was fascinated by aerospace and NASA and everything in the Mercury program. He landed a scholarship in football as a linebacker at Lenoir-Rhyne University in North Carolina. While there, he became interested in mountain sports. He received a degree in economics, but it was the late 1970s so he decided music was the place for him. He pursued and finished a degree at the College of Recording Arts in San Francisco.

But finally, in 1977, Lee said he was "exhausted of being a poor student working all the time. I found my way to The North Face."

Lee was a big, fit guy—a linebacker from North Carolina with an oversized personality. He was new to the team when we met at the Buckminster Fuller planning party. He was talking loudly about sports, and we hit it off. It was brief, but I remember immediately liking how he spoke out about things, how he loved sports, as I did, and how he loved to laugh.

"I remember Hap as very intense, engaged, and driven," said Lee. "And at The North Face I learned appreciation for more than just the widget. There is the brand, the quality, the big association with premium things, things that add value."

After I sold The North Face, Lee stayed on a little while but then he moved to Fila at the peak of its brand growth. The company had started an outdoor winter sports category and Lee was working directly with the chairman of the company to set that up. His understanding of brand then grew even more when he became a global director of apparel for Nike's outdoor brand, All Conditions Gear (ACG).

He left Nike to become a consultant, running Turlington Inc., and it was in that role that he partnered with Eight Inc. According to Lee, Eight Inc., among other things, "creates experiential retail environments."

In addition to Lee, three others were attending the meeting: Eric Anderson, Wilhelm Oehl, and Daniel Iacofono. Eric was a tall, intense, and quiet former owner of the snowboard binding company Switch; Wilhelm was a designer who was designing world leading retail stores; and Daniel was a facilitator for the consulting firm MIG, also working with Eight Inc.

Before the meeting, as I sat drinking tea and coffee with my sales manager, Shawn Biega, in Starbucks across the street from the site of the meeting, we saw the Eight team pull up in a Lincoln Towncar limousine. "That's how to show up for a meeting," said Shawn as we watched them exit the limo and walk across the street. Yeah, heavy hitters.

Our meeting room was a square corner-of-the-building room with three couches set at 90-degree angles. Our "room" was actually just a section of a maze of rooms and hallways on this top floor. Down at the other end of the floor way above San Francisco, behind a glass door, others were involved in a different meeting that also needed computers, PowerPoint presentations, and drawing boards.

In our room, the atmosphere was San Francisco casual—not a lot of ties. The facilitator of the meeting, the affable Daniel Iacofono, was busy drawing and writing on a large whiteboard in front of the three couches. Daniel "is nationally recognized as an expert and innovator in the areas of community participation, consensus building, and facilitation," according the MIG website. When I saw him in action, it was easy to see why the folks from Eight Inc. work with him.

After we all took our seats and did the obligatory introductions—there were about a dozen in the room—Dick proceeded to give an overview of the company while Daniel followed along on the whiteboard with bullet point words and amazing on-the-fly artwork with multicolored Sharpies. He was fun to watch. His hand moved rapidly.

Dick told the story of Ardica and its promise and early struggles. He spoke of going several years relying on angel investors. He outlined the technology, the military project of lessening a soldier's weight load, and he talked about Big Silicon and how "One day they came by and said, 'Let's see what you've got.'"

As Dick told the story of Ardica's history, technology, and strategy, two things became clear about him. He was incredibly intelligent, and painfully shy. He spoke quietly and often with his eyes down. The business leaders of our company were here—finance, sales, operations—as well as high-energy consultants who were dealing with Big Silicon on a daily basis. We were trying to figure out an amazing exciting future, and

Dick was talking in monotone. And yet when he said something about, for instance, the potential to get our energy from a wind farm, he boiled it down simply and eloquently to, "It's a thing of beauty."

He talked about how our technology was the best, our team was the best. "On the technical side, we're in good shape," he said.

But, there were still issues. Lots of issues.

We were trying to develop two different fuels and we had to choose the one to go with for the F-43 project by December 1st if we were to meet Big Silicon's stated deadlines. We would have to build facilities for production, get all certifications (for both building and shipping the fuel), develop the packaging and marketing collateral, and finance all of this.

One of the fuels, sodium borohydride, is a well-known compound that we had uniquely tweaked to work in tiny, miniaturized fuel cells for the best efficiency and remarkably high energy density. Our fuel controller patents worked very elegantly with this fuel solution and, we believed, were essential to anyone wanting to develop miniaturized, portable consumer electronic devices.

The other fuel, alane (made from aluminum) showed potential for greater energy density but was currently very expensive to produce, and no one, to our knowledge, had ever made this type of product in anything other than small laboratory test quantities for rockets. Yes, it was rocket fuel—really. Our research had shown the primary patents in this area were with Russian developments. If we were skillful, we believed we could have our own patent on this fuel for use in miniaturized fuel cells. And we had commenced the patent paperwork on this.

Even more exciting, we had patent applications started on making this fuel at a sustainable, clean fuel site. So, our vision was for us to make our fuel cell fuel at this location, thereby "bottling," storing, and distributing clean fuel. Such a patent coupled with a partnership with Big Silicon would be a home run. Of course, no one had yet made commercial quantities of alane, and there were some unique twists required to make it applicable to miniaturized fuel cells. There was, however, a great deal of hope inside Ardica about alane and progress was being made every day.

Dick then talked about our business and financial strategies. He said the company was close to closing on our financing—financing that we all were painfully aware had been dragging on for 18 months— but that the negotiations with Big Silicon (they may invest, they may want just a Joint Development Agreement, they may want something else) were still ongoing. He explained that while the financing and the negotiations were two separate activities, over the course of his negotiations in the last few months they had (for good or bad) become inextricably intertwined.

He discussed how when he first arrived he got government contracts and he also talked about our upcoming applications for government stimulus money. "The strategy is to go get Obama's money," he said. "Somebody's going to get it. It may as well be us."

And since Dick was good at getting government grants, we were pursuing three separate ones with different partners, on different projects in different geographic areas. Dick didn't go into details in the meeting but essentially we were pursuing, with partners, two $6 million grants and one $1 million grant. This money would be helpful but there were no guarantees and a lot of strings attached. Still, he assured us that it looked promising.

But in my experienced business view we needed more than stimulus product development money. We needed predictable levels of cash and cash flow to build our business—infrastructure, brand, marketing. And we needed to arrive at an efficient, executable plan with buy-off from the whole team. That's why we were having this strategy meeting, to find a way to leverage our exciting and revolutionary technology into products and sales and to set up an actual platform to build a world-class business. With the right plan and the right level of investment we should be able to take the pressure off of the day-to-day decision making (where we had been forced to focus). We could then begin shifting from focusing on the urgent to focusing on the vital.

Jim Retzlaff, our CFO, was the next to speak. He kept his history lesson short, stating the obvious. "Cash has been a key concern for the company since the beginning." He discussed how money issues had made the company "caught up in urgent trivialization and that stops us from the key things." For instance, he said, he discovered when he arrived in January that the company didn't even have a business license. Jim added that the funding was crucial. The company would finally have to have a real budget, he said, but the influx of money would allow the company to do some vital things.

The question, of course, was "What is vital?

ARDICA WAS FOCUSED ON THREE MARKETS: consumer goods; the U.S. Military (hybrid battery and fuel cell systems development for the Communications-Electronics, Research, Development and Engineering Center, "CERDEC" contract); and the F-43 program for fuel cell development for Big Silicon.

Things got interesting in the meeting when we started talking about products. That's when my sales and marketing team got involved.

Greg Nevolo, who used to be head of Red Bull's aviation marketing program and was now a key player on our marketing team, leaned forward on the couch as he gave a PowerPoint presentation about our many opportunities—what we were doing and what we were considering. He talked so fast that it was almost like he'd been drinking Red Bull by the pint, but he just had so much information to get across that he pushed it.

There was a lot in our big picture. Our existing Moshi power system was already garnering big interest, and we had top-level partners. The Moshi included the flexible seven-pack of lithium-ion batteries, a microprocessor brain the team cleverly designed, and something we called the Technology Connector that allowed any number of consumer electronic items to plug in and recharge off of it.

Among the questions, as we continued to refine and develop our market strategy, was: "Can one thing run everything?" Could we make one microprocessor (e.g., a printed circuit board) and make it interchangeable? Or could our Moshi system be modified to be variable in terms of devices it would power? In other words, could we make it of interchangeable size and capacity so that the batteries could be connected together, Lego-like. This was the "modular Moshi" I mentioned earlier.

The goal, as Greg, Shawn, and then I tried to articulate, was to have something agnostic—not just specific to *our* heaters and *our* electronic devices. One that was able to power lots of different things. This would ensure broad relevance and adaptability. And, importantly, something that allowed us to focus on being *the* dominating global portable power supply company, not just an end-device electronic company.

Daniel Iacofono, with his magic Sharpie, took over the discussion for a while and got our group to agree that what we were doing was "enabling lifestyle with green personal modular power."

I loved the tagline but I warned in the meeting that we must be careful using the word "green" without doing our homework, because every company has some compromise. We would be green, but if someone held us up to a microscope, we would have to be sure to be able to pass inspection before we touted it.

When I got my turn, I saw no need to rehash old history. Instead I began talking about maximizing the return for the shareholders' investment. As soon as I started, I realized that I live for such moments, to inspire and transfer my knowledge and experience to a team of brilliant people working on a dream. I simply wanted to offer guidance and I thought my years of experience in brand building and business development could help Ardica's brand in this, its infant stage.

We aspired to be a worldwide brand and the leader in the field of green portable power on the go. And one key decision that was being made in the negotiations with Big Silicon was whether *we* could be a branded product, so that everything we sold had a clearly visible "Ardica-enabled" on the side. Or whether we would be a private label fuel supplier for the F-43 and thus become solely dependent on our branded partner—in essence we would be hoping Big Silicon wouldn't develop the its own next generation F-43, whatever that might be.

The difference between the two options—a brand versus a private label supplier—as I demonstrated with numbers, charts and graphs, could mean as much as an additional $130 million in exit valuation if we chose the path to become a recognized brand. That was, we estimated, a difference of $10 per share by 2012.

I wanted to build a brand and build it quickly—not just because I am skilled at it, but also because of the extra $130 million it would mean for Ardica's shareholders. Our underlying idea was to partner with top-quality companies with strong brand identities, and then ride the coattails of these companies with their established reputations and credibility. We were building our brand "from the top down" by only working with the most important brands that were opinion leaders in sport, outdoor, and fashion apparel, and in the consumer electronics market. These were, in fact, different pyramids with different opinion leaders inside each one. We needed multiple partners—all undisputed opinion leaders in their respective niches. Getting Big Silicon on board with putting our name on the outside of the product was a key to making Ardica-Enabled: mimic the "Intel Inside" partnership that pushed so many computer companies forward.

Although we were still developing our exact fuel for our fuel cell, the complete power system—whether it was fuel cell, battery, or a hybrid combination of battery and fuel cell—was our "killer app." By being adaptable, micro-portable, flexible, wearable, and off the grid, it offered, as Greg said while leaning forward, "a once in a lifetime opportunity." No company yet had this space in the consumer's mind. If we could get it, we could dominate this market niche.

There were also, as I pointed out, opportunities for failure at both ends of the extreme:

- We could try too much and get spread too thin and accomplish little or nothing.

- We could become solely a private label supplier to Big Silicon and miss the branding opportunity of a lifetime and all the huge opportunities with our commercial Moshi partners and the military. Or worse, Big Silicon could just cancel the F-43 project and we would miss everything.

We were determined not to fail. But we were not totally naïve. We were all excited about the future but we were aware, as Lee Turlington pointed out, "Role clarity is very important to success. You are creating the Manhattan Project."

As the meeting came to a close I was more excited than ever about Ardica's future, and we began to figure out how to moving forward. But one thing quietly nagged at me as it had for more than a year. Our latest round of fundraising had begun in January 2008 (yes, 2008, and yes, it had dragged on to June 2009) and still was not finished.

Jim described the funding as being an almost biblical game changer for the company. "I think of 'before funding' and 'after funding' as sort of like the difference between the B.C. and A.D. calendar," said Jim. "We won't have to watch our pennies as much. We'll more have to watch our dollars."

In our strategy meeting, Dick said the money was a week or so away. I hoped so.

15

"Let's cut right to the chase. They don't have the best guy in the world going to get the money," said Lee Turlington in a phone interviewafter the strategy meeting. "You need to rely on the sizzle as well as the steak."

Dick was our guy to get the money. Our story had lots of sizzle but somehow Dick had failed to bring that across. Lee says the story of our technology, branding efforts, partnerships, and possible partnership with Big Silicon along with the combined resumes of Dick and myself should have been able to attract investors. "The talent of the two—talk about something marketable to the main world," said Lee.

"The company has a remarkable and incredibly strong and talented engineering group," says Lee. "And it has an experienced and talented marketing and sales team and leadership. But the weakness is a lack of a clearly defined strategic plan and a lack of funding."

Meanwhile our management issues were becoming apparent to outsiders, and I feared they were becoming apparent also to investors. "I told Dick you have got to solve your differences [with Hap] to make this work," said Lee.

Our differences were much more than just in our backgrounds, military versus Berkeley. Or in our departments, engineering versus marketing. Sure, those were the prisms through which we each saw the world.

But in the company, people could feel us pulling it in different directions. The differences were especially apparent to everyone in the company with regard to how we valued the strategy meeting. And this, I think, spoke volumes about our management styles. I wanted to be inclusive. I valued many opinions, and I wanted synchronicity between the engineering department and the marketing department.

Dick did not want the two groups in the same meeting. This was clear to everyone. Quite simply, Dick lacked confidence in the strategic planning process. Because of his lack of confidence, strategic planning at Ardica stalled without proceeding into creating that plan that might have gotten us money. "We were successful at putting on paper what the big money opportunities and critical projects are," said Lee. "But we didn't delve any further."

He added that he saw our company essentially being run by "two guys who aren't necessarily on the same page...In most companies that are successful, one guy runs things. But open and inclusive usually wins out over closed and directional."

THE LONGEST EASTER

August 2009

16

Oｎ ｊｕｎｅ 26ｔｈ, our CFO, Jim Retzlaff asked in an email, "The time from Good Friday to Easter was two weeks (not three days), right?"

It was two weeks after he used the B.C./A.D. analogy in the strategy meeting about "before round B funding" and "after round B funding," and he was still waiting on money.

Two months after the strategy meeting, on August 12th, money still had not arrived. To use Jim's analogy as a metaphor, the body had not risen yet.

We continued to wait for round B to close, which led to lots of frustration on the team. This was not a five-person company of college kids anymore. The college kids were now grownups, there were other grownups on board as well, and these ongoing money problems, which were promised to be over months ago, led to some very interesting exchanges within the company. I was as frustrated as anyone. We needed money and, frankly, we should have had it a long time ago.

In January 2008, when Dick and I took over operations of the company, we set a goal of raising $5 million of new equity to sustain us, but we had different opinions on how to procure round B.

My sales director, Shawn Biega, and I introduced Dick to a professional investment banker, who was ready to do the raise. I advocated hiring a professional. In my extensive entrepreneurial experience, I had found fundraising to be a time-consuming and distracting process. It usually took at least six months of time that was better spent doing real work.

Dick disagreed. He preferred to raise the money himself and said that, with his contacts, it would be relatively easy. He also theorized to me and others that the A round investors might come into the B round.

Rounds of financing are labeled A, B, C, etc. to denote their natural sequence. An easy way to think about it is that the A round finances development, the B round finances the go-to-market/product launch and the C round finances the expansion of sales. Each round has some legal rights (including pricing) that vary, and therefore one round cannot be started without closing a previous round. In theory you can have as many rounds as you want, but in practice it is a bad idea to have too many rounds because it makes you less attractive to subsequent investors due to the complexities that arise from different investors with different rights in the different rounds. It also makes you look like you have been around *forever* and that your deal has been "shopped" numerous times. It connotes weakness, not strength. Therefore, making the B round big, and making it our last round, was our goal.

You can write and execute the round any way that investors will accept. We set the B round up to close all at once. You can also do a rolling close where you set a goal—say $5 million—but once you reach a reasonable amount—say $4 million—you close and then take any more as it comes in up to the pre-agreed $5 million. The advantage of this is that you have access to the money right away and the investors become shareholders at that point.

The usual argument for making a round close all at once is simple. No one wants to be in unless enough capital is raised to see the company through to success. If there isn't enough capital, an additional investor may be needed to save the company. This new investor can then dictate new terms, usually heavily weighted in his favor. I pushed for a rolling close after the $4 million plateau was reached because, frankly, we were out of money and needed cash quickly. In extreme cases the demands of the last investor in are draconian—what is called a "cram down." Investors fear being caught in a future cram down. That risk seemed less to me with $4 million in the bank than where we were at that moment.

Dick decided to do it his way. As CEO, it was his call to make and I don't think he had any doubts that he could get all the money—and very quickly. His approach was to seek out a multitude of small investors instead of seeking out one or two large investors. My experience was that this would be time-consuming for Dick and take longer than necessary for the company. But Dick was optimistic.

He approached fundraising one small investor at a time. This chasing small investments at the expense of discussions with large investors struck me as stepping over dollars to pick up pennies.

As for the use of a professional fundraiser, Dick said he didn't want to pay the high fees associated with an outside fundraising group. Even Jim Retzlaff had described the fees of fundraising groups as bordering on usury.

But sometimes cheap is expensive and expensive is cheap.

Time was passing and no money was coming in. By July 2008, my sales director, Shawn Biega, and I talked, and we felt we couldn't wait any longer, so we stepped in and pushed the process. Through our efforts with our friends and Ardica's friends and family, and combined with Dick, we raised a total of $1,260,000—Dick calls this the Hap Klopp Fund. In spring of 2009, eight months later, Jim Retzlaff and his family kicked in $200,000. Dick raised an additional $675,000. Then a short while after this, Dick raised $60,000 more. There was talk that we were about to get $75,000 more and then we would finally officially close.

That would make for a raise of $2.17 million over a period of 20 months, instead of the $5 million "in a couple of months" that was expected. Month after month, the team heard the same names of possible investors who were going to make up the balance of the B round. In the end, only a couple actually signed on.

But by August 2009, the B round was still not officially closed. Fortunately, even without closing the round we were able to access some of the money we took in by designating it as a loan that would convert into equity upon the close of the round. Our prestigious law firm helped but, given the complexity of this change, the firm had to work a lot more hours and, of course, they charged several thousand more dollars. The move also required us to pay interest on the loans rather than treat the money as equity.

We needed to close it quickly in order to allow us to aggressively move into some other way of finding the additional funding we had failed to secure. Why was our company, which was collaborating on developing a product with Big Silicon, and had high-level outdoor products customers such as Redwing, Sitka, and Mountain Hardwear, and which was doing apparel development with prestigious customers like Hugo Boss and Spyder, having trouble raising money? This was a legitimate question now spoken aloud by many in Ardica.

The answers were obtuse and complicated. But we were flat out of money. There was no time left for intellectualizing. The solution I pushed for was yet another round of fundraising, but this time the fundraising would be by a professional fundraising group, Legend Merchant Group orchestrated by myself. Legend are bankers who were introduced to us by friends of Shawn.

Frankly, the B round money we had collected would not be sufficient to pay for all past due expenses, let alone fund the all-out assault necessary to build the company and the all-important brand. We had to curtail many planned and budgeted activities—visits to customers, marketing, trade shows, product development, and even accounting—just to stay alive. This was not sustainable.

We had no extra time. We were now missing delivery of key products to partners and potential partners because we didn't have the money to pay some of our suppliers. As Greg wrote in an email, "Every day I receive another email from our vendors, begging, asking, yelling at us to pay them."

We were doing the best we could—some would say remarkably well—but we were jeopardizing our relationships with Mountain Hardwear, Sitka, and some very promising sample orders for 2010 with Spyder, Hugo Boss, and L.L. Bean. We were also in danger of missing a huge opportunity with Redwing. But we had recently learned that in order to be allowed into the oil and natural gas exploration field, we must pass something called "Intrinsic Safety," in order to ensure that our product wouldn't cause problems around explosive materials. I feared that we didn't even have time to research it further.

And shortly, I feared, we would be jeopardizing our ability to deliver on our promised developments to Big Silicon. We had spent too much energy managing who and when to pay, and then searching for vendors to replace those who no longer extended us credit. We needed, instead, to spend our energy executing.

I imagined that our influential and high-volume global partners we had cultivated—Hugo Boss, Spyder and Big Silicon—were, in fact, assessing our viability. They expected us to be a world-class supplier and partner, which meant operationally and financially meeting every promise, every timeline, and every request. But we were slipping, and thus risking those relationships.

Meanwhile, we waited for the rest of the money from investors to come in. Money that Dick told us had been promised. But promises are just words, and you can't pay bills with those. As promises go, we seemed to be passing them forward and that was troubling. Money issues were slithering through the company, department by department. In more than one case the issue was not just internally how to deal with the lack of resources, but explaining to folks outside of Ardica that we don't, at this moment, have money. *But we will. Trust us, we will.*

17

L ATE AUGUST. "I'm under an enormous amount of stress," said Jim
Retzlaff. "I'm in the middle of it. People contact me when they're
not paid."

On August 14th, we received the last of the promised investments.
Unfortunately it was only $75,000. And finally, 20 months into the pro-
cess of fundraising, we decided we had to finalize our B round and work
towards a new way of funding the company going forward. Closing the
B round was not simple and required more costly legal work from our
law firm. Because we did not reach the $5 million goal, we were legally
required to go back to all investors who had put up their money and ask
them for permission to close the round at the $2.1 million we had re-
ceived. We also asked them to convert their loans (money we had already
spent) to equity. Whew! They all saw a great future and agreed.

Onward. After all the hard work, we shouldn't have needed another
round of money, but we did, quite desperately.

As CFO, Jim was the obvious focal point for anger at our inability
to pay bills on schedule. Being an apologist was not a job he signed up
for, and the idea that this was still happening to Ardica in late August
2009 was beyond frustrating to me. Jim heard it every day. He and his
family had invested $200,000 in Ardica and so the pressure was personal
too. Yet despite all of the financial headaches and despite the unfulfilled

promise of a big round B close, Jim believed like an evangelist—a realistic evangelist who discovered after Easter that "I would say Jesus didn't rise. Jesus is dead."

It was true. The lackluster results of our round B now meant that we needed plan B.

But Jim believed in a second coming, like we all believed because our team was the best and the brightest and the most motivated…and we simply would not fail. All any of us had to do was look around and we knew this. Yet money creates tension…and "lack of money creates *so much* tension," said Jim.

The tension was like a throbbing headache pulsing through the company and then outward to our vendors and customers. "Since we don't have the money to buy supplies, we can't supply Montana," said Sergio Galvan, our manufacturing manager and the person in charge of setting up our Montana outsource factory to manufacture the Moshi. "They can't really function the way they were expected to."

Meanwhile Shawn Biega, our sales manager, said, "If we don't deliver, I don't know what I'm going to do with my life. My name will be mud in the industry."

The problem with money issues is that once they become evident they permeate a company. "This is the hardest issue I've ever been presented with," said marketing director Greg Nevolo. "I have no money to do anything."

Tibor Fabian, our CTO, said, "It forces you to question every day what is most important."

And though money issues forced everyone in the company to prioritize, the engineering side viewed the money issue differently than the sales and marketing side viewed it. Perspective explained everything.

"I'm glad I don't have to worry about it," said Martin Corpos, a design and product engineer. "It's not my job. I come to work every day and I get a paycheck every two weeks." Martin did a lot more than that but he stated the fact in a very specific way that is befitting an engineering mindset.

Even the engineers who are more involved in the money issues, specifically Tibor and Dan Braithwaite, who was placed in charge of the F-43 project, saw the money issues as mere obstacles, not hindrances. "We'll always find a way," said Dan. "There's no magic algorithm. You just weigh the details of the situation and the severity of the impact...Frankly, I've seen worse. It's definitely not the tightest spot we've been in. But the stakes are bigger, of course...I think life is hard. Let's not kid ourselves. I keep fighting hard. If you keep working hard, something good is going to happen. "

As much as I love optimism, this seemed more like blind optimism than anything based on numbers. Engineers and business people, it seemed, saw numbers in different ways. Nevertheless, engineers were also owed money and Tibor acknowledged, "My wife is grumpy about the money."

Still, Dan's "work hard, something good will happen philosophy is what we all believed. But recently there really had been something of a disconnect between engineering and sales and marketing. It was probably, more than anything, a disconnect between Dick and myself. Maybe we were both at fault. Money issues amplified everything.

"I worry," said Dan. "I'm concerned about how everybody is getting along."

Lee Turlington, one of the Eight Inc. consultants who facilitated our June strategy meeting, noticed the differences when we were first planning that meeting and especially "Dick's lack of confidence in the process" of strategic planning. Lee saw the competing visions and styles between Dick and me. And he said this, which is probably true: "Hap's not a perfect angel in the relationship."

But I was not trying to be a perfect angel. I was trying to save the company. Bankruptcy was a real possibility if we didn't get more money. Lee knew that. Everyone knew that. In fact Dick knew that I was trying to save the company—just as he was trying to save the company. At this point, though, it was becoming clear we had different visions, different styles, and different skill sets. Did our differences affect our ability to raise money? I didn't know, but they were certainly compounding the tension caused by that inability.

"I feel like I'm just going around the block again," said Miriam. She remembered the split between founders Tom Covington and Tobin Fisher and she saw some similarities in the situation with Dick and me. "Employees, to a degree, are choosing sides," she said.

Neither one of us wanted it that way, but we disagreed on important things and it affected almost everyone in the company. For instance, Lee described the June strategy meeting this way: "We basically had a group therapy session."

The idea of strategic planning is to get the entire team focused, laser-like, on a few specific goals. There is more to it than that, including deadlines and accountability assignments, but the goal is to get everyone working in unison. It's a noble goal. Unfortunately we were not there and our planning session, as Lee pointed out, hadn't gotten us there. It did, however, begin the essential (in my opinion) matter of dialogue in the company.

Dick, I think, placed a lower value on open ongoing dialogue. Remember, he was reluctant to have the meeting and then insisted on separate sessions for the engineers and the executive team. Sales and engineering, by design, were not in the same room at the same time. This was one thing we clearly disagreed upon.

Despite that disagreement, Dick said the strategy meeting accomplished exactly what I had hoped it would. "In the first place, the one thing that was new was the idea of closer integration between the marketing and sales guys and the technical guys on the army project and on these technical projects."

This new idea was actually an old one that the sales and marketing team had been raising for a while and, more than two months later, it remained an idea unimplemented. It seemed there was not enough time, resources, or, frankly commitment to finding a singularity of purpose.

We each wanted success. We all expected it and we were each working incredibly hard toward success but we had not begun executing a strategic plan because we didn't have a strategic plan. Lack of strategic plan, said Lee, was a big part of our inability to raise money.

Our differences had become apparent to both Dick and me. It was dawning on me that despite Dick's engineering brilliance, he was not comfortable building a complete business coupling invention with commercialization. I think he instead receded back to what he knew, organizing a project to build an invention rather than building a business. He believed the company could sell a project or a few patents that would come from that project for tens of millions of dollars or more.

Dick believed that our F-43 project for Big Silicon, backed by solid patents, fit that plan perfectly. All we had to do was work like hell to get Big Silicon to buy us. But this presupposes that they would make an actual decision to launch a product with our technology, a decision we'd been told wasn't coming until early- or mid-2010. The old saying is, "If you are a hammer, everything looks like a nail." And in Dick's case, he was gravitating to what he was comfortable with, which was the process of invention. That is great, but it needed to be paired with commercialization.

Unfortunately, I was having a hard time convincing Dick that we needed to build a total business—setting up an accounting system, shipping, infrastructure, and, most importantly, getting sales and building the Ardica brand. I wanted to do this because all industry figures showed that a company using this approach would greatly outstrip the valuation for a project-based entity that only held patents.

Underpinning almost every conversation was the lack of money, that capitalistic root of all evil. It seeped into all parts of the strategy meeting and subsequently, onto a lot of desks, especially Jim's, and onward to a lot of "please understand" phone calls that too many of our employees had to make.

Yes, we were Ardica and we were out to change the world…if we could only pay our bills.

18

"**M**AKING PAYROLL HAS BEEN A CHALLENGE," said Jim. Our situation was messy, exciting, and stressful for all the wrong reasons. We should have been ramping up production, not trying to find a way to pay our employees and pay for supplies. We should have been able to raise money, and our budgeting process should have been more disciplined than how Tibor described our current process: "It's like, almost, who spends it first."

This race to spend stemmed, of course, from the lack of capital. Waiting for round B to close and bring in the promised large influx of necessary cash was straining the company. "My fear for Ardica if they start to run out of money," said Lee, "is that they're going to start to lose their talent."

Lee was right to worry. People were considering leaving. And although lack of money was the symptom that could drive many out of the company, the cause of lack of money merely reflected a bigger problem. We lacked an overall strategic vision, a vision that would be compelling to investors, and we lacked a strategy to raise money. Dick had been in charge. He had made all the contacts and all the B round decisions. "They were wealthy friends of Dick," said Jim of Dick's contacts. "They liked the story and believed in Dick."

It didn't help that he was trying to raise money during one of the worst economic downturns in American history. The investors Dick approached, those wealthy personal friends, "have been hammered just like everybody else," said Jim.

Lee said, "the Angel environment [has been] completely unstable for the last 15 months. Even the highest-worth individuals have been drastically affected." The faltering economy clearly hurt the investors Dick was courting. As investment houses fell and credit markets dried up in September 2008, we were nine months into round B. The Hap Klopp Fund had brought in more than we were asked for, but with the economy collapsing, we waited on Dick to bring in the bigger portion of round B.

One potential investor in round B was a personal friend of Dick's from Pittsburgh who had previously invested in Ardica and had promised he would kick in at least $500,000 to $600,000. But each time he was pressed, he added new conditions. He finally invested $250,000, but mostly it was little investments from others that rolled in. And, there were numerous promises to invest differing amounts from almost a dozen people. Dick passed these along to the Ardica team, along with the myriad of follow-on stories on why it never worked out. Sometimes they just had to move the money from one account to the other, but it was complicated and could take a little while; one investor was working on a really big deal that would free up a lot of cash any day now, etc.

Dick believed the stories and the promises and passed them on. It was just a matter of getting everyone to agree on the same deal at the same time, he said to us. These were his negotiations and we all waited. From January 2008 through June 2009 and past the Strategy Meeting, we waited. And when round B finally closed on August 14th, 2009 with a whimper and not a bang, we were left to wonder what went wrong and, more importantly, what would we do next?

The problem, according to Dick, was that "investors do not sign up for the apparel part of the business by itself. You have to have the technical fuel cell to raise the money."

And Jim, who dealt on a secondary level with investors and was, like a lot of us, an investor himself, said from his perspective, "Investors do not believe in the jackets. They really believe in what we are doing with (Big Silicon)."

My take was a bit different. The investors were confused. Ardica's story kept changing (admittedly getting better), but the change confused them. First there were fuel cells for clothing. That changed to a battery array system (Moshi) for clothing. Then nine months into the process, we added Big Silicon to the equation.

I think we also appeared sketchy to some, or at least less than professional. For instance, we had no monthly financial statements because Dick believed they were unnecessary and too expensive to generate. Well, they were actually very necessary. More than one existing investor told me, "I've never seen a company with this much money invested that didn't have monthly financials."

And then there was the ever-evolving story surrounding Big Silicon. Ah yes, Big Silicon, the "high profile Silicon Valley technology firm" that we ever-so-vaguely described to potential investors. Big Silicon was the potential tipping point, our big chip that we should have played very carefully and also very quietly.

But from where I watched, it wasn't vague, it wasn't quiet, and nothing about our approach—in mentioning Big Silicon to investors or in negotiating with them —had been strategic. Therefore, it appeared our approach on both sides had backfired.

I believe that when Big Silicon first approached us, we had the leverage because we had what they wanted. It was that simple.

They had been looking elsewhere and would theoretically continue to look elsewhere, but they approached us and made it clear that we had the best approach to the science of developing fuel cells that they had found, and that they thought our idea could be developed to go to market. It could, as we knew, change the world.

We had what Big Silicon wanted.

At that moment, I believed, we needed a strategic approach to negotiating with them, launching a consumer brand, and raising money to fund all of this. We had no strategy. Instead of us making things happen, things began to happen.

First, as round B dragged on while we waited for investors to coordinate efforts in an "I'll-invest-if-he'll-invest" way, Dick began to sweeten the story, because he could. It was no longer just Ardica with revolutionary fuel cell technology launching from the platform of the army projects and Moshi battery system.

Now the story had a new ingredient: Big Silicon.

Adding them as a partner suddenly made our company more than just a great story and a great bet, but in the eyes of some almost a sure bet. It became a big part of Dick's investment pitch and potential investors were even more excited. But there was one caveat: they wanted to be sure that Big Silicon was serious.

Potential investors wanted a signed Joint Development Agreement (JDA). The JDA would serve many purposes. Perhaps most important to the investors would be that a formal piece of paper would prove the validity of our relationship and that it wasn't just some dream. On a more practical level it would define the rights and obligations of the two partners that would hopefully avoid future conflicts. Principal above those was the need to define who owned what rights to the patents that might flow from our joint efforts. But a JDA is complex and takes a lot of time, and negotiating with a savvy huge Silicon Valley company is predictably thorough, rigorous, and complicated. Our circular logic began.

There were meetings with Dick's investor friends and early development meetings with representatives of Big Silicon. Dick remained convinced that the elements were going to come together. He convinced us all. I introduced him to friends of mine who might invest, including one from Salt Lake City, Utah. "He's a personal friend of Hap's. He was going to invest $100,000 but in the end he fell out because we didn't have the agreement signed yet on F-43," said Dick.

The more the F-43 was sold as topic A, the more it hurt round B.

"I kept hearing any day now, we're signing the deal. The deal is going to close," said Jim. "We always thought these wealthy people were going to come through. I believed that, even so much as saying to people, 'It's going to happen tomorrow.'"

Throughout the company, day after day and week after week and month after month, the word spread that the deal was about to close. Marketing director Greg Nevolo described a "running joke among employees that it's always going to close next week."

And Miriam noted, "Whether it's a project or round B, two weeks later you hear the same thing again." Good things remained always just around the corner.

Meanwhile, the two deals, a JDA with Big Silicon and round B, became intertwined. The financing became contingent on the JDA with Big Silicon, while Big Silicon needed us to be able to prove we were a viable partner and supplier. So Dick decided to ask Big Silicon to be an investor. As part of Dick's pursuit of Big Silicon's investment he had to show them our out-of-date financial statements. Thus, they now knew our precarious financial situation and the reason we needed to raise some money fast. In essence they now knew they could just wait until we went bankrupt, buy our patents at discount, and hire a few of our people while the rest of the employees became unemployed.

During this time, employees were using personal credit cards for company expenses because the company had no money. Others tried to use the company credit card, only to discover it bounced. Dick calmly assured the team they would be paid back as soon as the rest of round B closed.

In this startup with ambitious and lofty goals, there were a million things going on. We were setting up a factory in Montana, getting safety certifications, pursuing patents, lowering costs by buying less expensive components for the Moshi and making them work, testing equipment in real world situations, selling, marketing, paying vendors, and developing partnerships, all while Dan and Tibor and the other engineers were doing the actual science and design work. Without a plan, forward was a direction with too many arrows, and without money, forward looked a lot like neutral.

Yet we kept pushing and somehow we moved every project forward despite the obstacles. As Dan says, "There's always stuff you can do to improve. There's always a solution. It depends how far you're willing to go to prove it."

"All of our projects are related," Dan said. "They're all working towards the same technological principle of portable power."

And Greg added, "Everybody wants to be part of a game-changing company. We're all still engaged."

The idea of seeding the market and creating the Ardica brand for the fuel cell to fit seamlessly into, while riding along on the good name of other top brands such as Mountain Hardwear, Hugo Boss, Spyder, and eventually Big Silicon was the plan that, if executed, would make us a worldwide brand. But doing this required capital. And the design of the fuel cell project also required a lot of resources. We all knew the opportunity was enormous. However, Dan rightly pointed out that, "You're never going to be in a startup where you're going to have infinite resources. Finite resources are a fact of life."

19

COMPETITION FOR RESOURCES in a startup is a fact of life. If you want to make it you had better have some resilience and ingenuity. The engineers had figured methods to design their way through money problems even though Tibor admitted "because you don't have enough money, you end up wasting your time." And wasting time wasn't exactly the best use of a PhD like Tibor. However, he believed our company needed tighter budgeting, especially when there wasn't enough money. When asked how do you tell someone in the company that they can't do something, he responded simply, "How do you talk to your daughter and tell her that she can't eat chocolate every day?" When he said it, he grinned and raised his eyebrows as if to add, in his Eastern European engineering-organized way, "C'mon!"

The first two times Tibor was interviewed for this book were during lunch. In both instances he ate a Mexican salad from a takeout place across the street from our building. It seemed he never wasted time. While a question was asked, he'd take a bite and then he'd finish chewing and look up, his clear eyes staring into yours and answer in a straightforward way, always insightful. He used English, not his first language, although by virtue of living in San Francisco it was now his primary language. His words were always precise, pointed, and passionate. He was also logical, methodically attacking the Mexican salad and then stopping to say something like, "I'm not going to beat myself to death that I couldn't bend the laws of physics. But I'm trying…When you wake up in the morning and you're excited about what you're going to do that day; I'm like a little geek in heaven." As he finished the sentence, his grin was contagious.

When Greg Nevolo had time to interview for this book, he also was multi-tasking and also not wasting a moment. But as marketing director, the words flew in a torrent out of him. Once, at a dinner party at my house for the marketing team, Greg sat folding and refolding a red napkin, listening to a story, probably thinking about two others, and tapping his foot while changing his sitting position every couple of minutes. Energy and passion explode from him. "We have to build a brand," he declared. "Everything I've learned in my whole life is to create an emotional connection for the customers. It has to be real. *This is the coolest thing I've ever seen.* You can't put shit on a plate and say this is the coolest shit I've ever seen." The Moshi and all that it signaled for the future, was the coolest thing the sales and marketing team had ever seen—a game-changing product.

Greg and Tibor, with equal passions and wildly divergent skill sets, were the necessary ingredients for a successful company. But those two skill sets of engineering and sales and marketing were involved in not just the personal struggle of mine and Dick's competing visions for the company. The engineers and the sales and marketing team were in some way choosing strategic sides in the management struggle, but the bigger question that we were in the midst of was a philosophical one: Do you sell what you have designed? Or do you design what you can sell?

"Maybe it's a classic struggle in an organization," said Jim. "The tension between sales and engineering. The salesman want to sell and make the customer happy but the problem is the engineers are tasked with making the changes the customer wants." And underlying that, as Jim knew too well, were the financial issues. In his role as CFO, Jim had one of the few neutral views and yet it was high enough up to see the big picture. "I'm Switzerland," he said.

But he was also observant, and if he had the time and resources he could have easily just followed the money. But he didn't have time or resources to actually generate monthly financials, so he could only speak anecdotally. "The engineers want to spend $1,000 on gadgets and nuts and bolts and might not be able to, and yet the sales and marketing team goes to a trade show and spends $12,000 for what looks like a party," says Jim. "It looks like Hap's team has spent a lion's share of the money that has come into the company."

"Looks like" are the operative words here. With no up-to-date monthly financials, the only numbers generated were those I generated myself for sales and marketing expenditures. So I knew what our team had spent. And from the figures I had generated I could see that it was far less than had been spent in other parts of the company—lawyers for example. Or lobbyists. And, in fact, I bet no one thought of employee salary and benefits as expenses, but they were our biggest expense. Those brilliant engineers, after all, when they were paid, were well-paid.

But, in fact, our team had spent some money and we had used that money to seed the worldwide market with the Ardica name. We had been out in the field explaining how our product works and how big of a coup it was to get our unknown brand onto the skiwear of the United States Olympic team alongside Spyder, the well known and respected brand. We had received orders and placement for our product in some of the most prestigious sports and apparel retailers in the country: REI, L.L. Bean, Cabelas, The Territory Ahead, and Backcountry.com. It was a list of retailers most brands, not to mention a new one, would die for. What we had accomplished in a mere 20 months was mind-boggling, considering that we were only now actually about to launch our first product.

Yes we had spent some money, but far from a lion's share of the money. And we got bang for our buck. While a standard industry rollout of a new product, including advertising and trade shows, could cost $250,000, we were able to leverage our contacts and get our products into the hands of some of the most famous and respected people in the industry, all for about $30,000. It was money well spent. We were getting national press and recognition from top influencers, including Olympic skiers Lindsey Vonn, Ted Ligety, and Julia Mancuso. The marketing and selling was working wonderfully, but we all expected round B to be bigger and close sooner. We thought there would be more money so that proportionally the sales and marketing share would have been an even smaller percentage. This lack of money as well as the tension between Dick and myself had caused the marketing budget to be an even bigger source of tension than its usual drama-producing role in most companies.

Everything at Ardica was at such an *almost* stage. We were balanced on a high wire and half the company thought the other half was leaning too far to one side. Meanwhile the other half kept trying to tell the first side that if you'd just let us reach a little further we could grab a balloon to carry us to the sky. Neither side understood the other completely, but we somehow held the balance.

20

DIFFERENT PEOPLE OFFERED the same assessment, but Shawn said it best: "On more than one occasion, Eric saved the company."

Eric Folsom, our manufacturing and outsourcing manager, was located logistically, figuratively, and literally in the middle. His desk was just inside the large open doorway that separated the South Side, sales and marketing, from the North Side, the engineering side. He sat on the North Side, the engineering side, at a desk that you passed going in either direction through the door. If Jim Retzlaff, our CFO, could claim to be Switzerland, then Eric was located in the DMZ. He was tall with dark hair, a thinnish build and the droopy eyes of someone who worked too many odd hours. He made things happen that, by all rights, shouldn't have happened. "I've got to deal with the consequences of unpaid bills," said Eric.

While Dick and I disagreed on the vision, and then the lack of money brought our disagreements out of our own heads and into the company atmosphere, and while the engineering and sales teams each seemed to implicitly pick sides, Eric Folsom quietly went about saving the company by dealing with everything else.

"My title varies," he said. "Some days I am design manufacturing officer, or safety compliance officer, or shipping manager, or head of manufacturing outsourcing. So I guess I am Manufacturing Outsourcing Shipping Art Inventory Compliance Officer." He put "MOSAIC" on his business card.

Launching our new Moshi product to a worldwide, if limited, audience with a miniscule budget was a daunting task. Add in the fact that the Moshi was a portable power system requiring lots of different kinds of costly safety compliance certifications and the task became more complicated. To put it in perspective, the 2009 costs of certifications to Ardica exceeded all advertising and trade show costs combined.

Meanwhile, we tried to cut costs while also making slight design modifications, plus we had to get the various parts to ship on time from factories across the world, especially China, to an assembly plant in Montana, and then get the finished product to brand partners on time to meet critical deadlines. Eric was in charge of all of that.

So far, he had managed to meet deadlines, or find a way to position us to expect to meet deadlines, with unpaid bills ringing in his ears. It was an incredible amount to put on his plate, and almost everything he did could seem, on first glance, to be overwhelmingly complex. And it was all, in fact, overwhelmingly important.

For instance, safety compliance is an alphabet-soup maze of necessary and recommended certifications for the use, shipping, Hazmat-rules disposal, and electronic safety of our product. Testing, with consumer safety in mind, had to be performed on all Ardica products entering the marketplace.

And the standards of different countries must be met by a global brand, which we planned to be. If you look on many electronic products, you will see initials like CSA, TUV, UL, and others stamped on. In order to get these stamps of approval, which are essentially entry points into any marketplace, your product must undergo lots of destructive testing. Basically, if it's hard to destroy your product—or nothing bad happens, like a fire or an explosion when you do destroy your product—that is good. If your product is able to withstand heat and cold and humidity and gravity and all sorts of other possible conditions that a laboratory can come up with, the product theoretically eventually gets the stamp of approval.

More than one stamp is necessary because, for instance, the CSA stamp is Canadian, while the TUV is typically needed in the E.U., and the UL stamp, which means United Laboratories (a private lab that tests for government standards), is needed in the United States. Among the things they check for are materials (issues like fire retardancy), electrical safety, and warnings that should be applied to the product.

But there is more. For our Moshi heated jacket system, it needs to pass another test required by the Department of Transportation. This part consists of eight tests:

- Altitude simulation
- Thermal test (extreme hot and cold, cycled 10 times, swinging every 30 minutes)
- Vibration test
- Shock
- External short circuit
- Impact
- Overcharge
- Forced discharge

In addition, the Moshi's alphabet soup appetite required FCC certification (or EMC testing, as it is called). In this process, the product was taken into a controlled environment and an antenna is used to find out what it was actually radiating. "This process is important to make sure you are not going to cause any disruption in the emergency frequency and also with TV signals and anything else," said Eric. The results of this test generally lead to restructuring parts of your printed circuit board (PCB) and sometimes adding ferrites, a sort of magnet, to reduce what's known as electrical noise (electrical impulses that spread outward).

This represented just a small portion of the things that Eric had to keep up with while Dick and I bickered about the future of the company. By the way, our fundraising sluggishness did not exactly make things easier for anyone, especially the guy who worked in the DMZ.

Eric Folsom was raised in Milwaukee, Wisconsin—actually in five different cities in Wisconsin, although he at first calls it all just Milwaukee. He is distinctively straightforward. "My dad was a hatchet man. They'd ship him from business to business and he'd have to come in and tell a company that there was a big layoff."

Nowadays, they'd call that a turnaround specialist.

Anyway, after a high school career that was wrapped around a lot of skydiving, Eric entered the navy as an aviation electronics technician, and for a while it was good, and then he had "a mid-life crisis almost." Unable to convince himself that electronics was for him, he decided to pursue his second hobby, culinary arts. In January 2003, he realized he wanted to go to culinary school, so he asked an Admiral for help in getting out and into culinary school.

"He said, 'Cook me your best meal,'" recalled Eric.

Eric cooked the Admiral cornish game hens with bearnaise sauce. But he had to improvise by, for instance, fermenting alcohol from apple juice because, of course, alcohol is not carried on a navy ship. Well, the Admiral liked the meal, gave the recommendation, and Eric went to culinary arts school. In March 2004, he graduated. But a few months working in a few different restaurants convinced him that although he loved to cook, he didn't actually like working in the business.

That year, in 2004, he returned to his roots in electronics by taking a job with Systron Donner, in the San Francisco area, which makes aerospace instrumentation. "I learned a lot from the job," he said. "How to re-engineer a lot of things."

In May 2005, he went to work as a product engineer for Tilia, a food-packaging conglomerate that manufactured things such as toasters, electrical woks, panini grills, and waffle irons. "I got to take things apart and destroy the crap out of them," said Eric. "I got to evaluate things from a chef's standpoint."

He also learned to build control systems for audio-visual equipment.

"It was a glorified remote control embedded in the wall."

Eventually, the San Francisco Tilia office closed because a rival company bought the parent company. Eric was laid off but landed a new job as a manufacturing engineer at SP Controls. While there, he helped the company land projects that his boss didn't want to pursue. How did he do it? "I learned Mandarin," said Eric.

So by the time Eric arrived at Ardica in February 2009, he was well-rounded and ready to take on the many roles we threw at him. For instance, he said, "When I leave here, my day doesn't stop." Instead, he goes to talk to his Chinese vendors, in Mandarin, by phone at 2 am San Francisco time.

"When I came to work here, I knew this company did not have the typical mentality. Here, everybody's motivated," said Eric.

One charm of a startup is its collective motivation. And yet within that collective is the need for individual action taken with initiative and often under great stress. We all understood. Eric just happened to be responsible for lots of individual actions without a lot of authority. He still pulled it off. It was really amazing.

Eric handled much more than the alphabet-soup certifications necessary to sell our product. He was also finding and working with vendors to make sure everything shipped on time as requested.

He tried to build a two-week buffer into our delivery times, but our money situation had impacted his timelines. "It's happened twice," said Eric. "Two vendors told us they wouldn't continue until they got paid."

Yes, Eric Folsom also dealt with the consequences of unpaid bills.

21

I F VENDORS DIDN'T DELIVER, we didn't deliver. Our sales team, which put its name on the line based on delivery, would feel like, and maybe be treated like, dirt. But if the vendors didn't deliver, it could wipe out more than the sales team. Without product and income, this R&D company, which brought in our sales team in order to become a consumer product firm, may have had to fold up shop under an increasing mountain of debt. Our science, that of Dan and Tibor specifically, was potentially game-changing, but under the circumstances it might have been viewed as merely "nice" and stolen for pennies on the dollar. Lots rode on these vendors delivering.

"I do my little dance," said Eric. "Sometimes I have to look for another vendor."

Or sometimes it took a team effort. For instance, one Chinese company, which had a San Jose office, prevented its factory from shipping some parts until they were paid. "Dick was able to smooth over some of the financial woes," said Eric. "They released bits and pieces, but not everything. They wouldn't ship the backpack cable." Of course, selling a product requires that the product have all the parts, and the backpack cable was an integral part of the Moshi system. But Eric was dealing with a vendor that was "pissed off we haven't paid them."

So Eric was resourceful. He contacted his old boss, the one he worked for when he learned Mandarin, and told of his dilemma. "He said, 'No problem. I know this guy in Taipei.'" After contacting his friend's contact, Eric set up a time to come visit. Eric knew the big picture of business, and he knew the subtleties. He knew, for instance, that the custom in China is to always bring gifts. He showed up in Taipei with a bottle of wine and hung out on the boardwalk with his new friend and his friend's wife and child. And like that, Eric built a relationship that saved a deadline.

But a move like Eric's can, from afar, be difficult to understand. When a company has no money and the engineers are fighting for components to do their work, a bottle of wine as a gift can seem frivolous. It was the opposite of that, but perception has a way of appearing as reality.

Saving the company had taken more than just Eric's hard work and charm, of course. "Thank goodness for our vendors, who so far truly believe in us," said Jim.

The vendors believed because of Jim, and Eric, and all of the people in front of them and behind them. We were Ardica and we would do whatever it took.

"It's stressful," said Sergio Galvan, our manufacturing manager, of trying to get materials to produce our product when we still owe money. "We have to call people up and tell them, 'It's coming.'"

Sergio, who was charged with educating, training, and setting up our subcontracted, outsourced manufacturing at the plant in Montana, was also located in the Swiss part of the DMZ. His desk was next to Eric's. While Eric's desk bordered the "hallway" that controlled the flow between engineering and sales and marketing, Sergio's desk bordered Eric's. He just dealt with consequences further down the line, but like Jim and Eric, he found himself forced to apologize.

"I've had the credit card bounce four or five times," he said. When his phone rings, he said, "I try to call them all back to let them know I haven't forgotten them...We're always waiting for something. You can't just call someone asking for 2,000 pieces. So you put so much energy into getting them to work with you. You have to sweet talk them. I'm trying to make it personal and make it succeed."

It *was* personal. It was personal to all of us. Thankfully our vendors got it, and our great staff got it. But the issues were obvious from all perspectives.

"Part of the problem is how well we're organized. Communication doesn't flow as well as it should. If we don't manage a budget for the project and have a better system of communication," said Sergio, "I see it continuing this way of spending more money than we need to."

Sergio understood the challenges of all things Ardica, and except for the money part he seemed to really love it. He carried with him the perpetual smile of someone energized by what he did, and determined not to fail. "I don't think anything is impossible," he said. "I try to reduce it to its simplest steps."

But because of money issues, Sergio said that nothing was happening as it was designed to happen. "Someone will ask, 'What's the output per day?' But it's hard to tell you. We don't always have the material to start at the beginning of the day."

Like almost everyone in the company, Sergio had been tasked with something akin to the impossible, and a lot of the difficulty had to do with money. In fact, the reason we were even assembling the Moshi in Montana, rather than Northern California or almost anywhere more cost effective, was our pursuit of federal stimulus money. It was one of our three planned applications for funds.

"That's another live and learn experience," said Jim. "We originally budgeted the stimulus money to come in April or May…now the latest estimate is November. The stimulus is complicated. Our projects are intertwined with other massive projects. We are a subcontractor below a subcontractor." And because we budgeted for that money and it had not come in, the financial hole had gotten bigger.

Dick had been working with our Washington, D.C. lobbyists to get three different government grants. We needed specific kinds of partners for certain parts of the work we were doing. Politics also played a role in where money would be sent. We collaborated with three different groups to apply for three grants for three different projects, spread out geographically in Arkansas, Montana, and Texas.

In Texas, our partner was BnB Energy Partners. When the background work was done, Dick believed we could apply for a $6 million grant to be spread over 18 months. The money would be split between BnB and Ardica. The concept was to develop clean energy wind farms that could immediately, and locally, convert their power into clean Ardica fuel for our fuel cells. But Dick also thought he might want to shift production to New Mexico and use solar. If so, our Texas application and our parallel lobbying might have been for naught. It had, though, taken a lot of time and money from us.

In Arkansas, we asked for a $1 million grant spread out over 18 months. We were a small component of a large state government project aimed at improving the electrical power grid as well as reducing dependence on it. Our partners, besides the state of Arkansas, included Stanford University and Carnegie Mellon.

The third—or maybe the first, depending on perspective—of our stimulus grant applications was to be in Montana. Dick's plan was that we would receive, in conjunction with a company called MSE, $6 million spread over three years. Ardica and MSE, which had previously received a number of DOE grants, would split the money. The grant was to establish domestic manufacturing and assembly of the Moshi power system and the technology connector. The grant would help in the development of skills, jigs, tools, and engineering that would produce power systems which, in the long run, would be price competitive with offshore production. The money would also subsidize our short-term expenses to be price competitive out of the gate.

Dick led us to manufacture in Montana when he was pursuing an investor who decided not to invest. That particular non-investor, however, lived in Washington, D.C. and helped connect government grants to companies from his home state of Montana. He suggested we partner up with the clean energy firm in Montana he formerly headed, MSE, and mutually pursue the grant. For this, we used our Washington, D.C. lobbyist.

Manufacturing in Montana sure looked like a good concept—low cost, domestic labor, reasonably close to our California offices, and a supplier allowing us to meet the requirements of the Berry Amendment, which dictates that suppliers to the government manufacture products in the U.S.

But the stimulus money had not come in, and, in reality, had only been applied for in one state, Arkansas. Dick had been busy with other projects such as fundraising, and didn't have time to finalize the other grant applications. Still, he had maintained singular control over all of them.

And there was another problem. When Sergio went to Montana to help set up the factory, he found an under-trained workforce. "The workers apparently had no background," said Sergio. "They shouldn't have to watch me to learn to solder." He originally went to Montana for a three-day training session. He ended up staying two weeks. He found, besides the under-trained staff, a big compressor in the middle of the floor taking up 70% of the space, and no system for organizing or tracking inventory.

Sergio, like all of us, worked with what he was given, which for him was an ill-equipped factory in Butte, Montana. He described the situation as frustrating. He knew enough about costs to add, "I think manufacturing in Montana is expensive." But his job was to make it work in the old copper boomtown.

A city of about 30,000, Butte sits in a natural bowl in the Rocky Mountains in the western part of the state. The old mining town was historically known for its saloons and red light district, but when Sergio showed up one of the first things he did was visit the gravesite of one its most famous residents, motorcycle daredevil Evel Knievel.

When he isn't working for Ardica at about the same speed, Sergio Galvan, 40, races motorcycles at about 140 miles per hour. "I'm hands on," he said. "I understand technical assembling, how things fit together, and tolerances. I have an understanding of engineering and why they do things."

He came to work at Ardica, like a lot of our staff, by answering an ad we had placed on Craigslist. Sergio was born and raised in San Francisco and spent a number of years working for the city. His first job was testing electronic parking meters and the job then evolved into operations manager. His next job was at the Pacific Stock Exchange working in the computer operations department. And then he answered our ad.

Sergio came in when Plan A was the fuel cell. "They were looking for an assembler. It was so vague," said Sergio. "The dynamic back then was very different than it is now. They had small deadlines for presentations."

He came in and interviewed and found he loved the company, the facility, and the people. But what impressed him the most was the job assembling the prototype fuel cells. "It was like being in science class without the teacher," he said.

Figuring out how to do things when there is no script "is all about creativity," said Sergio, who knew a bit about creative endeavors. He played in a rock band, and he also painted artwork when he wasn't racing motorcycles or working for Ardica. Sergio was another well-rounded Ardica employee, which made him a perfect choice to promote to manufacturing manager when we created that position.

Now his job was to advise and mentor MSE on setting up the Montana operation and he was also the supervisor of four assemblers in our own fourth floor facility. The four assemblers were generalists. They worked on prototypes, helping Sergio create our methods and procedures. They also produced items that we couldn't get subcontracted. On this day, they were cutting and then sealing the foam around the lithium-ion batteries to create the Moshi, which was then assembled with the backpack cable and technology connector in Montana. Our four local assemblers were Chinese women who speak broken English, but Sergio managed to communicate with them about what he needed doing and what tools they needed to use. "We've developed our own style. The tools are color- coded. For instance, silver means crescent wrench."

Solutions can be simple or complex, but Sergio noted that Ardica had an all-for-one approach of "creative people who will help you solve a problem."

Nevertheless, when the problem was not enough money, creativity by itself wasn't going to pay the bills. And getting money can be sometimes— but not always—more complex than color-coding the crescent wrench.

22

ETTING MONEY REQUIRES proving you can make money. We could make money; I could prove it. But it wasn't up to me to prove it. It was up to Dick, or at least it had been as we teetered towards bankruptcy. Because of my fiduciary responsibility to shareholders and employees, I couldn't defer to Dick any longer on financing and financial management. So many of his efforts to raise money had fallen short. It had become a do-or-die situation for the company. We actually faced bankruptcy. I could see the edge of the cliff and realized that we might get there in less than a month.

If I didn't do something immediately—despite all the fantastic opportunities we had—the company could fold. I knew this as fact. Many of the Ardica team were also painfully aware how bad our situation was. Yet Dick was defensive about the situation, and eternally optimistic. I love optimism but I thought if we didn't do something quickly, we would be letting everyone down—employees, shareholders, and customers. The lack of money and Dick's failure to raise it had put a strain on our relationship.

We were now dealing with a lack of trust. Perhaps this lack of trust went both ways. I hoped it didn't but I feared it did. I did not have confidence in Dick's financial leadership, and I worried about his lack of business experience. I was sure he sensed it and so I imagine he felt something akin to pressure from me and maybe felt some animosity towards me. I was trying to save the company, save the employees jobs, fulfill our commitment to customers and, in doing so, fulfill my managerial responsibilities to our shareholders. And I wanted Ardica to make a lot of money for everyone's benefit. I meant no harm. I thought he knew that, but sometimes I wondered.

I wondered why we didn't have up-to-date financials. I wondered why he wouldn't hold any Board meetings even though I'd requested them. And, most importantly, I wondered why Dick, the CEO, and Fritz, the Chairman of the Board, weren't more worried about the fact that we still had no money. Did they know something I didn't?

People—good people like Eric Folsom and Sergio Galvan and many others, my colleagues and friends—were caught up in all of this. It made me sad. It made me angry. It left me no course other than to act to get us out of this financial crisis.

Holding the balance and moving everyone forward was an immense challenge, and a lot of it had to do with getting the entire team to understand what it takes to become a consumer product—and not just an R&D—firm. It requires making what you can sell, not just trying to sell what you can make. And we had discovered in our brief time of approaching the market that our idea of portable miniaturized power looked like a winner. But we had to strike fast in order to become the true market leader and that's why money was so important. Sure, it takes money to become a market leader. But the benefits are enormous.

Dick was skeptical. "It's a great story," he said about our projected sales and profits. "But when you peel that onion, we're only going to make $20 or $30." Dick said we had bad margins and did not make money on the sale of the Moshi and, he added, "The sales and marketing budget alone is $1 million. It's a numbers game. It's easy to hype all those super brand names, and I like that too. But on the other hand, the batteries alone cost a lot of money."

But when you peeled away the onion, as Dick suggested, and really looked at the numbers and the story behind the numbers, there was a different story. Since Dick had not authorized the money for the CFO to generate financials, the reality was hidden. When he talked about the sales and marketing budget being $1 million, he was mixing up apples and oranges, because those numbers included manufacturing costs and expenses. I knew this because I generated the numbers myself. When he said batteries were expensive, he was correct. But if you make money on them, selling a lot is good.

One reality was that the expense of locating our assembly operation in Montana on the hope of getting stimulus money had resulted in unnecessary high costs. Preliminary quotes showed costs would be 50% lower if we had assembled in our own back yard in Silicon Valley, and 75% lower if we had assembled in China. This could be achieved by simply moving operations, which Dick resisted because, as he pointed out, it hurt our chances for stimulus funds.

The numbers showed the costs on our initial, small production at a break-even level, but when we increased to the volume levels our partners were projecting, the economies of scale got us a margin of more than 40% of the sales price.

The idea of pricing based on projected future costs is a standard business procedure studied in all business schools and used by many successful companies relying on what is known as the "manufacturing learning curve," the predictable reduction of manufacturing costs as volume and experience build up. Intel and Texas Instruments and many other companies have successfully and repeatedly employed this strategy. I'd explained this to several inside Ardica, including Dick. But so far he hadn't accepted this logic. This was the first manufacturing and operating company he had been involved with that actually made and sold consumer products, so this was new to him.

For the time being, the assembly of the Moshi stayed in Montana. But there were savings to be had and savings, in fact, that had already occurred. For instance, Eric had sourced a cheaper foam for the Moshi than we had been using, but that meant that Sergio had to find a different adhesive that would work in order to put the actual seven lithium-ion batteries between two pieces of sealed foam. It was a small example in an early stage of how our product costs could be cut in order to bring us more profitable margins. We had such an opportunity. This was business 101. Or it should have been.

Dick rightly suggested that our decision-making process wasn't yet fully implemented. I argued, again, that the issue was our lack of a strategic plan. But the real issue was our lack of money, and Lee Turlington, our Eight Inc. expert, pointed out that our lack of a strategic plan led to a lack of money. And the circular argument, whenever we chased it, seemed to always lead back to one core question: what was up with our Joint Development Agreement with Big Silicon?

"It's just taking some time," said Dick. "It's a matter of days or weeks kind of thing. Lawyers talking to lawyers. Go figure."

The F-43 project was covered in Big Silicon's cone of secrecy. "New" in Silicon Valley is always a big deal, and so in-development often means being developed in secrecy. The F-43 was part of that communication strategy of no information released before its time.

With that as a backdrop, and the belief that green portable power is a Holy Grail to the company, we had been quietly and secretly on the verge of an agreement with Big Silicon for months. There had been visits, talks, negotiations. Big Silicon even provided us with financial assistance to help with our development of both fuels: sodium borohydride and the more potent alane.

Dan said, "For each fuel, we've made advances. We've made advances in the design of the cartridges and understanding of the system…I'm pretty excited about the potential of the F-43 project. But you've got to temper that with the realization that you have a long way to go to get to market."

And Tibor added, "We have improved our synthesis of alane. We can produce larger amounts—four or five times what we've been doing before." But as for the deadline of trying launch a product in October 2010, he said, "those are harsh targets. It's unrealistic to think we'll have a finished product in a year." Yet that was the timeline Big Silicon had given us.

Dick had one complaint: the sales and marketing team "[kept] trying to sell the stuff that is still in development." But that was another misunderstanding. We weren't out to sell what was in development, but we did want to be in the know from the development people as to what they were developing so that when it was developed we were ready to roll.

In fact, we were trying to sell the Moshi, which is what we were brought in to sell. And yes, by some appearances, it was still in development. The reality of the Ardica that Dick was running was that things were always changing and no product was ever completely finished.

But he may have also been talking about our interest in the supposed Big Silicon agreement. It had been framed by Dick in a very vague manner to all of us, inside the company, as the deal that was going to save the company. Of course we were interested. But we weren't trying to sell the concept of a partnership with Big Silicon right then.

We just wanted to sell the Moshi, and have enough money to do it right.

23

I WAS HOME, but I was still tense. I wished that I didn't feel this tension. Some of it was the usual good tension of an entrepreneurial venture, but a lot of it was negative, expanding, and unnecessary tension.

I began to think there were people in the company who missed being simply an R&D firm, but the truth was that the stakes had been placed. The huge financial gain would only come from creating a business entity. Some wanted to simply sell the patents to whomever and take home a little money. But the real gain would come from commercializing the nascent technology, not selling it off.

It was not the easy way out, but it was the right way. I found myself trying to give a business education to those who seemed to not care very much. Most of the Ardica engineering team was just out of college with an NCAA business education—NCAA meaning "No Clue At All." I was trying to get the team to learn, but I felt a resistance from Dick, who also, unfortunately, was learning on the job. They were all so bright that if given the time and the tools they would have quickly grasped the business concepts. But there was no time, and no process for passing this information on to the team.

I contemplated this as I sat at my home desk and my eyes drifted to a small Lucite gift my wife, Margot, had given me years ago. On it are the words: "We are all faced with a series of great opportunities, brilliantly disguised as impossible situations."

Easter was over. Bankruptcy loomed. I shut off the light.

THE "STORY" AND THE BANKERS
September 2009

24

A BUSINESS LOOKING FOR MONEY IS A "STORY."
In the middle of August, James Palmer, a managing director of the Legend Merchant Group, leaned calmly back in a chair in our offices and said, "I've had initial conversations with potential investors. It's very easy to make your company sound very exciting." James came to us, along with Hector Chao, another managing director at Legend, on the recommendation of some friends of our sales manager Shawn Biega. Shawn, essentially, found the bankers who were going to, hopefully, raise the money to save the company.

The plan had two layers. First, there would be a bridge loan of $1.2 million to help us survive. And then there would be a follow-on institutional raise of $5 million to $10 million to be used to fund Ardica's runway to full commercialization and sustained profitability.

Given the fact that we didn't really have accurate forecasts of cash flow, figuring out how much money we needed to immediately raise was a fairly simple exercise. We needed to immediately raise enough money to survive and give us enough financial runway until we could get our act together and have a real professional fundraising.

Because creditors were contacting us every day we, had lots of data points to confirm the accuracy of our Accounts Payable. We then did an account-by-account evaluation to determine an optimal, stretched-out payment plan that would satisfy them while also keeping the cash demands on Ardica to a minimum. We added to that number the monthly burn rate (the amount of cash we were spending monthly) multiplied by the number of months until we thought we could do the formal fundraising. That became the number we settled on as a minimum we would need to raise.

This need for a professional fundraising group like Legend had been building, but in August, after living on financial fumes for months, it finally became clear to everyone that there were only two choices: bankruptcy or an investment banker to raise money for the company. With his own limited success raising money, Dick finally accepted the need for using an outside firm, and he found Legend acceptable. Dick had been trying and promising to raise $5 million for nearly 18 months but had raised only a small portion of that amount. So now even he accepted using Legend.

The reality was that there was no other choice. Experience is what you get when you don't get what you want, and Ardica's experience was getting no money using Dick's approach. And so we had to sell ourselves to the Legend team, who would be selling us. They were here because they had already vetted us against other opportunities they had. They were here to help, and yes, some of that helping would be helping themselves. They were paid to raise money, and we needed money.

Hector, who had the opposite of James's laid back demeanor, leaned forward and, with his hands moving in short, choppy movements like a politician making a point, explained that we needed a four-page executive summary. "Certain things are going to be unique to the story. I'd like to emphasize portable energy and I'd like to talk about how quickly you have gotten to where you are. I want to talk about your market and product strategies, not just apparel."

The story had to be detailed and exciting.

When they asked me to start telling them the story, I began with a fact: "Fifteen months ago, we didn't have shit." And then, with the assistance of Shawn, I rehashed all that Ardica had accomplished in that time and how we had targeted and signed up top partners in a variety of verticals such as backpacking, hunting, skiing, fashion, snowmobiling, etc. I knew it was an impressive list, especially given the speed with which we accomplished it.

We discussed branding and how we were getting our brand linked with other top commercial product brands. Then Hector talked about using images in the presentation to potential investors. "I believe in the power of images," he said. Hector and James seemed particularly interested in the marketability of the F-43 part of the story—clean tech.

James said he likes our "bent towards green energy" but added, "When I look at your catalog, I almost think that you're a clothing company."

Of course, we were much more than that. We re-emphasized the positioning of portable power. James leaned back in his chair. He appeared skeptical. Hector leaned forward and nodded. He took copious notes. They were an interesting team to watch work together. And I imagined they thought the same of Dick and me.

Dick seemed somewhat preoccupied that day. During our meeting, he had to leave the room for a number of phone calls. Whenever Dick took a call, it was always an interesting production. That day was no different. Dick actually carried two cell phones, one for his Pittsburgh contacts including his wife and Carnegie Mellon, and one for his San Francisco contacts including Ardica. When I first discovered this, I thought it was rather clever. However, it appeared somewhat confusing for Dick because both phones were exactly the same, with the same factory-installed ring tone. So when a phone rang, he had to dig through his pockets to find which of the two it was. And Dick was nearsighted so he had to stare at the phone within a few inches of his face to see who was calling. Each time the phone rang, he stepped from the room.

He returned and talked of the technology and the F-43 project. "The idea is that this has to be green fuel. Otherwise why bother? You can just plug into the wall."

But Hector said, "The only concern I have is that this is a milestone-driven story...you don't want to set expectations you can't meet."

James warned us to develop a patent strategy because, he pointed out, "It's very important to find the right person to manage your patent portfolio…Another company I visited was also a patent-rich company and they were so disorganized that it almost doubled the cost of maintaining their patent portfolio." These assets were important to potential investors, so it was important to present them in an organized way. "The more professional you appear, the better-positioned you are for fundraising.

After a bit more discussion about technology, Hector said, "Our role is to maximize value…We'll put you in front of the right people to tell the story. You've got to come up with a phenomenal story."

25

TWO WEEKS LATER in a 5:30 am phone call, Dick said that James and Hector from Legend "seem like good guys. I hope so…they've just got to get their story right."

Ah, the story. And that makes this the story of the story. Business is funny that way. "I've never seen a company coming to me needing money that didn't have a lot of positive things going for it," said James in a phone interview after the meeting. "Everybody comes to you with a story. It's whether you believe the story or not."

Our story was that for a long time we were basically Build A Better Mousetrap Inc. We were building better mousetraps but very few investors were interested in whiz-bang technology without a specific plan of how to market it. For a long time, Dick differed with me on this, and in his fundraising efforts he stressed the engineering. Plus, he simply cast about everywhere looking for money, rather than focusing on specific investors who were interested in our type of business. His theory was, if people have money to invest, they will want to invest in us.

The truth is that certain investors have sweet spots, areas where they are interested in putting their money. The reasons vary, but usually the investor has specialized knowledge and has experienced success investing in a particular area. And it fits well in their portfolio.

For instance, one potential investor our CFO Jim Retzlaff introduced to us was heavily invested in public storage. He was quite wealthy but we were very far from his sweet spot and, despite Dick's confident assurances that "at least $500,000" of this potential investor's money would be "locked up soon," the investment never came. Why? This particular investor was actually looking for money himself to put together for a syndicate to buy more public storage units. His present sweet spot was for businesses that had a predictable, positive cash flow. This was quite different from Ardica, a long-term cash-consuming entrepreneurial play. Dick, though, felt that the investor's wealth, along with their mutual love of airplanes (the man actually owned and flew a Russian MIG), would be able to overcome the sweet spot argument. It didn't.

For a year and a half, we had heard that money was about to arrive. Round B of $5 million "was closing any day now," Dick said on several different occasions. But it never happened and eventually employees began approaching me asking about money issues. Salary increases were promised but never materialized. Options were never granted as promised. I empathized with the employees because Dick had promised me salary, insurance reimbursements, and options, which also had not happened.

Stretching the truth seemed to be standard operating procedure. I tried not to believe it but evidence mounted. The potential investor that I had brought in from Utah called me to ask about a comment Dick had made to him in an effort to finalize the investment. He said that Dick told him we had an offer from Big Silicon to buy us for $50 million but we were holding out for $100 million. I answered that I thought, as a Board member, I would have heard of it. I had heard nothing of the sort.

In fact, in late July, I had lunch with Big Silicon's director of Mergers and Acquisitions, who told me he was concerned. Dick had asked them to invest in Ardica, to provide growth and development money. The M&A director from Big Silicon bluntly told that was a bad idea. He pointed out it could slow everything down, because his company didn't like to mix investing in companies with investments in development. One was focused on the concept stage of a company. The other, he said, was investing in the growth and execution stage of the company. He mentioned that Dick had asked him to call an existing Ardica investor who was in the process of considering investing in the upcoming B round. When the M&A director did contact our investor, the investor grilled him about Big Silicon's intention to directly invest in Ardica's B round of financing. Finally, the M&A director recounted that the investor said he would only invest in the next round if Big Silicon did too. Our little investor was holding Big Silicon's feet to the fire? I don't think so.

The M&A director, a former banker with Goldman Sachs, suggested that those waiting for Big Silicon to invest were hurting Ardica. "In my old days at Goldman Sachs we would just say to a reluctant investor, 'Why don't you not invest, then the company goes bankrupt and we will pick up the remaining assets?'" He went on to say, "Of course, we don't operate that way." He also pointed out that although Big Silicon loved what we were doing, until they were ready to go to market, the entire concept of the product could be shelved at any moment.

Yet Dick was telling investors that we had a $50 million offer and were holding out for $100 million.

This circular story brought us, somewhat desperately, to find Legend.

Shawn found Legend Merchant Bank through friends of his at another investment firm called Advanced Equity. Advanced Equity couldn't help us, but they said Legend could and they connected Shawn with James and Hector. "It shouldn't be hard at all," said Shawn. "I don't have problems getting money."

Shawn Biega, 39, was the quintessential salesman, which I recognized the first time I met him. It was about 1996 when I visited the office of the clothing company he created called Bombora. Shawn's gift for sales was why I brought him in to act as Ardica's sales director. When we met, we hit it off immediately. Actually, I felt a bit like a jet mechanic. His flow of energy just washed over me and over everyone around us. You can tell a great salesman within the first five minutes of meeting him—it has to do with demeanor, self-confidence, love of people, and passion. Shawn had all of these. I was impressed. At the end of those first five minutes, I knew that somewhere down the line Shawn and I would work together. I wanted to pair his unique skills with my experience.

Shawn offered a rare combination of skills and knowledge. He had a gift for marketing and brand building, a trained eye for selecting breakthrough products, and experience and familiarity with corporate finance. I sensed a business adventure in our future. He and I had similar thoughts on business and on life. He was so much more than a salesman. He was also a great friend, ethical to his core, and brimming with confidence. He was about 6'3" with dark wavy hair. His cherubic face was liable to break into a grin at any moment. He had a big personality. He was loud, brash, and he had the connections that found us our first actual customers.

Then, when called upon, he found Legend.

That was Shawn. By the time I met him, he was already an entrepreneur many times over, which is another thing that impressed me. He was a go-getter.

"I was always the guy mowing lawns," he recalled. He grew up in Danville, California, and then moved to Santa Barbara for college, and then Squaw Valley, California. When he was 14, his father started Tricor America, and Shawn got to fly all around the West delivering packages. He was also an avid skier. "I came up with the idea of opening an espresso bar at Squaw Valley," he said. "So I put together my first business. With a $20,000 investment, I was making $15,000 to $20,000 a month."

After a year and a half, Shawn sold the business and decided to attend film school. As a sponsored snowboarder who grew up ski racing, Shawn thought he could get into movies.

About this time, he was approached by the owner of Dogtown Skateboards asking if he wanted to help build the snowboard side of the Dogtown business. He joined them and helped grow the division from zero to $4 million quickly. But sometime about 1995, the original owner of Dogtown took on two partners and Shawn found himself "watching three grown, middle-aged men fighting all the time." So he left.

After Shawn left Dogtown, he went to Arnell Snowboards and ran West Coast sales. But Shawn's story wasn't completely linear. A lot of it included the phrase "While I was there, I also..." because Shawn, like most salesmen, wasn't linear. So while he was working for Arnell, he helped a company, Dita Eyewear, with sales and distribution. And while that was happening, he was also creating samples of clothing for a company he was calling Bombora. And that's when we met.

Bombora did well. Shawn saw his first order sell out, and that led to some tremendous growth. However, he became involved in a trademark dispute with a company in Australia. "The biggest lesson I learned was don't get into a lawsuit," he said. "I was cocky enough to think I had enough money to win the lawsuit." He folded the company and decided to try a completely new experience.

"I was always interested in the stock market. I wanted a job on Wall Street but I had no experience," he said. But Shawn, undeterred, was a bulldog when it came to his determination and persistence. He was hired at UBS on the institutional sales trading desk after "taking crazy tests... lots of math testing." He read three financial newspapers a day, was self-educated when it came to the markets, and was successful in a variety of walks of life.

After UBS, he went to Nutmeg Securities, which was listed on the Chicago Stock Exchange. "I was able to decipher lots of information very fast. I would digest the news, rip it open, and then answer how do we move on this price." But when he was asked to move to Chicago, Shawn was uncomfortable leaving his family and West Coast business contacts, so he left that business with a good education and a new entrepreneurial plan.

When he was with Bombora, he created a tagline "Beyond Coastal." So when he decided to create a sunscreen company, that was the name he chose. He found an old friend from high school who was a skier and the owner of a manufacturing facility, Abco Laboratories, a family business that had been around for half a century. With his friend's help, he tested sunscreen samples from all over the world and used that knowledge to create his own product.

He did it on barter. "If you help me, I'll help you," he said. He offered help in sales and marketing to the lab, and he had full access to the lab to create his own product, a clean, green, fragrance-free natural sunscreen that landed in boutique shops and new age markets like Whole Foods.

The more I knew Shawn the more I wanted to work with him. I was sure we could create something great together.

"Hap was always asking me to come join him in Canterbury," recalled Shawn of my efforts to get him to join the New Zealand-based rugby apparel company. But he was always busy.

Finally, the stars aligned in February 2008 when I found myself working for Ardica and I was able to convince Shawn to come join. And, as previously mentioned, the first thing he did, on his way to his first trade show for Ardica, was make our very first sale, to Mountain Hardwear. Ardica had been in business for more than four years and had never made a sale. Shawn made a sale on his first day. So with Shawn and me leading the way, we were finally developing a path to a new and revolutionary market. We had begun the process of creating the Ardica brand.

Our story was now believable.

But it took Shawn to get us to the right financial people, Legend Merchant Bank. And then we began to figure out what they wanted. "A big part of this, to me, is specifically Hap," said James. "Hap is more detailed than most. He said *here's my market strategy.* You'd be surprised how many executives have no idea what [information] to give you."

I knew how to build a business and make it successful, and I knew that my background would be key in finding a professional financial advisor. I also knew they wanted details to flesh out the business case for Ardica, and that they would be focused first on the needs of potential investors.

One thing investors look for as part of the story is buttoned-down financial controls and governance. Unfortunately, we didn't have that. We were still working on it. Our previous offering documents prepared by

Dick had financial statements that were six months old. We hadn't invested in this crucial information. In fact, even the usual monthly financial statements were not being generated despite my repeated requests for this operating data. The reality was that no financial reports of any kind were being generated. Nothing.

A report I eagerly pushed for, that I had used in my other companies, was a quick snapshot or "flash report," sometimes called a KPI (Key Performance Indicator), and alternately referred to as a "Dashboard." These flash reports are produced in the first few business days into the month, rather than the 15 to 20 business days usually required for full financial statements. These timely snapshots give managers a quick read of how things are progressing against the plan, and give managers an early warning system to allow time for making corrections and operating adjustments to changing business conditions. But we had never generated these reports.

So how were things progressing against the plan? Plan?

We had just then, for the sake of Legend, put together something faintly resembling a business plan. It wasn't a full-blown strategic plan by any stretch. Had our strategic meeting in June been more comprehensive, we might have been using that plan and been able to show it to Legend. But it wasn't. Even without that we were still able to demonstrate that we had a professional management team with profit and loss focus, at least on the sales and marketing side of the business. And we were able to claim great R&D and product development people, some killer intellectual property, and a recently developed go-to-market strategy by Shawn and myself that would get us traction.

Our PR plan was getting us noticed on tech blogs, in major magazines, and even in *The New York Times*. And we had revamped our offices to showcase our products and underscore our marketing approach to business, a development designed to convince every Ardica visitor (customers, investors, suppliers) of our new commercial focus for the business. And, of course, we still had the big dream of miniaturized fuel cells with their clean energy coming soon. Maybe.

All of these details were important to present to Legend. Including Shawn in the meeting with Legend was part of our strategy for dealing with Legend and very important. He had worked in the investment community and so he knew the financial drill. His inclusion was critical to putting the best face forward. They wanted details, and those were the sort of people they wanted to see in the company.

"In this environment, nothing is an easy sell," said James Palmer of Legend. "All the guys are looking at their current portfolio for something to sell off. But enough sizzle can still position the company right."

Shawn, who delivered sizzle without being asked, said, "To get the value at the end of the day, we need to make our name known worldwide."

"We see an opportunity for a company to take an idea and quickly establish a leadership position and be able to take a disproportionate share of the market available to them," said Hector Chao of Legend. He compared our opportunity to that of another startup he helped fund, Lexar Media. "They were developing flash memory devices that would allow the consumer to store data. They created a market by entering the market for digital storage…it was a great story. Everybody loved the story."

We were finally putting together a consumer products story instead of just the CVs of a few of our team, a few rough prototypes, and the detailed chemical composition of some of the fuels. Our previous attempts at telling our story, written by Dick, were almost 40 technical pages long, with a primary focus on our engineering. As Hector pointed out, "Sometimes it's hard for engineers to tell the story that generates excitement from potential investors."

26

THE LAY OF THE LAND WAS CLEAR. We needed money, and we needed it yesterday—money to cover the past debts that had piled up and sufficient operating capital to get us to the next stage with all of our products. But Legend believed rapidly getting all the capital we needed for 2010 and 2011 was impractical. First, because a sophisticated financing round usually takes six months—six months that we didn't have. And it would require a significant amount of due diligence on the company—due diligence that, at that moment, we would have probably flunked.

Moreover, it was impossible, at that moment, to forecast specifically how much money we would actually need. There was uncertainty about when we could actually have fuel cells come to market, uncertainty if Big Silicon was really going to introduce a product using our technologies, and also the unknown of how fast the burgeoning Moshi commercial business would grow.

The absence of this knowledge was more than just an Achilles heel in our pursuit of a large round of equity financing. This, coupled with our imperfect accounting made an immediate equity raise next to impossible. As James so succinctly put it to me: "You guys will have to get your act together. You will have to professionalize your company a lot more and show a significant order book before you are really ready to go see the big boys—the VCs and Private Equity players."

We weren't ready for the big boys, but Legend's money would help us get there. What Legend meant by that was that before they could do a professional equity fund raise, Ardica would have to have standard, auditable financials including supportable forecasts and budgets. We would have to finally publish an explainable organization chart with clear definition of responsibilities and authority. Plus, all sorts of other organizational cleanup was necessary, from product certifications to repaying employees their long past due company expenses. .

The decision was simple. With creditors literally and figuratively knocking at our door, we quickly agreed to do what Legend suggested in order to get a quick infusion of cash. We needed to immediately raise sufficient money to satisfy the creditors swirling around us and to also give us some runway into 2010. With this breathing space we could then position ourselves for that major round of financing, something Legend was calling the "institutional round," in early 2010.

The short-term solution Legend proposed was to do a bridge loan of $1.2 million. A bridge loan is exactly what it sounds like—a loan of money, not an equity investment. It is an infusion of money for a short- term period to create a financial bridge for a company until it does a larger round of equity financing. Or, alternately, until it finds someone to buy the whole company.

Legend suggested that a bridge loan was the right way to go initially for Ardica because it could be very quickly put together. The typical bridge loan investor made quick decisions and was less interested in the long-term story and the big upside for themselves. They would primarily be interested in the yield on their investment and in predictable near-term liquidity for their capital as well as the security and protection of their invested capital. The bridge loan was, in essence, the sweet spot for our type of needs.

Legend pointed out that institutional and equity investors, on the other hand, would be much more rigorous in their analysis of their prospective investment and focused more on things Ardica had not yet finalized—things like depth and experience of management, an exit plan for investors, what financial controls were in place, what the strategic plan of the company was, who the customers and suppliers were, and what the financial returns for investors might be.

What Legend proposed, and we readily accepted, was a 12-month bridge loan, which paid the lenders 10% interest and also gave them warrants to buy into the next round of financing at a 25% discount from the price we would sell at. As protection for their loan, the lenders would receive a first priority lien on all the intellectual property of the company through something called a UCC-1 filing with the State of California.

As this was evolving, additional unanticipated expenses starting showing up so we mutually agreed to up the targeted amount they would raise to $1.5 million. We kept Legend racing to bring the much-needed money in.

Legend's definition of what investors were looking for was much more detailed and differed markedly from what we had been offering.

Instead of details, plans, and strategies, when Dick's round B fundraising was stalling, his approach was to throw out offers of Board seats as if they were Halloween candy. He dangled the "Board seat" carrot in front of at least five people, one of whom invested but did not want the seat. As Legend explained to me, "being on the Board is not much of a priority for most of these investors. In fact, many would rather be an advisor with rights to sit in on the Board meetings than be an actual Board Director because of the liability involved."

Professionals raise money differently than we had been doing. They focus on the needs of potential investors. Legend immediately focused on reshaping the Ardica story to appeal to the likes of early-stage investors. They focused on what our offering document needed to look like to ensure that prospective investors would actually read it, including highlighting what actual financial information had to be included. They focused on the critical questions:

- What sort of financial deal would appeal to prospective investors?
- What type of investor would be interested in investing at this stage of the company?
- Who were the best people to "sell" Ardica to the investors?
- What was the Ardica story that could be neatly condensed into an "elevator pitch"?

Legend understood that the process of fundraising was actually one of selling. In this case, they were selling Ardica, not selling Ardica's products. But it was, still, selling. To address this Legend made a point of using Shawn and me, the only Ardica people with actual sales experience, as the front people in their presentations. And, as they explained, the story that was always most compelling to investors was the successful track record of the people involved. So they highlighted my successes at The North Face, and the sales and marketing team's experience with companies like Red Bull, Beyond Coastal, Ditta, Zinka, etc.

After our meeting with Legend, Hector and I put together five solid explanatory pages about Ardica that constituted the Executive Summary for the pursuit of bridge loan investors. We had reshaped the story. And then James and Hector looked in their Rolodex for bridge loan investors who would find us in their sweet spot. "The reason why [a bridge loan] is acceptable is that a little money can go a long way for the right company," James explained.

True to their word, on September 10th, just six days after we finished the Executive Summary, Hector said $600,000 should be available "in a day or two," and added, "The plan for a quick raise is to really take advantage of the opportunities available to [Ardica] now."

And the money arrived just as they said.

27

"IT FELT LIKE A HIT OF PURE OXYGEN after your head has been held under water for a half an hour," said our CFO Jim Retzlaff. "It was fantastic. We were very delinquent in paying most of our vendors. Sending checks to our vendors felt wonderful."

When the first bit of the bridge loan money from Legend came in, Jim and many others were clearly very happy and justifiably so. We had almost reached the edge of the cliff even though we were also on the verge of great successes. We owed people, we had let some people down on promised payments, and that was really painful. But we could breathe again and life at Ardica, though not yet the dream we all envisioned, was better. "The lack of money is killer," said Jim. "It's toxic…The vendors had gotten to the end of their rope. We would not be where we were without the charity and faith of our vendors. But they finally got to the point where they couldn't take any more."

Just before the money came in, Jim had been monitoring a stressful log of phone calls, invoices, and names of employees of other companies who had put their jobs on the line by vouching for our ability to pay. We had allies in other companies and we had been letting them down. Small vendors needing money for their own survival had not been paid. Jim was in constant contact, filled with perpetual hope. So when the first $600,000 loan finally came in he summed it up in a typically understated way: "It was enough to make a difference."

Paying vendors meant a lot of things besides simply stopping the flow of angry phone calls and emails coming our way. Most importantly, it meant our vendors would deliver to us, which in turn meant that we would deliver on time to Mountain Hardwear, which was then delivering their products to retailers in key stores for our October/November launch.

The money we got via Legend, in a very real sense, saved the company. A bridge loan is expensive money because it is risky. It doesn't have the security of a full round of financing and is not usually done with the same due diligence as an equity round. It gave us money to pay old debts. With the initial $600,000, Jim had begun doing exactly that. Now it was up to us to deliver what we said. But at least we could breathe, if only momentarily. Meanwhile, James and Hector of Legend were still trying to raise the additional money to complete the bridge round while getting all the pieces in place for the institutional round that would follow. James and Hector assured us the remaining $900,000 of the expected bridge loan would be in our hands in no more than 45 days. It was refreshing to work with professionals.

The proposed agreement with Big Silicon, in one of its many forms (a joint development agreement, or a total buyout), was a consideration for the bridge loan investors, who were getting warrants to buy some stock at a discount in the future. But it was only a consideration, not their primary motive. Our path to market, and branding, and especially the performance of our existing product—the Moshi and its two peripheral pieces, the backpack cable and the technology connector—were other important considerations. All of these things would become a lot more important when we talked to institutional investors for the next round, sometime in early 2010.

While Legend made a point of using Shawn and me as the front people in their presentations in order to move to the institutional round, it was going to take more than a few people's charisma.

"There are hurdles we are helping the company address," said Hector. Foremost among them were:

- Is the proper management team in place?
- What is the product strategy? How can the company roll out lots of units so it can make real money?
- How long can the company maintain a leadership position by keeping others away from its intellectual property?

"If you look at the boxes of issues the company has to address and you had to shade in the box," said Hector, "some boxes would be one-quarter full, some one-half full, some three-quarters full, and some 100%."

28

I S THE PROPER management team in place? Well...

Dick and I presented a united front to Legend. As Hector Chao from Legend said just as the bridge loan was closing, "The combination of leadership styles blends nicely. They have complementary styles. It's right now a team approach. As the company grows, the roles will have to be better defined. It will be interesting to see how the story goes."

So far, the story had gone wherever Dick wanted it to go, except into financial viability. Our management issues, it seemed, had brought us to needing Legend, and Dick continued to invent his own version of the truth. For instance, he told our law firm, to whom we owed a significant sum of money, that we couldn't pay them because "all the money had been spent by Hap on marketing," despite us paying virtually none of those marketing bills. He also conveniently contradicted himself whenever he thought it was necessary. He told everyone not to mention the name, Big Silicon, to anyone unless the other party had a non-disclosure agreement signed with Ardica. Then he went to the two largest electrical component suppliers in Silicon Valley and, in an effort to get extended terms, without any NDA, told them that we were working with Big Silicon. A case of do as I say, not as I do.

I wanted Dick to think strategically. Instead, I believe, he thought opportunistically, and then he used whatever facts he needed, even if they were confidential or non-existent, to coerce others into his way of thinking. He managed by instincts without financial statements, Board meetings, or employee reviews. I was more wedded to standard corporate governance.

Sometimes it seemed things would pop into his head and he would want to act immediately. In fact, the one expense he insisted the company pay for was an $80-a-month cell phone allowance for every employee. One thing all employees noticed was that Dick seemed to think that since Ardica paid the phone bill, it was fine for him to call at all hours, during dinners, on weekends, and even up until midnight to discuss whatever popped into his mind. Shawn told me that his wife jokingly asked if he had a new girlfriend. Jim's view was that Dick ran Ardica like he ran a navy ship on tour duty, expecting all employees to be on call at all times.

Legend knew our issues, so they gave us a strong admonition to spend the money slowly. Just before the $600,000 came in, Dick, Jim, and I met and developed a plan to spend the first $147,000 immediately to placate our most upset creditors. Then, we planned to get a team of our top employees together and mutually work out a plan to parcel out the rest of the money. The idea was to dovetail this money as best we could with other money that we thought, but weren't sure, would be coming in. Big Silicon, for instance, was supposed to be paying us $120,000 a month towards F-43 development, but they were 30 days past due and no one was sure why. We couldn't accurately predict when they would pay. We were also due $100,000 for sales of Moshi systems. But most of that was due in December, and it was only September. And then there would be the rest of the Legend raise to complete the bridge loan. So we, as Legend continually told us, needed to be careful with the money.

This is where the picture became surreal to me. One day after we received the $600,000 from Legend, I checked the bank account and discovered we only had $50,000 left. A payroll of $90,000 was due in a week and we were already, again, out of money. With this in my mind, I walked into the office in a really bad mood.

Jim was the first into the office. I quickly asked him how did we spend $550,000 when we had agreed to only spend $147,000?

His response was that "we didn't really spend $550,000, we only spent $480,000."

My question again was, "Okay, whatever the amount was, why didn't we stay to the spending plan of $147,000 as we had agreed with Legend?" I also pointed out that within the $147,000 planned spend was an allocation of $35,000 of needed reimbursements to employees for expenses they had incurred as far back as nine months ago, but I saw in the checkbook that none of that had been paid. I rambled on, picking up speed and volume. "Didn't we say that employees are our most important asset? That the number one priority in payments would be to the employees? How can we have spent all that money and still not taken care of the employees, to say nothing about not having enough money left in the back to meet the $90,000 payroll next week?"

Jim's frustrated comment was, "Dick said we had to do it?"

"What happened to our plan? What happened to our agreement? What happened to sanity? What is Legend going to say?" All these questions ran through my head. But Jim wasn't the issue so I tried to avoid riling him too much.

Jim, later in an interview, admitted that he believed that he was the issue. "I was so mad I wanted to punch Hap in the nose," he said.

I wasn't out to annoy him. I just wanted information. So I asked one more question. "You say only $480,000 was spent. If that were the case and our opening balance was effectively zero, the balance in the checkbook would still be $120,000, but it is only $50,000. What gives?"

Jim said, "I'm sure I only wrote checks for $480,000."

"Okay," I said. "I'll look at the books and try to figure out what the hell the difference is."

Ten minutes later I was back to him. "I've figured it out. The opening balance wasn't zero, it was a negative $70,000. I've checked the bank and there were two handwritten checks of $10,000 and $60,000 to our lobbyist from Dick Martin a couple of weeks ago. The checks were deposited right after the $600,000 landed in our account. Did you know about them?"

Jim's response was, "I didn't know anything about them. I think I should because I'm the CFO and because I'm responsible for keeping the books. But, this is the first I ever heard."

This was typical, and an example of why Dick and I had a rift. He advocated secrecy and "need to know" inside the company. I believed in transparency and open communication. He was a micromanager without any overall plan. I believed in establishing a plan with budgets and agreed-to milestones and objectives, and then the delegation of the commensurate authority and responsibility. As his way to control everything, Dick proposed that he personally oversee every decision, and personally approve, in advance, every expenditure that exceeded $50. I didn't find that practical or appropriate for a company spending millions of dollars each year. I was used to establishing budgets with input from the employees, and then holding them to that spending plan.

"Part of the problem is that we essentially have two CEOs, two chiefs," said Jim. And yet, he said that the company needed both of us to stay on our path. "They both bring wildly different skill sets." The idea, in theory, was great, Jim said. "Hap would focus on the consumer side and Dick would focus on the science side…but it's hard when you've got two people running the show."

The theory behind two chiefs was that we would combine our own unique skills into one cohesive vision. The reality was that we had dramatically opposed views on how to manage a business. I was running my team one way and Dick was running his another. Dick believed in opportunism, I believed in strategy. Dick believed everything was a disconnected project, I believed in building an integrated business around a brand for the long run.

He had an ad hoc compensation scheme based on an individual's personal needs. I had always used a company-wide, balanced scheme of compensation based on contribution—one that had motivational components, including bonuses based on hitting or exceeding plans.

Dick shot from the hip, managing without financial statements, board meetings or employee reviews. Moreover, Dick focused on opportunism and looking for a quick payout, like an early buyout from Big Silicon. My experience had been that building for the long run was the best way to run a business, letting the financial exit from the company take care of itself.

And for sure a compounding factor had been the cash situation.

Dick had what I believe was a totally unrealistic belief that Big Silicon was going to buy the company for tens of millions of dollars, maybe even $100 million. In my view that would have been a miracle at this point, because they wouldn't decide if the product which would incorporate our technology would be in their line for at least ten more months. They hadn't even decided if ours was a technology they had to have. They knew we were not talking to anyone else, so there was no competitive tension for them to make a preemptive offer. And we did not yet have a finished working product.

But his wishful thinking allowed him to avoid worrying about running out of cash or planning for the long term. He just focused on meeting the next payroll to get us to some acquisition date. As he became deluded by this improbable acquisition scenario, he started trying to focus Ardica on becoming solely a private-label component supplier for Big Silicon.

He discounted all the sales and marketing efforts to build the brand and sell commercial products like the Moshi systems. I kept trying to tell him innovative companies were the ones that command the highest value. And innovation was the combination of invention and commercialization, not just invention. But my words continued to be ignored.

Lord Acton said, "Power corrupts and absolute power corrupts absolutely." Well, false logic corrupts even more.

I did admire Dick. The problem I had was that my admiration was not for his business experience or his management skills but for his accomplishments, his lack of fear of the unknown, and his ability to ply the government waters for money. Up until the last few weeks of September, I would have said I was admiring of his grace under pressure. But that seemed to have succumbed.

It had been such a crooked path—the way we ended up working with Legend. Many times, the team was assured that investors were coming in "right away" but they never materialized. Lack of money led to big disagreements between Dick and me, dating back to my attempt to develop a strategic plan. A plan that would have allowed us to prioritize our goals and parcel out limited cash where it would do the most good. There are a lot of moving parts in any business, including Ardica's, which need to mesh to be efficient. Unfortunately, we were not yet a fine-tuned machine.

In fact, I had come to believe that we needed a leadership change. Greg Nevolo, Ardica's marketing director, put it this way: "Every single person is frustrated financially because there is somebody in the company who is put in the position where he is expected to go beyond his core competency." In essence, Dick was in over his head when he got himself involved in finance, accounting, and payment negotiation.

And it had become apparent to me and many others in the company that the issue holding us back was leadership. In late August, in fact, as Dick's round B was still not closed and we were finally reaching out to Legend, I did something I didn't want to do but which I felt compelled to do. I asked for Dick's resignation as CEO.

This was a hard thing to do. Dick and I, though we hadn't known each other, came into the company at the same time from very different backgrounds but with a similar overriding goal to guide a young team towards greatness. The theory, as many have pointed out and as we both recognized, was that we would blend our own skills to lead the company. Instead, it had become a battle of wills. If it was just that, I could have lived with it. But there was more.

I was repeatedly approached by people inside the company asking me questions about the state of the company, including when the B round would close. Our strategy devolved into something resembling hoping for luck. Our cash was virtually non-existent. Dick spent his time out on the road trying to get money. Morale was sinking. Our CFO, Jim, was almost as hard to find as Dick. The pressure he faced was enormous. People in the company were begging me to do something.

Finally after a number of sleepless nights, I wrote a letter to Dr. Prinz, the Chairman of the Board, asking for a meeting in order to come up with a new management structure. I cited a number of reasons why Dick had proven unqualified to run the Ardica business, including our continued lack of financial statements, Dick's lack of understanding of sales and marketing, his very limited knowledge of manufacturing, and his inexperience with consumer goods. Bluntly stated, he lacked experience, charisma, and leadership. Not surprisingly, our bankers had pointed out to me that those were serious hindrances to raising money.

Fritz said he had decided to stick with Dick as CEO. He said that Dick was still working on all potential investors for round B, and they may come in. Fritz implored me to have patience. Now, as we began working with Legend, Ardica was in a very strange place.

Legend was here for the opportunity, and a good part of that, I think, was because of Shawn and me. Dick had reluctantly gone along with bringing in Legend because he had exhausted all of his financial options. Meanwhile, inside the company, no one felt comfortable with the status quo. We had a calm surface but just below that were simmering disagreements on how to run the company, on the goals for the company, and on how to spend the limited money we were getting from Legend.

"We essentially have co-CEOs," said Jim. "That's effectively how it is working...it's a little demoralizing for me. Everything is so dysfunctional... Dick and Hap have some serious issues. Everybody can feel it." Jim, who has had to pay bills with money that doesn't exist, was caught in the middle of everything. In a moment of frustration, he admitted, "I'm annoyed at everybody." Then he reiterated, "I'm basically pissed off at everybody."

And even though Hector and James of Legend saw Dick and me as something of a united team, Jim was angry because, as he put it, "Hap spilled too much dirty laundry" when talking with Legend. In fact, I had told the truth about our management struggles to James and Hector. Sure, I couched it in ways that showed how we could work it out. But I am not one to do anything but the right thing. The truth wasn't dirty laundry. It's what we were legally responsible to tell. Legend was our partner in this fundraising. They were putting their name and reputation on the line to raise money; as such, we needed to share everything and make sure they encountered no surprises.

Truth was an issue for Dick. The "imminent" round B closing, promised for 18 months with nothing having come to fruition, was the most pertinent example. But promises that didn't come true were becoming a hallmark of his leadership. I wished it weren't so.

Shawn put it bluntly. "The company needs new leadership. There's two cooks in the kitchen and you can't have two chefs." The problem with two chefs is that we also have two recipes. "One guy wants to build a third party supplier," said Greg, "and one guy wants to build a brand."

I was the guy who wanted to build the brand.

29

A T THIS POINT, the book project was canceled.

The management fight had come to this. Dick was no longer cooperating with the book. He ordered the engineers to stop cooperating and was, in fact, doing his best to stop all work on telling the story of Ardica. Ostensibly, his reasoning was threefold:

To avoid saying anything about Big Silicon, in case it might upset them (even if the book was to be released after we jointly launched a product or we went our separate ways);

To save money owed to my co-author to finish the book ($9,000, which was less than 5% of Ardica's one month's wages);

To save time of employees (who talked to me and my co-author perhaps for an hour once every two months).

Dick went to Fritz Prinz for support on the decision to cancel the book—my book. Fritz agreed, four days before Christmas.

There we were. The story of Ardica was one of heroes and struggles, but our Captain Queeg had let paranoia and a delusional version of the truth try to hide the real warts-and-all version that showed very clearly that entrepreneurial businesses are messy. He somehow confused a long-term book with a newspaper and worried about information being released prematurely. He worried that things hadn't gone exactly as planned and more than once while being interviewed for this book he defensively asked, "Where are we going with this?" He was used to being in charge and never being asked any questions.

There are inevitable ups and downs in a startup, and that was the idea of this book. Yes, I wanted to write about a dream coming true. I never wanted this to become a cautionary tale. But what I wanted most, what I was sure would attract attention to Ardica for all the right reasons, was to write the truth about the brilliant people at Ardica.

Starting a business is difficult. There are inevitable struggles between sales and engineering, between finance and marketing. Much of this I anticipated and had experienced before, but Dick brought a whole new dynamic for me. I thought his incredible resume combined with my business background would make for interesting reading and a remarkable business adventure, one worth chronicling in a book. I thought he knew the ups and downs were inevitable in an entrepreneurial business, and that there would be constant conflicting demands for limited financial and human resources. This would be a real business story, exciting and authentic. And it would be about life in Silicon Valley.

But the micromanaging CEO, Dick Martin, lost control of the story, which, like all true stories, went where it wanted to go. The calendar turned and events happened—or, more accurately, didn't happen as he expected. And so he decided to cancel this book as originally conceived. Cooperation of half the company had disappeared and some of those who did cooperate did so with a rebellious attitude. They were rebelling and cooperating on my behalf, and I appreciated it. They understood that no company stands on a pedestal, but the truth actually does. And if this book became successful, everyone would know of Ardica. This remained, despite it all, an homage to the excitement of entrepreneurship.

And so the tension in the company continued to mount: fuel cells versus batteries, tactical thinking versus strategic thinking, secrecy versus transparency, short-term home runs versus long-term business building. Dick versus Hap.

Legend did bring in the remaining $900,000 they had promised. It felt as though we had slipped through the eye of the needle and now had enough financial fuel for the next few months. But I still didn't feel close to being at ease.

The need to present a united front to Legend and the bridge loan investors had brought us together, but just below this calm surface was tension and disagreement. Disagreement on how to run the company, disagreement on the goals for the company, and even percolating disagreement on how to spend the limited money we were getting. I was excited about the remaining bridge money coming in, but I was concerned. A house divided against itself cannot stand.

GOING LIVE, BRAND NEW
November–December 2009

30

W IPED OUT BY A RED-EYE FLIGHT that started their trip and then a grueling series of sales visits in Montreal that were followed by the kind of late-night carousing that can ultimately create the friendship that leads to a sale, Shawn Biega and Rich Walwood collapsed on their respective beds in their hotel room in Manhattan. If it's Friday afternoon, it must be Manhattan. "Dude, we've slept seven hours in the last 72," said Shawn to a visitor.

Shawn and Rich were our salesmen on the road, and in New York they were essentially launching our product.

The launch in New York City was the initial sales launch of products to consumers. We chose Paragon Sports in Manhattan because it is arguably the most influential sporting goods retailer in the U.S. Paragon influences other retailers who regularly shop their store to see what the new, hot products are. It also influences a lot of the media that is headquartered in New York City as editors regularly go to Paragon to see what is in and even to get products to put in their publications.

Paragon. This was it.

Of course, "it" had been going on for a long time, even before our August sales meeting when Dick stopped in to say, "It is truly exciting to think we have products going out in the stores. I'm confident now that we have a pretty solid product...the challenge to us is for you guys [the sales and marketing team] to come up with the margins we need."

He kept harping on margins so after the meeting I showed him a Harvard Business Review article I'd come across that explained what we were doing in succinct terms. Written by Mark Leslie and Charles A. Holloway, the article "The Learning Curve" said, "High tech companies routinely 'price on the learning curve'–that is they deliberately set selling prices low on the early manufacturing runs to stimulate volume that will underwrite their efforts to gain enough experience to lower costs and ultimately reap higher profits." But business logic didn't make a dent in Dick's engineering mindset.

When he stepped into our meeting, it was a pre-Easter (pre-Legend money) gathering and our sales and marketing team was trying to figure out how to positively shock the world while doing it with almost no money. Since it seemed impossible, our team all signed up. That was our mindset. Of course, grumbling among us was amplified by cash worries and Dick's visit did nothing to calm us. But as I said in the meeting, we were there for the purpose of building a long-term enduring brand. We would do our part.

So in New York, three months later, Shawn and Rich were on a mission. Because it was a sales launch and Dick Martin had no real interest in sales, he didn't want to spend the time and money to attend. It was up to Shawn and Rich.

Shawn was the tall guy with a big-talking demeanor, and he naturally used the words "dude," "rad," and "gnarly" as if he was 17 on the beach in Malibu. He was, instead, 40 and in the very hip, urban Hudson Hotel in New York City. Rich was the other tall guy. He has reddish hair and Elvis Costello eyeglasses and a laid back yet straightforward demeanor that appeared a great complement to Shawn. They were two tall guys working in unison trying to perform the tallest of sales tasks—get the crew at the premium sporting goods store in America excited about our unknown product.

That was for the next day. For now, they had to catch up on their rest.

As they lay around upon arriving in New York, talk wandered to the Ardica struggles—the financial challenges and the management issues between Dick and me. I was 3,000 miles away working to resolve all of this. They were exhausted, and worried that the company was in trouble. Shawn's eyes were closing. The question was asked: "If things are so bad for Ardica, why are you here? Why are you putting yourself through this?"

"We ask ourselves that all the time," said Rich. Shawn nodded affirmatively.

Five hours later, they were awake and in the hotel bar socializing with some friends of Rich's who grew up with him in Milton, Massachusetts. One friend now lived in New York, and another drove down from Massachusetts. The sales guys were out for a little relaxation and as the night pushed forward, despite the visit from personal friends, there was shop talk. It ran down two parallel rails—worries and optimism. They were worried about the company. They were optimistic about chances to sell the product.

As Rich talked, from across the room a leggy blond boldly walked up to Shawn, looked up at the tallest guy in the room and declared that she noticed him and wanted to meet him. They talked briefly and she walked away, apparently disappointed that Shawn was married.

Six hours later in a diner around the corner from the hotel, Shawn's first meal of the night was consumed, a turkey club. Prior to that, Shawn's nutrition had for the prior 12 hours consisted of Ketel One vodka. As he finished his sandwich and the night finally drew to a close he laughed about the woman who came up to him. He let out an audible sigh and stared out into nowhere. He talked about missing his wife and his two young boys, ages six and two. It was 3 am in New York. His family was back in California now, sound asleep.

"It's a tough life," he said. "Being on the road isn't easy."

31

Building a brand from thin air is any company's dream. It was *this company's* plan. Sending Shawn and Rich to New York to help launch our product was just one culmination of months of marketing, selling, and planning that had begun, essentially, when I came into the company and hired Shawn. At the time, Ardica had not even registered its brand name or logo. We started, truly, from thin air.

Initially, we focused our sales efforts on our partners Mountain Hardwear and Sitka. Until we sent the team to New York, we hadn't actually started selling our products to consumers. But we were already building our brand. Everything we did—literally everything—became a part of building our brand. The way our office looked, the way our packaging looked, and the way we answered the phone were all part of the brand. My team understood this. We'd all done this before but every company is unique.

Ardica was more than that. This was a once-in-a-lifetime opportunity. We were atop the wave that would be the next new thing, energy— lightweight, portable, and increasingly green energy. It was up to us to put it together. Each application of our launch skills and experience had to be tailored to fit the situation.

We had done a lot of unique things, but one specific thing we did was break the sales of our products into two parts. We sold the electronics and wires to our brand partners to embed in their garments. When they did this, they were licensed to describe their product as "Ardica-enabled"—meaning the product was primed with wires, controllers, and heaters to provide heat on demand, and a USB cord for charging or running electronic gadgets.

The important part, for us, was that in order to complete the package the consumer also needed to buy our independent power system, the Moshi, which was sold and packaged separately. We sold the embedded components at a break-even level to our partners in order to ease the acceptance of the price of the Moshi. By doing this we were employing, essentially, the razor and razor blade strategy.

Since we were selling the Moshi directly to retailers to sell to consumers rather than selling to our partners, who would then sell to retailers to sell to consumers, we were eliminating one markup. This was a significant price difference. Plus, by using our own high-quality packaging and operating instructions, we were able to get our brand and logo in front of consumers. This was all part of our "no detail is too small" strategy in which everything we did was intended to build the brand.

A brand, from an internal standpoint, is an agreed-upon definition of who we are as a company. I'd been pushing the idea of brand, with varying results, to everyone in the company since I arrived. The sales and marketing team got it. They even joked to me about not wanting to hear another of my "silo talks" or, since I interchanged the metaphors, I was also asked, "are we going to hear about the damn pyramid again?"

Yes, in fact. The top of the pyramid (or the top of the silo, if you prefer) was where the influencers were and, of course, if you could influence the influencers, you then had influence in the entire market silo. The opinion leaders at the top of the silo were limited in number, but extraordinarily influential. People in the silos were aspirational, meaning they looked "above" them in the silos to see what to buy or wear. That is why in the hunting world we were in a partnership with Sitka, and in the outdoor world we were with Mountain Hardwear. It is why in fashion we were working with Hugo Boss, in skiing we were working with Spyder, and in electronic consumer goods we were working with Big Silicon. And that is why we had a Trendsetter program for influential individuals.

This approach is similar to what Regis McKenna was talking about in his February 1991 Harvard Business Review article, "Marketing is Everything." In that article he pointed out that the first Macintosh computer from Apple was ill-equipped to overthrow IBM. It had small memory, a black and white screen and no software. But as McKenna pointed out, "For all those deficiencies, however, the Mac had two strengths that more than compensated: it was incredibly easy to use and it had a user group that was prepared to praise Mac publicly as it launched and to advise Apple privately on how to improve it… Months before launching Mac, Apple gave a sample of the product to 100 influential users to comment on. It also… gave demos of Macs to industry insiders and analysts. The dialogue with customers and media praise were worth more than any advertising could buy." The Mac exploded on the scene and had immediate credibility and following.

In our sales meeting in August, I went over all of this. Then a month later, I did it again for the engineers, with the sales team in the room too.

The meeting with the engineers didn't go as well as with the sales team. "It was pretty disappointing," said Shawn afterward. "It was a room of about 15 people and nobody paid attention to Hap. There were no questions. No one said anything."

Shawn paused and added, "We're always trying to engage them. But Dick has only been talking to Dan and Tibor."

So here was the thing. We had been trying to create a unified message for ourselves and for the world, but half the company, under the leadership of the CEO, seemed preoccupied or even uninterested.

"I think the real problem is Hap and Dick," said Shawn bluntly. "There's Hap's boys and there's Dick's boys. But there can't be two chiefs. That's my opinion." Meanwhile, in the middle of our quiet and unspoken but obvious tension was the brand. "There are a lot of challenges," said Shawn. "It would be nice if the company were a little more excited."

Shawn, the excitable one, kept us going, and we had already done remarkable things to build the Ardica brand. Our side of the company was excited because we saw the opportunity. But the engineers were wary instead of excited, because when they saw money being spent they seemed to expect an immediate return. We tried to explain that a brand takes time to build, but it would be enduring, and the growing awareness was already becoming apparent to anyone who looked.

Meanwhile, our transparency was counterbalanced by a deepening secrecy from Dick about the F-43 project and our future ability to market the fuel cell technology. In August, the only thing Dick said in our meeting was that "The whole fuel cell market won't be good until we get the fuel squared away...we have made some breakthroughs to make it cheaper and repeatable." And that was apparently all we needed to know. We didn't hear about milestones reached or milestones in front of us. We didn't hear about products or the progress with Big Silicon. We were kept, it seemed, deliberately in the dark.

But we were building a brand. We needed all the information we could get. We wanted synergy. Instead, we got Dick standing with his hand in his pocket, talking in a monotone about engineering, and staring at the floor. *Our leader!*

At that pre-Easter strategy meeting, after Dick walked out, we talked for two days about how to build our brand, including how to present ourselves at trade shows that we probably couldn't afford to attend. Of course, we needed to attend trade shows because that was where we made our initial sales contacts. We brought in Adam Rodriguez and Martin Corpos, two engineers working on the Moshi and Technology Connector project to understand where we actually were in the finalizing of the product for the market. We wanted a firm assurance of the date we would have a final product so we, in turn, could responsibly assure our partners that we would deliver the finished product we had shown on time. And, that it would be totally reliable, because we all know that a key pillar of brand building is a corporation's reliability.

But the engineers said there were issues with getting the product finished on time. Adam described "fighting fires" on various things while getting the product finished and Martin added, "There's a lot of room for improvement." It wasn't exactly comforting.

In fact, we needed to build a perfect product in spec and on time. I didn't get the sense that the engineers understood how essential that step was to the success of our brand. While we discussed how to lower the price and improve the product in the future, we did so with the understanding that we were on the verge of going to market with what we had. And though our launch was small, it was filled with fanfare. We were, indeed, building a brand.

In fact, given what we started with, we were suddenly the dog that caught the bus. How did *that* happen?

It happened because although the entire company didn't have a plan, the sales and marketing team did, and we created our own synchronicity. We had set out systematically more than a year prior working to get the word out about our company and our product.

One of the first things I did when I joined Ardica was to institute a Trendsetter Program to test the product and start seeding the Ardica name in the actual marketplace with highly respected individual opinion leaders. It was run by my old friend and colleague from The North Face, John Kirschner.

"I am the one that gets it out of the laboratory," said John. "The Trendsetter Program has three main purposes. It is product testing and product feedback by people who have no connection to the company. Their only connection is to me. Second, it is to create buzz in the ski industry. And third, to enhance sales through our retail customers."

The idea was for John to get a Moshi-heated jacket, labeled "Ardica-enabled," into the hands of honest, visible users of the product. "All the people who get the product know how the deal works," said John. "They don't lend it to anybody…if they like it they tell everybody. If they don't like it, they tell me."

Getting these unique jackets made for us was a lot harder than it sounds. It required us to design and build a garment of our very own with our own materials and specifications. We then needed to source the products in Asia and have them integrated with the sourcing of our Moshi components. Getting manufacturers in Asia to make short runs of limited numbers of garments was incredibly difficult, especially when we had to hit the same deadlines as all the other fall outerwear marketers in the world. There it was again—pressure and tension—on one more front.

32

I HAD BEEN USING Trendsetter Programs since my time with The North Face and I had found that these programs provided valuable information when launching something new. It was one piece of a larger puzzle, providing crucial user feedback from the most demanding users in the market at the critical development stage. The important part, of course, was getting the right feedback from the right people.

That's where John Kirschner came in. John, who lived in Vail and was a leading Vail ski instructor, was very plugged in to the outdoor world, including rescue people, top ski instructors, ski and outdoor salesmen, a very visible ski resort president, and the vice president of a ski boot company. Just knowing the people, of course, wasn't enough to get them to participate as trendsetters. According to John, the product "has to be something that works really well, is attractive, and is made of *unobtanium.*"

He explained. "In all of sports, the guy who feels really cool is the guy who has something his buddy can't get. His buddy can get it next year at retail. Of course, there's a fine line between exclusivity and loneliness." Trendsetters are visible, influential people who understand the concept. "That's why I handpick the people," he said.

John grew up in Beverly, Massachusetts, north of Boston. He proudly and often described himself as a member of "The Tribe." His parents moved to Massachusetts in 1938 after fleeing Nazi Germany. His father was in the leather business, selling fine suedes.

While growing up, he skied and loved it and when he graduated from college, as he explained, "I wanted to go skiing for a year." That was more than 30 years ago.

I first met John Kirschner through a mutual friend in Vail, where John was living. He had gravitated to Vail after graduating from Northeastern University with a degree in education as an English major. His goals were to be a disc jockey, an English teacher, and a ski instructor. When I met him, I found him to be funny and outgoing, incredibly thoughtful and sincere. We became fast friends. Then when I came back to Berkeley, my phone started ringing. John wanted to work for The North Face. He called again. And again. And again. And finally he just loaded up his car and drove from Vail to Berkeley. I hired him as project manager.

"Hap wanted me to implement a key dealer program where we would pay more attention to our best customers," recalled John. Soon, John showed an incomparable level of initiative and was instrumental in suggesting The North Face start a ski wear division. He recognized that "there really weren't any barriers other than that we weren't doing it." Plus, he said he saw that "every garment we made was in dark blue or tan. I saw we needed to make something in red."

John understood the DNA of our brand, what it could and could not do. We started to get traction. "The best thing about Hap," said John, "was that he let you run your own division and make your own mistakes and then pay for them." John didn't make a lot of mistakes. "I learned about being a supplier of wholesale ski wear, running a sales rep force, financial parameters, and I had a lot of fun and did business with a lot of great people," recalled John from those North Face days.

Eventually, he left Berkeley after tiring of city living and pining for life back in the mountains. He worked for four years in Sun Valley, Idaho before moving back to Vail to start a consulting business and resumed teaching skiing. He had been there a long time and made a lot of connections, and so when Ardica wanted to start a Trendsetter Program, John was a natural to approach.

I actually originally approached John before I got actively involved in Ardica and when Tom and Tobin were running the company. When the company was just starting to think about selling a fuel-cell heated jacket. This was before Dan designed the Moshi on a cocktail napkin. "Two winters ago, I had a hydrogen fuel-cell powered vest," recalled John, who was among the first to discover for sure that the product wasn't ready. "Product testing before me was walking into the cooler at Safeway," he said. John had trouble getting paid and the product wasn't ready, so he just stopped collaborating with Ardica.

But then I became involved in the day-to-day management and I called him again.

As John told it, "Hap was getting more involved. Shawn had just been hired and then Rich and Greg came in. There were actually people who understood sales and products." So back he came to do more field testing and another Trendsetter Program.

In the winter of 2008-2009, the first Moshis were sent out for testing. Of 60 sent out, according to John, 20 failed. "The batteries failed or the connectors were bogus. We had to duct tape the connectors." Even with those prototype issues, John found interest. "I'd be honest with people. But this is so unique that they were all intrigued."

Still, he noted, "Had we not put them out there testing last year, we would have made some very costly mistakes. It's easier to fix 20 than 2,000."

While the Trendsetter Program was useful in getting the name out and fixing mistakes, the rest of the team was working in unison on other parallel paths creating the same message. We were all building the Ardica brand, the world's next great brand for active outdoor customers. The next Gore-Tex if you will. This was wearable technology, and we wanted to be the best damn company in the business. Not just for the ego of being the best. We knew from our extensive industry experience that the brands that are the best have the greatest longevity and are an annuity for future business. And, great revered brands end up increasing the market value of companies as much as five to ten times over those with a monotone brand.

Greg Nevolo was working on unique packaging, graphics, and visual merchandising for the brand, all with our unique orange color, one that, as it turns out, is very difficult to replicate and, hence, a bit costly. Rich Walwood was putting together displays of our technology for getting our message across, including a tough steel Halliburton briefcase to highlight our electronics for prospective partners, and in-store displays to do the same for retail consumers. Shawn was working with the P.R. firm, honing our message and helping set up story lines to get our company really noticed.

Everything our team had done had been to create momentum going forward. Yet we all understood that, despite our amazing success, launching a product and a brand wouldn't happen overnight. We were looking for input from customers in order to improve our future product while building our brand.

This was why we ran a trendsetter program. And it's why we sent Shawn and Rich to New York. We were taking on the burden of directly selling to certain key stores, allowing us to train and educate the salespeople. Electronics in clothing was pretty new and not something that every garment salesman felt comfortable with. Plus the salesmen we used through our partners actually had hundreds of products they were selling. Counting on them to get enough time to really focus on the launch of the Ardica product was difficult. On the other hand, we only had one product to sell, so we could focus laser-like on selling and educating. Put another way, if we didn't sell, we would be out of business. "Do it right or die" has a way of focusing you when you are selling.

Not only are many garment salespeople uncomfortable selling electronics, many otherwise excellent salespeople are also uncomfortable pioneering a new product. Maybe they want to sell products which they already know and know can be sold quickly, thereby putting a lot of commission money in their pockets right away. Or maybe they only want to sell products where they don't have to worry about anything going wrong. There is an old sales adage that goes, "pioneers get all the arrows." Of course this thinking didn't apply to all salespeople. Some were perfectly suited for pioneering sales, but we didn't want to rely on this probability. Rather we wanted to use our team that was focused, driven, and skilled at pioneering sales.

33

PARAGON SPORTS WAS LOCATED at the corner of 18th and Broadway in Manhattan. Yes, we were actually launching our Mountain Hardwear partnership in a real store on Broadway.

Specifically, we were launching on one-third of a 5'x3" rack on the second floor of the four-story, 30,000-square-foot, fourth-generation family owned Paragon Sports—a one-of-a-kind leading edge retailer. The fact that we had only a few square feet to work with was disappointing. The fact that we were on Broadway, in Paragon, was exciting.

"I think I just waited on Courtney Love," said one of the salesmen at one point during the day. Paragon is that kind of place in that type of location where the former wife of deceased rock icon Kurt Cobain may or may not have shopped. Customers from all over the world, including pop culture icons and Hollywood celebrities, came in to the store.

But that was later. At about 11:05 am, they were in a cab heading to Paragon, already a bit late for a prep meeting with the Mountain Hardwear rep. "Dude, call RJ [the rep] and tell him we're on our way," Shawn said from the front seat to Rich, who was in the back.

"No one is holding their breath waiting for the Ardica guys," said Rich. "We'll be there in two minutes."

The driver, Shawn discovered while riding next to him and befriending him like he befriends everyone, was from Turkey. "Oh, I've been to

Turkey," said Shawn. "Istanbul." The driver shared where he was from and then suddenly in front of the cab was a mess of a traffic jam with a police flasher going and five buses and many cars piling up in front of them. Shawn suddenly turned to his new Turkish friend and demanded, "Come on, dude, take a left. Go now!" The driver, inspired, turned left. Shawn then inspired the driver to not see a red light and get the cab to the Paragon within what seemed like a New York minute.

Inside the store, there was a long line of people waiting to pay. Rich led the way to the second floor and into the maze of racks.

On the website NYC.com, a blogger named BC from the Lower East Side described Paragon this way: "The place was almost maddeningly busy and you're well advised to ask one of the innumerable clerks strategically positioned all over the store where your department is upon entry; otherwise you will wander aimlessly up and down stairs looking at more stuff than you planned to and feel overwhelmed by all the shopper activity going on around you."

At the top of the stairs, Rich started towards the huge North Face display along one wall, past Marmot plopped in the middle, and then he found, across from the ultra-warm-looking Canada Goose jackets with a coyote fur hood, Mountain Hardwear's small slice of valuable second floor real estate. At the end of one of Mountain Hardwear's racks was Ardica's Moshi on a silver stand over the words "Heat, Power, Charge." The Grand Opening.

Standing by the rack waiting with a casual smile was RJ Turner, the Northeastern sales rep for Mountain Hardwear. He was talking to a couple of sales associates from Paragon when Shawn and Rich walked up, introduced themselves and then situated themselves near the rack. On the way to the store, Shawn and Rich were asked if there was a plan for when they got to the store, and the answer was there was no need for a plan. They'd done this before.

The goal of the day was to educate and excite the staff. The secondary goal of the day was to sell some coats. The theory, by coming to New York in mid-November, was that the weather would be cold and people would be coming into Paragon anxiously looking for a warm jacket. The reality was the weather was 55 degrees with a light rain.

Nevertheless, the publicity generated for our product in *The New York Times*, *Popular Science*, and other publications had already generated some buzz even without a fully educated staff. Two weeks before, when the coats first arrived, there were 12 men's and 12 women's coats. There were now 5 men's coats left and 11 women's coats left on the rack.

According to Margo Donohue, the director of the New York office of Ardica's public relations firm, editors are always looking to be the first to discover something cool and so getting publicity for the Ardica was fairly easy because the product was leading edge. Margo and I had visited the publishers in June to set up articles for November and December publications. Now, Margo visited Paragon to meet Shawn and Rich to learn more about our product and our sales methods.

And so at one point, crowded around our small chunk of retail space, there were our two salesmen, Margo, RJ, and three Paragon sales associates. Other Paragon sales associates wandered by in what seemed a random order of one, or two, or three at a time.

The training was casual and friendly. Rich sipped coffee. It looked like hardly anything was happening. Along the way Shawn said this does that and Rich echoed the sentiment and expanded it into that does this. In reality, they were without fanfare explaining our product to the sales staff but were simple and direct. And the sales staff understood immediately. It looked like hardly anything was happening, but it happened. Professionalism is making the difficult look easy and selling is all about making a sale without the buyer actually realizing they are being sold. A key part of being a great salesman is being a great listener. And that was a key part of what the team of Shawn and Rich were doing.

Having two people selling works particularly well because while one is talking the other can be listening—listening for what the customer (in this case both the retailer and the end consumer) want. Then later they can feed this information back to the product development group for the next round of products. In other words: to be successful requires designing what the customer wants, not what we want them to want. But, it is important to know that not every customer can articulate exactly what they want, so a great salesman has to be a particularly astute listener and draw their own conclusions.

Lawrence Mollicone, a sales associate with the name tag "Larry," was among the first to see the product that day and also the most enthusiastic. He even figured out the question a customer would ask that would lead him to show the customer the Mountain Hardwear heated jacket. "If they said, 'I want something really light that's not too puffy and will keep me warm,' I would show them this."

As Larry bemoaned an earlier heated fleece jacket put out by The North Face, Rich explained that while being significantly lighter and more compact, our product actually came with a printed circuit board embedded in it, providing artificial intelligence to control devices like phones and MP3 players. And, of course, the really compelling part was that because it was embedded in a jacket, it provided power on the go. The North Face product only provided heat. Even RJ, who was there to sell Mountain Hardwear jackets, said, "I think the heat part is a lot more of a novelty than the ability to power things up."

Larry echoed the sentiment. He pointed to the jacket and said, "I want one of these."

Then he pointed to the Moshi and emphasized, "I *need* one of these."

Larry had explanations for things, and he predicted that the Moshi would be hot. The reason why more men's coats sold, he said, is that "Women are not as quick as men to buy into technology. That one that sold may have just been a gift." This was a feedback nugget since our initial assumption was that women usually seek warmer clothing and therefore we felt they would actually be more enthusiastic about the heat. Learning is an iterative process.

Men are more interested in early technology than women, suggested

Larry and he added, "The early adopters definitely will want to have this now." Larry considered himself one of these early adopters and added the only concern he or others might have would be the price. But in order to be in sales in Paragon, he said it is important that he not just know about the product but also use it. He said he buys lots of items at Paragon and intended to get a Moshi immediately.

Paragon sales associate Sergio Vazqueze said his lead question to a customer was, "How will you be using it?" He added that the department is fun to work in because the customers are educated and are avid readers of outdoor media. He said the Mountain Hardwear jacket heated by the Moshi is a cutting edge product that will "appeal to hikers and campers in remote locations." The "gearheads" will love it, he said. "If you could put a satellite antenna attached to that coat, you could sell it," he added.

Sergio pointed out that he is not a salesman. His role is instead to help and educate the customer. "With these kind of leading edge products, our role is figuring out what the customer wants and then reacting to it." Sergio, who was working as an industrial designer on a 1,700-acre resort in Costa Rica until the economy went down, came to Paragon because he needed a job and he liked the atmosphere. And that's what was interesting about this store. It was not staffed with a typical teenage staff muttering "whatever" in a suburban American mall. These were adults, engaged and educated adults.

Getting these adults excited to sell our product in this primetime Manhattan store was very important. But there was a lot of competition here. A huge chunk of real estate was taken up by the The North Face. And even in the Mountain Hardwear line there were numerous options. RJ Turner of Mountain Hardwear said of our Moshi, "I don't think the product is ready yet. I think next year's design will be better." But he added that if the price came down and the design became sleeker, it would be a huge winner. "Just look at how excited the staff is about it." Later, Ted Ganio, director of Mountain Hardwear product development, was asked if he thought the product was ready and he said yes. "Anybody who thinks you can produce a perfect product out of the gate has never been in product development," said Ganio. "We are sold out to retailers," he said, and added, "our business next year will be three to five times what it is this year, easy."

In the background, the store's stereo system played the Rolling Stones song "You Can't Always Get What You Want." About that time, a man in a gray suit appeared and started watching as a sales associate tried on the jacket. When asked, the man declined to give his name but said he was a stock market investor working in New York. "I kind of have a reaction of this just makes sense," said the man. He added that the price seemed a little steep. He did not buy.

But then a boy walking by with his family noticed all the people standing around and soon Shawn and the boy's mother and one of the sales associates were having a conversation. The boy tried the jacket on and he loved it. Mom asked the price and didn't blink. Shawn talked about more features and when Mom asked the boy what he thought, he said he loved it. But then…the coat quit working.

A wire got kinked up or something. It wasn't the Moshi, it was part of the Mountain Hardwear unit. That's why Shawn was in the store on this first day. He began fidgeting with the jacket. It was also why RJ Turner from Mountain Hardwear was in the store.

"Where's RJ?" asked Shawn.

Then he asked again, louder. "Where's RJ?" Meanwhile, the family stood quietly by watching as Shawn tried to get the jacket to warm up again. RJ was nowhere to be found. The mother thanked Shawn for his effort. RJ, who lives in Scranton, Pennsylvania, had apparently already started his drive home, and a sale was lost. It wasn't the end of the world, but it was a missed opportunity.

Another customer who was interested but did not buy was Daniel Young of New York. He liked the heat element the most. "Being in the city, you walk into a subway train and it's sometimes warm and then you go out and it's cold. I like being able to control your environment."

Nick Traina, a Paragon sales associate who was also a college student wanting to go into marketing, said he was impressed by the Moshi. "I just see this as a part of everyday life. I think in ten years this will be everywhere." By the time Nick had his turn to learn about the Moshi, the day was almost over for Rich and Shawn.

As they finally stood outside the store waiting for a taxi, Rich said Nick's reaction was exactly what he was looking for. "The day went really great," said Rich. "We didn't sell anything, but we will."

A couple of weeks later, Rich was back in San Francisco concentrating on a new promotional event, our design contest. During a break, he had a few minutes to reflect back on his trip with Shawn to the East Coast— Montreal, New York, and then Maine to visit L.L. Bean. The New York trip, with the goal of educating the staff, was a success, he said. "Sales is going to be the ultimate quantifier," he said. "We can judge that after Christmas."

Shawn described the approach in Paragon as a "subtle sell." He described the East Coast trip as successful in educating numerous stores about the product, as was the trip to L.L. Bean in Maine where they were "going through a lot of paperwork" to set up a partnership line for next year. Shawn and Rich, by doing this year-early work, were seeding the market in a sophisticated way that required detailed sales skills. But as the market continued to get seeded, Shawn said he worried about the company meeting deadlines. It was the concern of every salesman in every startup—maybe in almost every company: Can we deliver what I just promised?

The education process flowed in two directions. As we started to deal with some larger companies we found that we were more scrutinized. The trip to L.L. Bean, said Rich, was an example of exactly that. "We've been talking with them for six months about developing a couple of products," he said. "That trip was more for them than us. They wanted to vet our internal systems… They walked us through every single department.

They took us to the legal department to make sure we are insured and certified. They took us to customer service to ensure we can match up to their policy of superior service and integrity… it raises the bar for us… To some degree we were taken to school on their processes."

34

R ED LIGHT? What red light? Rich Walwood needed sushi. It was a little before 5 pm on December 5th when Rich started accumulating undetected traffic violations in San Francisco for the sake of Ardica, and for the sake of putting on the best possible presentation of our Design Contest. The contest had been planned for more than six months, the finalists were in town, all the employees and investors and other friends of the company were going to be here, and Rich was in charge of pulling it all together. The event started at 5 pm. "We'll be there at 4:59," Rich announced assuredly to his helper that afternoon.

Until a few hours before the party, work throughout the company did not halt. Rich, with Miriam Dower's help, had planned the party, but nothing had been set up until that day, and it was still being set up. I helped others put the final touches on the room, and Rich went off to pick up sushi, beer, and posters from Kinkos announcing the contest. The first stop was the birthplace of the Moshi, the Moshi Moshi restaurant. But when Rich pulled up to the intersection, the light was red. The restaurant was across the intersection but suddenly his white Volvo found a way across the intersection. "I'm in a hurry," he said. He explained it using the same four words when he crossed the once-again-red light intersection in the opposite direction with six huge trays of sushi and four cases of beer loaded in the back of his old station wagon. Red light? Apparently just a suggestion.

Later, grabbing the posters from Kinkos, Rich realized the store was on the opposite side of Market Street and so he simply did a city U-turn and parked where a meter was—for only a moment. He could have racked up enough points to lose his license, and get a parking ticket, in the span of 15 minutes. With a trunk full of beer, the temptation at that point was to open one and tempt fate completely. But Rich hurried into Ardica to finish setting up, and then got back to his car to change out of his grubby clothes into what he called his "Superman costume"—dressier clothes. After all, he understands presentation, and the design contest was an integral part of our introduction to the design world. The time for action was here.

The idea of the contest was to challenge designers from around the world to come up with innovative uses for our Moshi, and then present the winners with prizes. The hope was also to present the Moshi to the world. Given our goals, it seemed natural to put Rich Walwood and his eye for retailing and presentation in charge of running the event.

Rich grew up as the entrepreneurial-minded son of an architect. His father designed commercial buildings, churches, houses, and office buildings, and Rich was the neighborhood kid you could ask to get your bicycle modified or maybe to buy fireworks. "I had an entrepreneurial spirit," recalled Rich. "I was always doing stuff on the side."

When he graduated from Boston College High School, he wanted a change of scenery. So he chose the Midwest, majoring in journalism at Marquette University in Milwaukee. And then he switched to architecture at the University of Wisconsin before moving back to Boston to attend Boston Architectural College.

"I started selling clothing to support myself through school," said Rich of the beginning of his retail career. But the beginning didn't last long, as he went to work with a friend who was in the masonry restoration business. "I joined the bricklayer's union. I laid some brick," said Rich. "I was 23, 24 years old. It was a bitch, hard work, but the money was great so I did it for a while."

But then one day in 1989 while at a friend's wedding in Panama, Rich had "a tropical epiphany" that led him to find less backbreaking ways to make money. He returned to Boston and worked as a bike messenger for a couple of years, but then a friend asked him to help deliver a 61-foot sloop from Newport, Rhode Island to Key West, Florida.

Once in Key West, he was asked to help run a sailboat charter business and do some bartending on a boat as well. And so he settled into Key West life, which included "a new crop of girls every week, lots of drinking, and other things as well." It's the kind of life that can wear even a young man out, and when Rich was offered an opportunity to go to San Diego and work at the America's Cup Race, he jumped at it. In May of 1992, Rich woke up with a girl he just met, convinced her to rent a car, and drove to San Diego.

He found his way to the merchandising program of the America3— "America Cubed"—sailboat in the America's Cup. "Our first goal was to outfit the team and from that we had a fulfillment program in which we solicited donations and then gave a gift. It evolved into us having a retail store on our own."

Rich became a merchandising coordinator for the America Cubed brand that began opening retail stores and doing licensing deals on things such as clothing, watches, and shoes. It was a shooting star of a business that lasted three years. By the time it closed in 1995, Rich had learned a lot about merchandising.

After a few months of vacation in Mexico and Spain, he found a friend who was selling the t-shirt half of a wetsuit business. Rich and a friend purchased the "Red Ink" print shop and turned out some black financial statements by visiting trade shows while concentrating on the surf and skateboard market. The company showed solid growth for more than a decade while concentrating most of its efforts on the Japanese market. But the Japanese economy hit a wall in 2000. His partner left the business and "the energy of two people was cut in half."

With a bunch of extra inventory in his basement, Rich opened a retail store in San Diego and operated it for two years. During that time he attended trade shows and met a lot of sales reps. One was Shawn Biega, who at the time was running his own sunscreen and lip balm company, Beyond Coastal. At that show, Shawn introduced Rich to me briefly. We exchanged phone numbers and stayed in touch.

Meanwhile Rich ended up representing other lines as an independent sales rep as well as his own line. In his travels he came across a brand of sunscreen, Zinka, that he remembered as popular featuring neon colors in the 1980s. He tracked down the original owner of the brand and ended up working with the owner's daughter-in-law. "I said, 'I can help you package this and I can help you sell it,'" recalled Rich. He started as an independent sales rep/consultant and he ended up running and growing Zinka for five years. But when the growth wasn't rewarded, he left. "One of the first people I called was Shawn. But Shawn said, 'I wish you had called me six months ago. I just sold my company,'" recalled Rich.

But then Shawn mentioned Ardica, and Rich was immediately intrigued. As Rich said, "The technology was definitely interesting. It had legs in the marketplace. But in the back of my mind I thought I'd show up for work for a brand that was already established. It's an uphill battle trying to introduce something. But the idea of working with Shawn and working with Hap was very appealing."

He was hired within one day. Rich remembered coming in and "we talked for hours." He took the job even though he had a perfect spot to live in Los Angeles. "I had a killer house with a private beach." He left that to work with us. We picked him because he had a perfect set of skills that we needed. He was an entrepreneur, he was passionate, he had experience, and he loved making the messy and chaotic part of guiding a startup into a smoothly running, branded machine.

And now he was running traffic lights and doing U-turns on the streets of San Francisco for Ardica. We didn't assign him that. He took the job on himself. We actually assigned Miriam to be the point person on all logistics for our contest, and Rich to oversee the party and the PR associated with it. The event served a number of purposes—it was our design contest and holiday party. The design contest was our first opportunity to inform designers around the world about our groundbreaking product. We wanted to create buzz in the design community and hopefully get some new product ideas that could eventually go to market. In addition, it would get our brand name before the eyes of a lot of influential people. Since we used the web extensively for the execution of our contest, it was also one of the first legitimate opportunities to showcase our brand to the end consumers. We named the contest "Power to the People."

Our summer intern, Brian Payer, volunteered to help organize and run the contest. He had run contests previously, so he knew how best to set it up. But there was much more to it than the contest.

35

As a holiday party and a showcase for Ardica, we had to present the proper image of our company. It was a stage we created to give the world a tiny glimpse of who we were—minus all signs of the fuel cell business. The missing new technology of the F-43 and the secret negotiations with Big Silicon were hidden by all of us in secret compartments in our brains, not to be spoken of all night long. And all physical evidence was locked in our two rooms for chemical experiments, where the glass walls were papered over to obscure what was inside.

The engineers didn't clear anything from their work area until a few hours before the party started. That was when Rich and Miriam could prepare for the event and transform our office into a festive hall while maintaining our high-tech vibe. Meanwhile, we were also working in conjunction with our neighbor in the American Industrial Building, Blue Sky Studio, a professional photography studio on our same floor. Bill Delzell, the founder of Blue Sky, allowed us to use his extra studio space that we converted to a science fair-like atmosphere for the awards presentation.

It was a big night and we did everything we could to present our best face to the world. I obsessed over finishing the interior design on our office, to finish replacing the frat house look that had come from originally furnishing our office from the "Free" section of Craigslist and give our workplace a professional and high-tech look. The face you put out to the world, I've learned, is the face that the world interprets. Building a brand is always about consistency of image. You can't produce high-quality product in a garage, and you can't produce high-tech, commercially marketable products in a frat house atmosphere. In fact, our bankers, Legend Merchant Bank, told us that they decided to work with us rather than another fuel cell company partly because our office design demonstrated to them that we "get it"—not only how to develop products but also how to market, promote, package, and brand them. Clearly, the branding was beginning to work.

But we weren't finished as of the Friday before Saturday's party. Ben Damron, the project manager for Sand Studios and the lead interior architect on our office, was there with his crew of workmen renovating and upgrading the bathrooms and the conference room, personally pitching in on the last-minute details of scrubbing and painting the walls as well as completing the sign on our door.

We had originally hired Ben when we first started the redesign of our offices a year and a half earlier. Because of tight cash, we broke the project up into financially digestible parts, and we now brought him and the team back to actually allow us to meet San Francisco electrical and earthquake codes in the engineering area while finishing off the bathrooms and the conference room to match the functionality and aesthetic of the previous work. He'd already established our aesthetic by hanging ceiling-high banners with pictures of extreme sports on them and used them as dividers in our most public space. In a phone interview, he called the ceiling-high banners a "big gesture, a literal interpretation of what Ardica does."

Ben described the initial effort to design our space as "wanting something much more refined. More artistic than dynamic. I kept distilling, taking away more and more...My excitement about the project was drawn from the energy coming out of the employees. There's people walking around in lab coats with test equipment. It's an inspiring environment."

Miriam described the redesign as, "Making it look modern. It combines the industrial feel with a clean, techie, modern look."

Ben was inspired by the building that Dan picked out for its high ceilings and how they inspired creativity. Across the years, Ben the designer found synchronicity with Dan the engineer. When I went to Ben I offered him few constraints other than a tight budget and, importantly, a deadline—the day of the design contest. He said he'd meet it. On the morning of the party, work was still being done. In fact, a mirror in our bathroom had fallen on Friday but luckily didn't break. Maybe that meant seven years of good luck. It certainly meant the mirror had to be re-hung in a hurry.

Part of the renovation that was immediately necessary was dictated by the fact that we were just days away from a safety inspection by both the city of San Francisco and OSHA. We needed to redesign how we stored our hydrogen canisters and reroute some of our wiring to bring us up to San Francisco wiring and safety code. All of this went on during the week leading up to the party, which made daily work even more difficult for the engineers. Theirs is a job that required focus, and the noise wasn't helping.

Meanwhile, Rich had asked for help in preparing the area where we were holding the design contest and party, and that also took away from their focus. Rich was given the responsibility to put on the party, but because of the hard division of responsibilities that Dick had created between the engineers and the sales and marketing team, he had no authority to get the engineers to help. He could only use moral persuasion, which proved mostly ineffective. He was in a frustrating position, which led him to disobey common traffic laws in order to fulfill his obligation. Ben finished in time. The entire party was being thrown, it seemed, at the last second.

That wasn't true, of course. We had planned it for quite a while. I actually came up with the idea back in June, and our intern, Brian Payer, raised his hand and volunteered to help run the contest. Our sales and marketing team loved the idea and thought it was a great way to build the brand as well as get the word out to the design community about our robust power system. Rich and Miriam became the managers of the project, and Brian used the experience from other green technology contests to help us.

Brian was a summer intern who worked on our hydrogen delivery system for both the F-43 and army projects. "It is ridiculously more practical than what I learned in school," said Brian in June, when he was first interviewed for this book. "This is incredible, a hands-on research experience. I feel like I won the internship lottery." And he acted like it, volunteering for any task at hand and showing incredible enthusiasm and aptitude for all that he did take on, including, when the time came, to help with our Design Contest.

Brian, who was 25, grew up near Cleveland, Ohio. His dad was a professor of materials science engineering at Case Western Reserve University and Brian's interest in engineering was somewhat genetic, but he found his way to Ardica via Stanford University, where he got a bachelor's degree in chemical engineering and had now gone back to the University of California for a graduate degree in Engineering Entrepreneurship. He spent his summer between degree programs working for us in a lab coat and goggles creating a hydrogen-laden "pill" and then figuring a way to stop the process we used from "foaming and caking" into "soupy viscous garbage." In June, in the midst of it, he loved describing what he was doing and demonstrating and explaining what was happening. He was one of the lucky, determined ones who wouldn't let school get in the way of his education.

Brian was tall, 6'3" or so, and thin with a calm intensity, joyful yet serious eyes, and big ambitions. As a "garage project" he was working on developing a type of paper that could be printed on, erased, and printed on again—reusable paper.

And during the summer and then during his first semester of graduate school, Brian helped us set up the contest by creating a database of potential participants, doing an online template of the requirements for entry, and setting the criteria for judging.

While Rich was organizing the party and getting posters designed, and while Brian was setting up the contest, Miriam handled the logistics and most everything else. Others were involved too, including Brinn Wellise of Switchback, our public relations firm. "We put the word out to the media and to design schools," said Brinn. "We engaged Wired and Gizmodo… our role is media specialist."

Brinn described how there had been "tremendous traction" during the previous couple of months and she was correct. For instance, *Popular Science, Outdoor Life*, and *Canadian Ski* magazines all named our product one of the top products of 2009. In fact, for working with a startup with zero sales, Brinn had done a heroic job, and her pitching had garnered us press in dozens of outlets including online, on paper, and on-air. She began pitching our "Power to the People" contest in the summer.

By then, she had already been pitching stories about our company and our portable power system to her varied contacts across the media world, and with great success. She started in August of 2008. Shawn had worked with her on a number of other projects, and he suggested we work with her. Plus she and I had a number of mutual contacts so we immediately found a way to work together. Mostly because she was good.

"Our pitching is targeted and different," said Brinn. "There's a lot of individual pitching. Another tactic we used was we brought Hap out to New York for some one-on-one, desk-side meetings with editors." There were meetings with *Popular Mechanics, Maxim, Outdoor Life, Field & Stream, Prevention,* and *National Geographic Adventure.*

I remember it was a whirlwind trip in July 2009—three days, four meetings a day, all changing as we progressed. The purpose was to plant stories with long-lead media, publications who were writing for publication in November and December, just when we planned to launch the Ardica program in retail stores across America and in Canada and Europe. Margo Donohue, of Switchback, and I hopped in taxis going back and forth to various locations across Manhattan, trying to tell the Ardica story while framing it so it had interest for the specific magazine we were approaching. In some cases it was a story about heat, in others it was about wearable technologies. In some, it was about my background in the outdoor business. In one it was about brand, but this highly fashionable editor was as interested in admiring our watches as our actual pitch for Ardica.

That is PR—you can't control it. You can only guide it and go with the flow. Moreover, the summer of 2009 was a particularly strange and challenging time for print magazines, which were facing a tremendous number of cutbacks in personnel. Two years earlier, when I had been on a similar trip, every magazine had two or three writers ready to sit with me. Now the number was usually one, and these were time-starved writers. Fortunately, we were prepared with samples, handouts, and well-honed pitches so we could be as efficient as the writers required.

Perhaps the most bizarre point was when we went into a building where one of the magazines was formerly housed. It turned out that all the publications had moved. We started at floor eight and saw nothing but empty offices. Then we went to floor seven and all the way down to the lobby. It was a ghost town. Not a single person was there, just empty space. An eerie feeling, a sign of a changing times. Typically, the doorman knew nothing about where the company had gone and was less than helpful, so we set out scrambling to find the magazine. I was on my computer, Margo was calling information. The phone number for the company actually wasn't much good either because, due to cutbacks, no one was answering their phone. Finally, I found the address on the computer and we jumped back into a taxi sweating and swearing. When we arrived at the new offices, only about 20 minutes late, we were assured that being 20 minutes late is just like being exactly on time in New York City. So we began our pitch.

"I haven't heard a lot of skepticism," said Brinn. "I've heard a lot of editors say, 'I want to try that product.'" Brinn, who was based near Lake Tahoe, was especially tuned into the outdoor world, a world that is a comfort zone for Shawn and myself, and a natural place to launch our product given the influence of credible outdoor users and trendsetters.

And, it is an industry where consumers will gladly pay a real premium for quality products that enhance their experience, potentially save their lives, or just give them some cool products to talk about.

The list was as impressive as it was long. It was a great job by Switchback, because even before we had a product hit the shelf we were getting publicity, and by the time of the design contest in early December, we had been written up on influential blogs like Gizmodo, newspapers such as the *Wall Street Journal* and *New York Times*, and, as mentioned, we'd even been named one of the products of the year by *Popular Science* and *Outdoor Life*.

It was a snowball effect, as each bit of publicity led to something else. Even when it wasn't perfect, it was still always good and we learned from any criticisms. On November 16th, 2009, Lauren Goode wrote in the *Wall Street Journal*, "When it's generating heat, the jacket is quilted heaven for the gadget geek; a wearable, socially acceptable electric blanket that doesn't carry the infomercial stigma of, say, the Snuggie." At the end of her article she added, "I really enjoyed the heating function, but its device charging left much to be desired." She thought our technology connector took up too much room and she was disappointed it did not fit to her Samsung flip phone, one of 20% of devices it did not connect to.

But even that was a mostly great article, and we were still working on the technology connector and even considering scrapping the idea or outsourcing it. We actually encouraged outside input so we could learn and get better.

And that's why we put out the call to designers from outside the company, via the design contest, to come up with innovative uses of our product. "The goal for us is to alert the world, and specifically the design community that this new format for portable power exists," said Rich. "It's a way to reach out and generate some buzz."

36

THE EASIEST WAY TO EXCITE DESIGNERS is with a cash prize and a prestigious panel of judges. We provided both. We offered a $5,000 grand prize, a $2,000 second prize, and free airfare to San Francisco and lodging for the weekend for all nine finalists. And, importantly, we offered their designs access to an elite panel of judges:

- Dr. Fritz Prinz, Chairman of the Mechanical Engineering Department at Stanford University (also the Chairman of the Board of Ardica)
- David Kelley, founder of IDEO one of the world's leading industrial design firms and the originator of the Stanford University Design School
- Ted Ganio, VP of Product Development at Mountain Hardwear
- Joe Brown, Product Editor of *Wired Magazine*
- Brian Lam of Gizmodo, one of the world's leading technical blogs
- Myself, the founder of The North Face

In just a few weeks, we received more than 100 registrants and 17 completed concepts. The contest closed October 1st and the nine finalists were notified within a few weeks.

The finalist team leaders were:

- Saravanan Nagasundaram, a freelance designer from Bangalore, India, who suggested a heat wrap for back pain (He did not attend the event because of visa issues)
- Fabio Texeira dos Santos of the Universidade do Sul de Santa Catarina in Brazil, who suggested a wetsuit with a heating system (he dropped out because of intellectual property issues)
- Heng Fuu Yeh (Richard Yeh) of Studio Y and the Parsons School of Design in New York, who suggested a serving system to illuminate shot glasses.
- George Thomas of the University of Alabama, who suggested a portable car seat heater that can be moved from a car to chairs at home
- John Eng of the Rhode Island School of Design, who suggested a sleeping bag heating system
- Kyle McCrory of Virginia Tech who suggested a heated sleeping bag equipped with a flashlight and the ability to charge electronics
- Crosby Reinders of Virginia Tech, who suggested a ski patrol vest able to charge a number of items as well as provide heat to rescue personnel
- Matthew Mangati of Virginia Tech, who suggested a vest for photojournalists that powers their necessary technology
- Tony Smith of Virginia Tech, who suggested a powered respirator for coal miners

After the staff of Ardica picked the nine finalists in the conference room, aided by the help of several six packs of cold beer, Miriam was in charge of informing the finalists and arranging for travel and accommodations. She also planned the award ceremony and worked on a schematic layout of the event, giving it a science fair look. She worked on the guest list and coordinated the judges as well as the PR people. "Miriam was a huge player in making this possible," said Rich.

So while the event was being planned and Rich was getting posters designed and the finalists were fine-tuning their presentation, we decided to also engage Stage Two Consulting to hold a People's Choice Twitter vote and get more buzz in the digital world. They were not given much time, but we received more than a thousand votes in the contest, which translated into thousands of page views.

According to Jim Schaff, vice president of Stage Two, his firm worked in concert with Switchback as he did with other skilled PR firms, which mostly target more traditional media. Schaff remembered that I wanted to do more to increase our visibility in the tech community, and so he not only set up the Twitter vote but also began contacting influential bloggers outside of the mainstream. "We are supplementing your PR firm," said Schaff. "Because of the space we're in, the tech community takes us seriously."

When someone who is respected tells others to check something out, it's usually worth checking out, explained Schaff. For instance, he said, one of his influencers, Ken Yeung, told his 3,700 followers to check out our contest and "as a result you get access to some of their followers as well," said Schaff. This was the same effect that we got on skiers and mountaineers in the Trendsetters Program run by John Kirschner. This was synchronicity of brand and purpose. John was identifying and managing the Mountain Team, and Stage Two was helping identify and manage the Urban Team.

Stage Two was started by Jeremy Toeman, who was one of the creators of Slingbox, the successful TV-for-your-computer tool. He marketed Slingbox very effectively using social media and in 2006 he launched Stage Two. Schaff found his way to Stage Two after hiring the company for his own firm, which specialized in data storage. According to Schaff, the social media networking "went phenomenally well" and so when he left his company he gravitated to this new field. But even with the new rules and new go-to people, "It always comes down to product," said Schaff.

And for Schaff, the gadget folks loved the Moshi. In fact, he was hoping to get the product installed beyond the jackets into backpacks, which he thought would be a huge market for us. But in the world of social media, becoming viral is a key. He offered the example of a blender company that began putting videos of its blender blending wood and other not-normally-blended items as a way to think outside the box. The blender company, through their "Will It Blend?" YouTube videos, increased sales 350%, said Schaff.

Our design contest was not as viral, he admitted, but he said getting the word to young designers and the tech community would lead to good things. "It's a space that's driven by gadgets and disconnected devices, and the only unifying factor in all the devices people are carrying around is that they all need power," said Schaff.

The contest fit that theme and expanded on it by asking designers for new uses for our portable power system.

By the time Rich returned upstairs in his "Superman costume"— essentially a sport coat—the contestants were setting their displays up in front of the big room at Blue Sky Studios that we borrowed from Bill Delzell.

Bill was a great guy, a friendly neighbor and a fellow entrepreneur. The American Industrial Building that we were housed in has probably 100 small and burgeoning businesses, not unlike our own in terms of the stage of their business. But Bill had a well-established photography business with three studios. He shot catalog product photos for companies like Banana Republic, the Gap, and Williams-Sonoma. He also did portrait shots for aspiring models and even regularly shot the head shots for the annual Miss America contest. But, besides this, he was also developing a revolutionary new photography studio concept, a series of computer- controlled cameras, lights, and backgrounds that could reduce the number of people and the time required to do a photo shoot by a huge amount— initial tests showed a 75% reduction. This entrepreneurial concept was where we really intersected.

Shawn, Greg, Rich, and I all had spent time talking with Bill about his exciting idea and even using it for some of our product photography. It was easy to work with Bill. He was an easy-going and engaging guy.

So, when we needed extra space, it was natural to go to Bill and he immediately said yes. When he found out we were going to have numerous influential people from the design world, from tech blogs, and from well-known magazines, he even offered to keep his photo studio operating so we could photograph some of the winners and participants and also showcase his technology to any of our visitors who were interested.

Meanwhile, the big room where the engineers work had been transformed into a party room with a few well-placed red and green table cloths, some glittery pine cones, and lots of beer, sake, and wine. And sushi...yes, we kept pushing the Moshi–sushi connection. After all, branding is all about consistency. There was music and people were gathering. Our normally dressed down workers were almost dressed up, and for once the place felt tension-free. I was there with my wife, Margot, and others were arriving with their spouses too.

But there was one key person missing—our CEO, Dick Martin. His outgoing wife, who had a very successful Mary Kay distributorship, was there and having a grand time, but Dick was called away at the last minute on an East Coast trip, for reasons he never explained. She said he hoped to get there in time for the end of the party. The party had been planned for months and he was the CEO. It was odd. His wife, who lived in Pittsburgh, had come all the way out for the contest and party. I really felt it was too bad that Dick wasn't there, because this night, for once, all the tension had melted away. We—plural, as in all of us—were Ardica, and we still had dreams. Leader or not, we had dreams.

The big room at Blue Sky studios took on an in-process feel as the contestants in their oxford shirts and ties set up side by side, and some bloggers stood around and interviewed them while a photographer chronicled it all. Down the hall on the fourth floor of our old building, the big room at Ardica took on a cocktail party feel, but within an hour the party was moved to Blue Sky, where rows of chairs were set up and the students (all contestants who attended were students) were to give 90-second presentations.

First, I got up and briefly discussed our robust power system and how we wanted the world to think about it. I stated that we thought reaching out to designers was a great way to spread the word. Then Rich stood and introduced the contestants, who each spoke about their project. All were articulate, though some were nervous speaking to that room full of smart and amped-up people.

When they were interviewed before the presentation, each expressed a natural affinity for our Moshi and confidence that they'd come up with a useful and marketable product. "The ski patrol has all these devices they use," said Crosby Reinders, who designed the ski patrol vest. The ski vest won third prize.

Matt Saunders, part of Tony Smith's Virginia Tech team that built the powered respirator for coal miners, said his team watched documentaries on coal miners and talked to a friend who worked in the mines, and then they studied how difficult it was to work while using existing respirators. This was a product we surely had never thought about at Ardica, and it was a great use of our miniaturized and portable power system. It really did provide a socially valuable idea. In fact, the powered respirator for coal miners was so impressive it won the People's Choice Award as voted on the Twitter contest run by Stage Two.

Greg Lefevere part of Kyle McCrory's Virginia Tech team that built a heated sleeping bag equipped with a flashlight and charging capability, said his team gravitated towards camping based on what he saw on our website. The sleeping bag won first prize.

Rich thought all the contestants had great products but was especially impressed with the overall presentation of the sleeping bag that won first prize. "Their damn brochure looked better than ours," he said.

After the winning plaques were presented, the party moved back to the Ardica party room, where music was blaring, wine was flowing (as were shots of sake), and engineers and salespeople stood side by side, smiling. It was a great entrepreneurial moment. The engineers let loose—Dan danced on a desk, and Adam gave Tibor lessons in "rubber knees," a hands-on-knees 1980s dance move. "It couldn't have come any sooner," said Rich of the party. "It has been a little tense."

At the end of the party, Dick appeared.

THE SUGAR DADDY STRATEGY

December 2009–January 2010

37

"**D**EAR BOARD MEMBERS,...Demo and briefing scheduled for (the CEO of Big Silicon) today at 10:00 am." Dick Martin wrote theBoard on December 9th, 2009 and said our potential product had passed over all hurdles with Big Silicon's underlings, and a demonstration with the world renowned CEO was scheduled.

The implications seemed clear, Dick was saying a deal was on the verge of happening. Unfortunately, a deal of some sort was always on the verge of happening according to Dick, but none had come true in the two years he'd been trying to raise money. But now, again, a deal was seemingly upon us. Dick and Fritz were convinced that Big Silicon would buy us at a very high price. Both Legend and I voiced strong doubts that would happen. It seemed to us, based on our experience, that we were a long way from a deal. But our voices were drowned out. Dick and Fritz proceeded forward on their own.

In late November, Dick told the Board that he and Fritz, as Chairman, had communicated to Big Silicon that our proposed selling price would be $40 million plus an additional $10 million when Big Silicon hit $150 million in sales of the product using our technology and another $10 million when they hit $250 million in sales of that product. Dick said that, in response to this potential selling price of $60 million, Big Silicon executives had said was "that is definitely in the ballpark." Dick boldly told some Ardica employees that a deal would be done by the end of 2009. At the time, the CEO of Big Silicon was supposed to see a demonstration of our product. But he didn't see it. The demonstration was delayed. And then delayed again. I felt the fact that they had presented a financial sale price and proposal to Big Silicon without first consulting the Ardica Board of Directors was unsettling and represented a corporate governance issue.

Things were happening, but neither the Board nor I had been told exactly what. There was a scramble to produce alane, the high-density fuel that we were working on, at a price that was acceptable. Dick said we are almost there. Based on what some employees were saying to me, I was skeptical. I asked Dick if our scramble to produce alane meant that Big Silicon had indicated they wouldn't accept our initial fuel, sodium borohydride. He didn't answer. In reality, Big Silicon hadn't even decided to put our product in their line. But Dick insisted the negotiations for the sale of our company were almost complete. He told Shawn, "You are going to have yourself a great Christmas present when this closes!"

So on December 9th, when the CEO of Big Silicon theoretically saw our product (I don't actually know for sure that he did), Dick's optimism was high. The next day, he told me that the CEO had now delegated negotiations to members of his team. Dick said it was "just part of their negotiating strategy."

Meanwhile, our negotiating strategy seemed to be let's shoot from the hip. In fact, we didn't actually have a strategy. Dick and Fritz offered up hopeful numbers backed by a brief analysis saying, in essence, Big Silicon would introduce our product and buy a huge number from us. So that bit of wishful thinking was worth $60 million. I explained that, in my view, this was a bit like borrowing their watch to tell them the time of day.

Still, since both Dick and Fritz were talking specific numbers, I wondered if an impending offer was actually real? Had Ardica really somehow found the winning lottery ticket? I hoped so. I doubted it, but I hoped so.

Legend and I strongly suggested that the corporate governance on this wasn't being handled properly. After much pressure, Dick finally agreed to schedule a Board meeting. We had a lot to discuss, including my proposal to hire an outsider to give an objective opinion on the transaction compensation issues as well as a negotiating strategy. One other issue that had been percolating was the idea of finally ending the management schism and simply splitting the company into two parts, the fuel cell side and the Moshi side. Of course, nothing was simple and the numbers Fritz and Dick put on the value of the Moshi side were skewed very high, probably due to the same rose-colored glasses they used to value the potential of the deal with Big Silicon.

I proposed that the Board get professional advice from an advisor. We needed advice on how to proceed with a potential sale of the fuel cell business, and how to split off the Moshi products, which Big Silicon, we were told, was not interested in acquiring. We needed advice on valuing the company.

The Board interviewed a number of candidates for the advisory role and then narrowed it to two, one recommended by Legend, and one recommended by our law firm.

By this point, our Legend money had mostly been burned through and many people, including employees, were again owed lots of money. Our sales reps had not been paid commissions in three months. Shawn Biega and Greg Nevolo were threatening to resign. But, as the story continued to go, Dick kept promising that a deal with Big Silicon was imminent and he refused to consider an alternative in case it didn't happen. Our back-up plan of having Legend raise a sizable institutional round was in limbo because Legend had not received enough information from us to prepare for the institutional round. When I looked into it, I found that had Dick actually told our CFO, Jim Retzlaff, to hold off generating information. Due diligence preparation and fundraising apparently was not a priority when Big Silicon was sure to show up and save the day.

Of course, money was still needed and we still didn't have money. This shortfall forced us to cancel any big presence at trade shows and greatly inhibited seeing customers. And it potentially threatened our relationships with our key customers Hugo Boss, L.L. Bean, Mountain Hardwear, and Sitka. But our situation continued to be double-sided as, despite all our internal issues, we were generating fabulous publicity and garnering numerous industry awards for the Moshi apparel system. Plus we continued selling Moshis as fast as we could get them. This was a problem, since we couldn't pay our vendors to get the additional Moshis to sell. We needed a runway of money until we either got an institutional raise completed or sold the company to someone. But we were living hand-to-mouth with a strategy best defined as "dreams come true, don't they?"

What an odd place to be. In fact, what an odd place to continue to be. Hope isn't much of a strategy.

Three days before Christmas, Dick called me while he was on his way to the office. Big Silicon had, he said, "given an offer of $20 million." I pressed for details and he admitted it "wasn't a term sheet." I asked what it was and he said that $20 million was a firm price. He then added that he and Fritz thought they could get the price up to $25 million.

The next day, on December 23rd, we had a Board meeting to discuss the "offer" and hire the advisor/consultant we had chosen. The consensus of the Board was to choose Dave Epstein, who was recommended by our law firm. He was smart, with a Silicon Valley background, and had experience with finances, which was a real contrast to Ardica. He brought an outside perspective. In fact, we thought bringing in any advisor was necessary to satisfy our director's governance requirements. He was sure to generate information to get us off our butts. Epstein proposed a daily fee. The Board, as a group, felt that if a deal was imminent, as reported by Dick and Fritz, there was no need for a long-term commitment from an advisor. The proposed longer-term advisor's commitment, which had been made by the consultant who was recommended by Legend, was unnecessary and probably too expensive. Dick and Fritz were confident we didn't need or want long-term advice.

Fritz also took this moment to suggest to the Board that the company should stop investing in developing the Moshi side of the business because the purchase of Ardica was about to happen. He suggested that if the Ardica brand business were to go on past the sale of Ardica to Big Silicon, we should find someone to buy the Moshi side and/or I personally invest in it outside of Ardica. He knew that I would be interested in that side of the business. He suggested it was worth $5 million because that was what he thought was invested. In fact, the amount invested was far less, but that argument was actually irrelevant. The true value is only what someone will pay for it. And the value is only there if the marketing team is there. And that became iffier by the repetitious daily promise of Big Silicon's impending purchase, being only a day away. Every day, it seemed, it was only a day away.

On the morning of December 24th, 2009, Fritz wrote to Big Silicon requesting that they "provide a fair offer, in writing, and include all the key terms."

Fritz and Dick were clearly dreaming of a very green Christmas and the dreamer in me was hoping they were right. But the business person in me was worrying that something was missing from their logic—mainly logic.

On Sunday, December 27th Big Silicon wrote back to Fritz to say that, in thinking about Ardica, Our "valuation is firmly below $20 million at this time...Thus, we think the best next step is for you to think about selling below $20 million."

This wasn't $60 million, or $40 million or even, actually, $20 million. It was "firmly below" $20 million. Although Dick and Fritz had Christmastime visions dollars dancing in their heads, I found this to be a very predictable response from a company like Big Silicon. I had told both Dick and Fritz that a sale was premature and all we could expect at this time was a lowball offer. There were four reasons, I believe, why we received the low-level "offer," which actually wasn't really an offer but rather a suggestion of a possible offer. The four reasons that I saw were:

1. Big Silicon had not yet decided if the product that our components and fuel were supposed to drive was even going to market. If for

sure they were going to market with our product and were totally dependent on us, Fritz's valuation of $40 million plus bonus payments when sales thresholds were reached could have made sense. His suggestion was apparently parried by the potential acquirer, Big Silicon, who said, "We don't know *when* or *if* we will introduce the product." This was immediately followed by a suggested drop in potential valuation by 70%. (Yet they remained interested in our technology, or why talk at all about an offer?)

2. There was no competitive tension. Without competing bidders, there was no pressure on Big Silicon to act fast or aggressively. They were Big Silicon, but they weren't the only Big Silicon around – yet we acted like they were.

3. We had confused them by offering two fuels, one which is more desirable but further down the line. Now that they knew a better, lighter, more miniaturized solution might exist, it could be the only thing they wanted, and we could not yet deliver it.

4. The fact that when Dick asked them to consider being an investor in the B round, we had shown them Ardica's financials. This meant they knew we were under tremendous financial pressure and could not hold out very long for a higher price. Dick, in effect, had shown them our poker hand. The fact that we still begged them every month for our development payments probably confirmed to them that we were in no better shape financially than the financials we had shown them during the B round.

From my perspective, given our cash-strapped situation and the fact that we had made zero progress on providing financial information to Legend, if we could get $20 million, it would be a godsend. But the negotiating price was stated as "firmly below" that number and so the question became, should we negotiate? Or were we just negotiating against ourselves?

Fritz and Dick remained confident. Fritz even suggested to the Board, "let's play hardball and just walk away. Then they will come back with a higher price."

Au contraire. As I stated above, Big Silicon had four very specific points of leverage, while we had squandered many of ours. With no money and a $90,000 payroll due every two weeks, the pressure was clearly on us. Given the hole we were in, I believed we should negotiate towards $20 million (if we could get it) while also rapidly preparing for an institutional round of financing as a logical Plan B. In reality, much of the due diligence required for an institutional round would also be required by Big Silicon in an acquisition, so this would not be double work. And it would prepare us for two possibilities. Right now, we were prepared for neither.

In a subtle way, preparing for an institutional round would increase the competitive tension because Big Silicon, which was actually encouraging us to find alternative sources of funding, would recognize that we would be talking to strategic investors, maybe even some of their competitors, as well as financial investors. These strategic investors would surely only be interested in buying us if they got an exclusive to all of our technology.

This recommendation to re-energize the institutional round of fundraising, of course, led to the trickiest thing of all. Namely, to pull off an institutional round, we needed structural changes: a different CEO, and a new Board composed of experienced and sophisticated business people. We also needed to convince the sales and marketing team to stick around. I was now spending more and more of my time in non-productive conversation with my team, trying to overcome their mounting dissension over being so fed up they wanted to leave the company. Some of their comments were rational. Some were emotional. Many were laced with expletives, as they tried to find a reason to stay without a new CEO.

So as the end of the year approached and Ardica hadn't been bought for $60 million as we were led to believe, Dick unveiled his new plan. This newest Plan B, which he told me he had been working on all along just in case Big Silicon dragged on a little longer, was to raise $625,000 in equity from a bunch of his friends. This would tide us over, he assured me. "Not to worry," he said. "Those funds will be here during the holidays." When the funds hadn't arrived as promised over the holidays, I confronted him with the fact that we were literally out of cash. He said, "You know, it's hard to get to people during the holidays." Speaking of holidays, it was like Easter all over again. Or Groundhog Day.

38

O N THE SECOND WEEKEND of January 2010 Rich Walwood
opened an email from a customer and, he recalled, "I'm just
thinking, oh shit, this is the email I never wanted to get. It's
catastrophic basically."

The customer, Rich explained later, had found a hotspot on his
Mountain Hardwear jacket where the wires crossed in the heater, and
it had melted through the lining of the jacket. "He just wanted to let us
know," said Rich. "In fact, he loved his coat. He wanted it fixed or replaced."

Rich decided to be cautiously optimistic. Likewise, I suggested that
opportunity is sometimes disguised as catastrophe and that we needed
to approach it that way. Meanwhile, Dick talked to the supplier who
assembled the heaters and sent Eric Folsom, our manufacturing and outsourcing manager, to visit the supplier. The immediate plan Dick came
up with was to do x-ray analysis of the returned products we received to
look inside and see what was wrong, because the heaters were embedded
in the jackets and therefore not visible to the naked eye. Dick proved
once again to be very good in a crisis. Unfortunately, he was not so good
at avoiding a crisis.

Rich's first thought was that one bad jacket might indicate more, and
that could be catastrophic. But he also knew that until this jacket problem surfaced, the few problems discovered had been minor or caused by

operator error. Although we wanted a perfect product, at least some of us understood that a brand new product in a new category might need tweaking.

The need for some tweaking was clear back in July when our marketing manager, Greg Nevolo, discovered while on a trip to Europe that the middle "charge" light on our coat did not come on, as promised in our brochure, when it was charging a device. Greg expressed concern that, although this was a cosmetic issue, customers might incorrectly conclude that their device was not charging. Rich agreed and called it a "potential nightmare" but design engineer Adam Rodriguez calmly explained that any new device would have bugs. It turned out to not really be a big deal and it was corrected by some inserts into the product's directions.

In early December, another glitch showed its face. A writer from the *Chicago Tribune,* who had been field testing the jacket, discovered her battery only stayed charged for a little more than an hour on high heat. In our manual, which Greg wrote and circulated for editing throughout the company, we had described our heat as lasting three hours.

We discovered that because Trendsetter feedback said the jacket needed to be warmer, the engineers had reset the level of the heat in the jackets we sold. But the engineers never told sales and marketing about the change. The engineers increased the heat level by resetting the power flowing to the heater, but this increased power resulted in directly decreased power running time. It was a simple adjustment, but the crucial information never got passed along and there was a lot of finger pointing. In the end, we made a few changes to the website and to the brochure. We reduced the stated battery run time to what was the correct run time. Fortunately, by this time we had enough sample product with users in the field who told us the reduced run time was acceptable, so we didn't have any need to let a document stay in the field that was overstating what we could do. The problem was resolved. In many ways, what we were going through was the classic path along a manufacturing learning curve. This was real life experience playing out along the curve.

Fear of impending doom had become standard operating procedure in recent months. But most of that was due to the ongoing money concerns.

Worries about product failures bringing down the company were never prevalent, but fears of missing deadlines and not paying vendors were. Some of these were natural in a startup. The ongoing money issues and management struggles over the direction of the company, however, had a distinct flavor.

"After the holiday party and design contest, Dick proceeded to blame myself and Rich," said Miriam. "We were the reason the company had no money. I heard from him for two weeks that we bought a ton of booze and we didn't need to buy so much alcohol. After the party, some people took home bottles of wine," she said, and that upset Dick, who claimed that the party was to blame for the company's money woes. Not to mention that the party not only boosted morale, eased the tension, and brought the company a ton of great publicity that most company holiday parties would never dream of getting. He was only concerned that a few employees ended up with a free bottle of wine from the party. A party that he, as CEO, had skipped most of. Morale boosting, obviously, was not near the top of his to-do list.

Blaming the small budget of the holiday party for all the company's woes was a continuation of Dick missing the point or, perhaps, misrepresenting the facts. Somehow, in his eyes, the improvements to the design of our offices were also "party expenses." These were actually capital expenditures for improvements that helped change our image from frat house to high tech. Plus, one third of the cost of those were for electrical upgrades to get us up to safety code. Safety—the ultimate party expense. I was growing weary of it all.

There were too many things going on that I didn't like. There was still the absence of standard financial reports to run the company on a daily basis. Not only did we need them to manage the business, but they were also a requirement per our agreement with Legend Merchant Bank.

Dick and I disagreed on seemingly everything but the most urgent problem. Yes, we agreed, we needed money. Yes, we agreed, a burnt coat was bad. After that, we were parallel but disconnected trains. His track went north. And my track also went north, I believed that we both had a vision of success. But we had two very different ideas on how to get there. I also believed that while both our visions were lofty, mine was at least backed by facts. And it seemed that Dick the engineer didn't like my facts. I didn't really know what to do, although I knew what I had to focus on because my sales and marketing team had begun a not-so-quiet revolt against Dick's leadership. It had been festering.

39

JAMES PALMER of Legend was a bit angry at our Ardica team. For one thing, he was receiving conflicting directions on raising money. He offered and the Board agreed that Legend would raise $425,000 more to add to our bridge loan to give us desperately needed short-term operating capital. But Dick only took $125,000. Just enough to meet the next looming payroll. Then he unilaterally told James that he didn't want the rest. He gave no clear reason, and he did not consult the Board.

James had sent his family skiing for the holidays while he stayed in San Francisco to raise money for Ardica. "Frustrating!" he wrote in one email. With that as background, Dick avoided James and the money. It was weird. At first, all Dick would say to James was that he would get back to him and coordinate it later. Understandably to me, this made James angry and he explained to Dick that the money was not something you could just turn on and off like a switch. Besides, the Board had already approved the $425,000 addition to the bridge loan, and the money was very necessary, with or without Dick's equity money. But Dick thought the $625,000 he had been pursuing was on the way, and he apparently didn't want the company any more indebted to Legend.

James was also upset that the advisor he recommended, Jeff Scheinrock, had not been chosen. When James asked to discuss this issue, Fritz showed up an hour late. Yet despite some flashes of anger, James remained surprisingly positive. Perhaps it was because that is his nature, or perhaps it was because if he did an institutional round he would be paid handsomely.

The advisor we did hire, Dave Epstein, said of Legend, "I don't want to talk to them because they are the enemy." Dave told me that "Dick doesn't trust Legend. Dick's plan was to buy out Legend with all the money he could raise." This, of course, would require Dick raising $1.625 million to buy out Legend, and then more money for operating expenses. In fact, if Dick raised the elusive $625,000, it wouldn't even cover our current expenses. It certainly wouldn't buy out Legend. We currently owed about $700,000 and had $300,000 of operating expenses each month. Our current estimates were that we needed an additional $1 million to cover our operating expenses through the spring. Adding all these rough numbers together indicated we needed at least $3.4 million. Dick was unable to raise $1 million over 18 months. We needed help.

Epstein stated that, in his opinion, when Big Silicon suggested negotiating "firmly below $20 million," they were actually talking about something less than $10 million and perhaps as low as $1 or $2 million. Maybe he was right. But they must have been somewhat interested or why would they have even considered negotiating? Yes, I understood as I wrote that, that I was sounding like Dick and Fritz. It's how Big Silicon mastered using the carrot. It's actually just business. A sober look doesn't mean you can't still be intoxicated.

Lots of things remained mysterious, primarily because the standard operating procedure of our CEO continued to be secretive. After telling people that a deal was going to happen by the first of the year—and it didn't—he never bothered to explain anything more. It just passed. Even the engineers, who generally got more input than the rest of the Ardica team, were left in the dark. Sure, they sensed something but he never told anyone of the non-offer offer—that is, the offer to negotiate if we were willing to talk about a price firmly below $20 million. And so no bills were being paid, and no information was being shared. Tick, tick, tick.

40

THE TIME BOMB OF LOOMING BANKRUPTCY was getting noisier by the day. In the engineering room, Dan Braithwaite kept his head down. Determination? Of course, that was Dan, but he also had a distinct hangdog look. Tibor Fabian also appeared stressed, but it was hard to completely determine their moods anymore. They no longer cooperated with this book, and they didn't talk to me much. Shawn, though, talked to them and then Shawn talked to me. It's very much, as James once pointed out, like high school all over again. And, to me, the cool kids in the engineering room look very stressed.

The sales and marketing team didn't need anyone to interpret their moods. For instance, Shawn was owed $20,000 in commissions and expenses, and he had been owed the money for months. That's cause for a bad mood. In a meeting with Shawn and me, Dick said he could only pay $1,500 of the $20,000 to Shawn. Dick also asked that Shawn pay his own way to trade shows and conventions and then get reimbursed. Since both Shawn and I had gone six months without being reimbursed one nickel, this seemed like a bad idea. So Dick then suggested that Shawn take Dick's corporate card, with the name "Dick Martin" on it, and use it at trade shows and while visiting potential customers across North America and Europe. Dick somehow didn't seem to realize that Shawn might have to show an ID that matched the credit card to use it. Finally, after haggling, we agreed to get Shawn a corporate card with his own name on it. Of course, this too would have to be paid at some point, but Dick pointed out this saved us from paying cash now. This was just one of many he-doesn't-get-it issues the sales and marketing team had with the CEO.

"I'm not going to stay if the CEO is not out," said Greg Nevolo. Greg was openly rebellious, wildly independent and, at that point, oozing with negative passion. As the time bomb of bankruptcy ticked, and the CEO remained secretive yet blindly optimistic that his eggs-in-one-basket strategy counting on an immediate sale to Big Silicon was brilliant, Greg had become the loudest voice shouting that the emperor had no clothes. Actually, the CEO wore the same clothes—black Izod shirt, ink-stained whitish chinos and black orthopedic shoes—every day in a very military-like way. Yes, the commander wears a uniform. We all got it. Greg especially.

For months now, Greg had been working like a maniac and feeling underappreciated, ill-informed, and financially restricted in his ability to execute. The money issues affected him quite hard since he was a marketing manager often on the road and in need of company support. Back in August, when another payroll was paid late and the automatic deductions taken from Greg's personal account for his personal bills were, in turn, halted, Greg wrote a letter to Jim, the CFO, and he copied it to Dick, Fritz, and me, among others. It said, in part, "I don't appreciate how the leadership of this company continues to FUCK with the well-being of the 20+ employees that are committed to the success of this company."

Referring to that letter later, Greg said, "I went off the deep end. I unloaded both barrels of the shotgun. But it's about being upfront. Don't wait until an hour before something happens to tell me. It's about delivering accurate and relevant information so we can make decisions."

That payroll glitch, which now appeared to be a small glitch in comparison to our current situation, inspired this written comment from Fritz back to Greg: "No doubt the company has a liquidity problem at the moment, but every effort is made to correct that…Like many small companies Ardica is in a fragile state. I am asking that you remain patient and supportive for a little longer. Change will come shortly." It was an August promise.

So Greg dug in and kept conceiving of brilliant marketing designs, while doing his part to nourish relationships with key customers, especially Hugo Boss in Germany. The passion that had led Greg to write that letter was the passion we saw when we hired him. We were an energy company and Greg was an energetic guy.

Greg Nevolo, who was 38, grew up on the west side of Los Angeles, a place he described as "Venice Beach, Santa Monica, and Malibu." He was a self-proclaimed skateboard and surfboard fanatic who also loved to ski. When he was growing up, his parents took him skiing often. Despite those earthly thrill-seeking pleasures, Greg's sights were in the stars. When the first *Star Wars* movie came out, Greg saw it 30 times. But although those were living-vicarious moments, as a child he learned to pilot an airplane and he dreamed of being an astronaut. "If I could go back in time, I would instantly enroll in the Air Force, but at the time: no way, the military wasn't for me. I have a problem with authority." Of course, Greg still had a problem with authority. That was one of his most endearing traits.

Another was his intelligence. "When I was in high school, I found out a very interesting thing about myself. I never had to study and I could get a B." His father, a corporate lawyer, was often on the road, so he was raised mostly by his mom. He was always in trouble in high school and, after his family moved to San Francisco, he attended the Brothers of the Holy Cross Religious School where he was constantly in trouble for "talking during mass, planting a smoke bomb during a dance, talking during class, and general inappropriate behavior." In other words, he was developing a perfect personality for a great marketer.

Despite his expansive personality, Greg was developing another side as well. It happened during his junior year in high school. "I worked at The North Face retail store in Palo Alto and I took a climb for my first time.

That was the moment my lifetime with the mountains was solidified…I was scared shitless. I was scared of heights. That climb got me over my fear of heights and all of a sudden my world opened up. It seemed at the time that everybody's missing this."

He briefly tried college at San Luis Obispo and declared a major of "yeah right." On vacation while skiing at Lake Tahoe, he realized that not only was he a good athlete, he was also a great skier. So he began competing in ski events. "I started winning events…and sponsors started paying me to travel." He was taken to Alaska, for instance, and got to ski completely fresh snow, "6,000 feet of vertical skiing, the best skiing you can ever do." By 24, he was being flown to Europe and he was hooked on the lifestyle. His question became: "how to market myself to companies?"

While he pondered this, he had plenty of time to sit and think and talk while waiting for good skiing weather. He recalled a conversation with some pilots who told him he should go flying while he waited. "All of a sudden, helicopters came into my life," said Greg.

In 2002, his mother succumbed to a four-year battle with breast cancer. "I took care of my mom the last five months of her life. That was the most extraordinary moment of my life. I was there for my mom. It was an extraordinary awakening to what matters in life." When his mother passed away, he took his inheritance and went to flight school.

His career as a paid skier, Greg soon learned, was to have a short shelf life. In 2003, Greg partially tore the ACL in his knee in an accident, of which he says, "I should have died. I didn't die. It was a huge wake-up call."

After he recovered, as he matter-of-factly stated, "I discovered that I had a talent for building ski jumps." He built them with a Snowcat, "a humongous thing with a blade on it; you could destroy things." But instead of destroying, he built ski jumps and began to make a new name for himself. He was hired by ESPN to work from camera platforms and make sure they were set up to get the right shot. One adventure led to another. He began skydiving and then base jumping, all variations on flying and getting air. He found sponsorship for his base jumping from

Sobe, the drink company. "This brought me into the energy drink world."

About this time, Red Bull contacted him about being a project manager "to get a helicopter to Nepal and land it on Mount Everest. Reflecting, Greg said, "Everything I've done is a pretty insane, random thing." So when he was hired by Red Bull he was asked, "What can you do that is representative of Red Bull? Here's an unlimited checkbook." Greg came up with the idea of a helicopter that flew upside down.

From this, Greg developed the idea that marketing was "giving people an experience they will never forget." The Red Bull job was "a dream job for a while," but then there was a power struggle for how to do things and, he noticed, there was "stress involved in the party lifestyle nonstop." When he left in 2007, he was one of 32 people to leave within a 15- day period, he says. Though it was time to move on, he says he learned an immense amount about marketing and how to make an emotional connection with consumers. So after taking a year off, he hooked up with an old friend he had known for 15 years, Shawn Biega.

When offered the opportunity to join up with Ardica, Greg jumped at the chance to work with Shawn. "We complement each other. We argue a lot, but we keep each other even and steady. We call each other on bullshit."

Greg called everyone on bullshit, even if it's the CEO. A self-described "total spaz," Greg has an internal engine that is always revved to the hilt. Back in October, he called the company "totally dysfunctional and fucked up," and he made sure his opinions were made very public throughout the company.

And despite his loud complaints, he was able to passionately see the opportunity Ardica had created, but he was becoming increasingly worried that it would all be lost. On the other hand, he enthusiastically acknowledged that the marketing efforts to get Ardica products into Spyder and Hugo Boss products showed that the company's marketing was really headed in the right direction. For instance, he says that Ardica branding on a Hugo Boss jacket gave pure credibility because "when that day happens, Ardica is as good as Hugo Boss."

But, as he said more than once, "I'm riding it out to see what happens."

What usually happened was nothing happened. In late January, Fritz directed the Board's consultant, Dave Epstein to meet with Big Silicon. Epstein reported that they believed Fritz would not accept anything less than $20 million. Based on how Fritz had briefed us previously, this belief seemed valid. According to Epstein, they said $20 million was considerably higher than Big Silicon valued Ardica, and therefore they were "probably" going to drop the whole purchase discussion. Epstein called his meeting with Big Silicon "a total waste of time."

Finally, on January 28th, Greg announced to the sales and marketing team his plans to leave the company and start anew. He asked us all to join him. "I want to have fun, enjoy my life, and work as part of a successful team, creating again another game changing idea. We must be living every day as if it is our last," Greg wrote. "Without risk, there is no reward. I can see it in your eyes, hear it in your voice, read it in your emails, we are all ready."

Greg was right. We were all ready to leave. In fact, I had begun working on my resignation letter. It was clear to me that Dick and I could not coexist. If he wouldn't leave, I had to.

LET'S SAVE OUR ASS
February 2010

41

THE SECOND BURNED JACKET was secondhand news. At the Ski Industries of America show in Denver, Rich learned that a woman had returned what she called a "melted" jacket to a store in Utah. On January 30th, Rich wrote, "We have a potential shit storm on our hands and we need to be prepared to face it immediately with some explanations and a recommended course of action." Written in the subject line of his email were the words "Burning Down The House."

"Someone [from Mountain Hardwear] came up to me at the show and asked, 'Hey, did you hear?'" recalled Rich about how he heard of the second burned coat. "The rumor at the show was that the coat had melted and the lady got burned." After 11 phone calls, Rich reached the customer, and she was not burned. In fact, she loved her coat and wanted another one.

Rich kept hoping those two failed jackets were weird coincidences. But three more coats were returned not long after, and by then the management team had sprung into action. Our attorney began looking into liability issues, and Dick began working with our insurance company and with the supplier of the heaters that failed. Meanwhile, I began formulating a plan to tell our partners, retailers, and jacket buyers.

I had learned long ago that a recall is not the worst thing in the world. In fact, if handled properly it can even enhance a company's reputation.

But I'd also suspected from my previous dealings with Dick that, despite our momentary convergence of focus on the jacket problem, we would approach the solution from different perspectives. I'd grown tired of it. So, on February 3rd, I submitted a letter proposing that I leave the company by March 1st. I drew a line in the sand. I'd had enough. "I believe the company can no longer continue with you and I co-running Ardica. This is causing a lot of friction and divisiveness..." I wrote in the letter to Dick. I proposed that I leave the company, get reimbursed the

$125,000 in unpaid salary and expenses that I was owed, and get to keep the options I had been granted. I offered an alternative proposal: namely that Dick leave the company and I become CEO. I firmly believed this was the better solution, but it was one I was reasonably certain he would reject because he seemed obsessed by the need to have the title. This wasn't important to me. As I wrote Dick, "My goal and my only goal remains the same—to make Ardica highly successful. It is in this spirit that I propose the above."

It was time. Our battle was driving the company apart and preventing success. Miriam said, "More and more people are not showing up. Dick's here when Hap's not here. Jim shows up whenever he doesn't want to work from home. There's not any excitement about the company. Not any excitement."

Instead, there was tension and a recall. As the investigation into the recall grew, it quickly became clear that the problem was not with the Moshi power system, the system created and built by Ardica. The problem was in the heating element in the jackets, specifically the connections. The first thought was that the wires were crossing, but "it turns out that it is more of an issue of crimping the wires done at the connection point," said Miriam. "The wires weren't always crimped as well as they should have been. The hand tool that the wires were crimped with wasn't calibrated to a standard crimp."

Whose fault was it? Our supplier, engineering, manufacturing, outsourcing? There was plenty of blame to go around but, said Rich,

"Nobody's going to get fired. That's not how we do things at Ardica."

About the time of the recall, Eric Folsom, manufacturing and outsourcing manager, was willing to be interviewed for this book, but he was ordered by Dick not to comment. The engineers had been cut off from all comment.

On the other hand, the sales and marketing team was bitter and angry and willing to voice their discontent. Greg, who was leaving, said bluntly, "fifteen engineers need to be fired."

And Shawn Biega said, "The engineers are scrambling like hell right now to fix the heater problem. They always have excuses." Meanwhile, he said, "I can't sell anything. It's pretty fucked up. I feel so burned. I've had headaches the last few days, dude."

So how did we get here? Were we just entrepreneurial Keystone Cops? Perhaps we just combined inexperience, hubris, and remarkably bad judgment. Dick liked to regularly say, "I've run nuclear ships and that's serious stuff. This Ardica stuff is really child's play." Well, the way we played like children has gotten us into some serious trouble. Instead of a strategic approach to consumer products, Dick's idea was instead to appoint our young design engineer, Martin Corpos, to be our point person on all of our manufacturing.

Martin was not an electrical engineer. He was not a trained quality control person. He did not have experience in any of the usual quality control techniques or anything to do with commercial manufacturing. Instead, he was a loyal employee, a warm and engaging person who had been involved with the jacket since his first day on the job as Ardica's first intern.

Martin Corpos, 28, met Dan Braithwaite shooting pool on campus at Stanford. Ardica "had been around for a year and they were hiring interns for the summer," recalled Martin. Martin described to Dan the atmosphere he was looking for, which amounted to "not cubicles," and he was encouraged to submit a resume. "My task was to focus on the jacket," said Martin. While the fuel for the fuel cell was the main focus of most in the company, "the jacket was the one thing nobody was working on," he said. That was in 2005, and since then Martin had learned a lot about jackets. Quality control for manufacturing, however, was an entirely different step in the process. It had been thrust upon him by Dick.

Martin had been almost universally described to me by those in our company as a "boy scout," and the moniker fit. He was thin with short dark hair, three-quarters Mexican and one-quarter Filipino with a laid-back California demeanor. He was well-mannered, intelligent, and happy to help in any way. Martin grew up in San Carlos, California, where "I took a lot of the steps laid out in front of me." His father was a civil engineer and his two older brothers, Matt and Mike, both went on to be engineers. "I've never really been one to say, Oh, I want to be this when I grow up. The closest thing was, all right, I'll do mechanical engineering, that sounds great."

The public high school in his hometown was the setting of the 1995 movie *Dangerous Minds*. Instead he went to Sacred Heart Preparatory School where he excelled at math and science, although he remembered, "I started to get a little roughed up by chemistry." But his high school taught him a number of disciplines for engineering. In a prototype design contest, he built a catapult. "My senior year, my physics teacher said, 'You're pretty good at this, you should try mechanical engineering.'" And that sounded great.

He couldn't decide where he wanted to go to school so he researched a number of mechanical engineering programs and narrowed his choice to Princeton or Stanford. In state or out of state, that was the question. So he took a trip to New Jersey and visited Princeton, where someone "told me, 'you're from California. It's cold out here.'" Stanford's weather won.

Martin loved his Stanford education, loved that Ardica was essentially a Stanford company, and remained involved with the school five years after graduating. "I volunteer a lot with the Stanford Alumni Association...I help plan events."

It was at Stanford that he learned many different disciplines outside of straight engineering, and this certainly helped prepare him for his many roles at Ardica. His intro classes taught him the collaborative process of "putting our minds together and learning how to work together," which was a perfect training for the hectic ways of a startup. Martin rounded out his engineering background by minoring in archeology. He went on two archeology digs, to Peru and Turkey. "It was a lot of work, mostly manual labor," he said. He did a lot of digging. He was taught how to excavate and analyze what he found, how to bag and photograph samples. The adventure was terrific. In Peru he spent eight weeks in a valley 10,000 feet above sea level. "I enjoyed the history and the problem solving," he said. "A lot depends on the context in which you found something."

And that statement could perhaps summarize what I thought of our jacket recall situation. A lot depended on context. Martin, the Stanford kid with the mechanical engineering degree, was asked from the beginning of his tenure at Ardica to step outside of his educational background into, essentially, electrical engineering. When he was assigned the jacket that no one was working on, "They had a really rudimentary heater, a copper wire attached to a connector," said Martin. "We needed to make it durable and cost effective." He had to learn how to source wires and "how to solder really well." At first, Martin says, "we were buying jackets off the shelf and just modifying them." And then they learned how garments are constructed and began making their own. To his credit, Martin rose to the challenge, learned, and helped create a product ready for market. "The day I stop learning at the job is the day I will start to look elsewhere," he said. It was exactly the right attitude. I applaud him. But as the company continued to push Martin into areas outside of his comfort zone, those areas became bigger and more complex and, well, more foreign. Recently, Dick sent Martin to Asia to help our partners learn to cut and sew our garments together. That was fine, and again Martin did well.

But Martin had no manufacturing experience. He didn't know the details of the quality control process. He was just a proud Stanford alumnus without any real world experience except his learning on the job. So I recommended to Dick that, based on my 20 years of overseeing garment manufacturing when I ran The North Face, we needed professional protocols in place and an experienced person on site. I felt we needed more manufacturing oversight, more real world experience. Dick opposed this idea.

I asked Eric Folsom, our manufacturing and outsourcing manager, where he fit in this process. He had quality and manufacturing experience on his resume, although not in apparel. He told me that he had proposed to Dick that he would go to factories in Asia and establish quality control and stay there to oversee initial production. Dick told him, "No, you can't do that. We don't have enough money for you to travel."

Instead, he had Martin, who was already in Asia to help with the making of the jackets, nominally take care of quality control. Eric is older and a bit more outspoken than Martin. I suspect that Dick liked Corpos to take care of things because, like a boy scout, Martin was not one to talk back.

It was a sad situation for which Martin and Eric were being improperly blamed by some in the company. The truth was that our situation was a result of the lack of leadership, the lack of funds, and the lack of a plan. Or maybe it was something more. Maybe some of our geniuses weren't as smart as originally thought. As problems evolved, and well before the recall, we had considered outsourcing some of our design. "But in our environment," as Greg said, "egos just get in the way."

42

OUR BRIGHT YOUNG ENGINEERS were always willing to take on new tasks and attack the most difficult design problems, but they lacked the real world experience to know how to follow a design through to the crucial final stage of manufacturing. In reality, most of our brilliant team quickly became bored once they got beyond the creativity phase of product development.

On one hand, this had always been a huge part of the appeal of Ardica. *We could do anything!* On the other hand, such hubris displayed across multiple functions required that there were no weak links, no bad luck, and more than zero money. It's double-edged. For instance, our hubris brought us to create and even initially sell a fuel cell system for heated jackets that wasn't ready. Yet it was that same hubris that allowed the Ardica team to immediately create a replacement power system we actually could make and deliver, a lithium-ion battery-based power pack. As I reflect now, it seemed that, by default, this had been our strategy. *We could do anything!* This "strategy" had led Greg to comment that Ardica was composed of "the dumbest smart people I've ever met."

It was clear to me that we were so late in the production cycle with our garment brand partners that we didn't have time to hire and train the type of employees inclined to give attention to the final details of a product and actual production. In December, I talked with Maynard

Holliday, our Fuel Cell System Production Manager, about this problem. I also talked with Hector Chao of Legend about this, and both he and Maynard suggested the same solution—outsource the task to engineering firms that had offices in both the San Francisco area and Asia. Ones that specialized in this sort of work on a project basis. Ironically they both knew and suggested the same firm, D2M.

I invited D2M to come in and make a proposal to our team. The universal response from Dick and the engineers was, "They are too expensive. Why do we need people like this? They seem overqualified." My guess was that not far below the surface was some fear of the unknown and some competitive knee-jerk reaction. And, even as young a company as Ardica was, there was some of that fatal, protectionist attitude of "it should all be made by our own people," which had already solidly rooted itself in our firm.

But Maynard and I didn't give up. He went to another similar firm, Speck Design, the company he had worked for prior to joining Ardica and asked them to give us a "friends and family" discount rate. Because of their respect for Maynard and their friendship, they did, and said they would do the whole project for $18,000—one half of which, however, needed to be paid upon commencement of the job. Since this proposal from Speck addressed the principal argument of cost that had been put up as the reason not to hire D2M, the team including Martin, Adam, Dick, and Dan reluctantly agreed to sign them up.

Unfortunately, despite signing them up, Speck never got started because either Dick couldn't find the money to write the $9,000 check or his resistance to the concept of hiring someone outside the company stopped this solution from ever being implemented. So, now we were facing a recall that could easily cost Ardica over $200,000: $9,000 vs. $200,000? The decision did not seem difficult to me.

The opportunity, as Greg and I and others had pointed out, was huge. But we did too much winging it and not enough planning. The sales team could sell the product with a few design changes but as Design Engineer

Kyle Hagin pointed out, "There is a disconnect between what we know how to do and what they think we know how to do."

Yet Greg said, when he went out to sell the Moshi, "Every single person in the world says I like that but..." The issues vary, said Greg, but often the comment is, "The product is cool. It's cool at the wrong price."

Price was actually only one of the issues we'd run into, and although it was perceived as an obstacle that could keep us from reaching the masses, I believed future iterations would bring the price down and the functionality up. It's the natural law of the manufacturing learning curve. But Dick believed that adhering to this was a blind act of faith. In fact, I was convinced that his own all-in reliance on Big Silicon buying us was actually the blind act of faith. A product going through cost-down iterations while gaining economies of scale was a common path to success.

By now, the split between Dick and me was evident in almost all issues in the company. And as talk of splitting the company into the fuel cell side, run by Dick, and the consumer products side, run by me, continued to be floated, I found real value in the possibility of outsourcing some design. Our history and the makeup of our team almost dictated that we should do some outsourcing. Greg, who favored outsourcing, says our engineers got products close but not finished. Outsourcing could get us to the finish line, said Greg.

43

A PRIME EXAMPLE of our "we can do anything" philosophy leading us astray was our previous insistence on designing our invented concept of a Technology Connector—the Swiss Army Knife of charger tips that could connect and therefore power a variety of different phones and MP3 players. The idea was to be able to power up 80% of the products on the market. A 1-1/2 inch by 1-1/2 inch thin plastic square case was created to hold the five connectors that would simply be uncapped for connection. The idea would be to uncap the one to fit your device and leave the others covered. Your device attachment would connect seamlessly from the Technology Connector to the wire leading to our Moshi and, viola, you would be charging. Brilliant!

Brilliant, except that our team at Ardica designed something that never really worked correctly. We discovered that the product design was so complex that it could not be produced using injection molding, which was needed for mass production at competitive prices. But the idea was so damn brilliant that we just kept throwing money at it. And time. Some things we fixed. Some we did not. In June, when I started writing this book, it was to be part of our product line. It no longer was. The story of the Technology Connector was related, as least in spirit, to our current recall.

"My first day on the job," remembered Kyle Hagin, "Adam [design engineer Adam Rodriguez] said, 'Here's the schematic for the Technology Connector. It's supposed to charge devices. You are redesigning the whole board.' So I ended up redesigning 200 pieces. Cutting, trimming, soldering in jumper wires. It was a hack job but we pulled it off in one week. And it was working."

Next, the company designed a second Technology Connector and, Kyle said, "I designed the electronics inside…there's a little microprocessor that controls everything." It turned out that what Kyle designed worked flawlessly. However, there were problems with the connection points bending or not adhering. There was no way to really produce it. Eventually, after tens if not hundreds of thousands of dollars in design and promotion, the Technology Connector was scrapped.

I believe our problems went back to our haphazard lack of focus, which could be traced to our lack of follow-up to our strategy meeting. Kyle says, "I am pretty much involved in every project." Kyle really was brilliant, but the management style that had placed him on every project was not. The management style that had placed him in charge of fixing one of our biggest problems on his first day on the job was not. And even though Kyle had succeeded at all of his tasks, I believe we could have made better use of his time by focusing his brilliance. Again, though, it was double-edged, because someone like Kyle only came to a company like Ardica because of the opportunities we offered.

Kyle, 25, was one of the few Ardica engineers without a Stanford pedigree. Instead, he was a proud alum of the University of Florida who recognized the opportunities in the Bay Area and uprooted his life to join our quest. Kyle was very special.

He was born shortly after his mother left the Air Force. His father stayed in the Air Force as an aviation technician working on electronics for aircraft while the family moved around from Florida to New York to Turkey to Mississippi to South Carolina and onward. His father rose in the ranks of the Air Force to be a maintenance supervisor working on the T-17 cargo plane. Kyle served an internship with his father, a supervisor of 1,200 people. It was just part of his diverse and valuable education.

"I always wanted to be a surgeon, like a brain surgeon," said Kyle.

"I didn't come close." After realizing he didn't want to "make a mistake in that world," Kyle thought of entering the world of aviation he had learned to love from being around his father. He attended Embry-Riddle Aeronautical University in Daytona Beach, Florida, and studied to be a pilot. But two realizations occurred at the time. Becoming a pilot is very expensive, and "I was getting 100s in physics and math."

He then transferred to Daytona Beach Community College to take advantage of a state law that said anyone who completed an Associate of Arts degree could get into a state school. At the community college, "I had a physics teacher that was really amazing. It was a five-credit course and I did it in six weeks…it was really intense. The professor came from the University of Florida and he felt it had the best electrical engineering program.

For two years Kyle attended the University of Florida in Gainesville, which is "smack dab in the middle" of northern Florida. He graduated in 2006 and then took a job in Tallahassee, where he worked for one year and ten months at a company that made fuel distribution systems involving credit cards and gas pumps. In early 2008, he came to a conference in San Francisco and stayed with his brother, who lived in the area. He quickly discovered "There were an amazing amount of companies out here and they all do what I want to do." He went back to Tallahassee and began plotting another visit. On September 23rd, 2008, he left Tallahassee and drove to San Francisco. He gave himself three weeks to find a job. "I was a pretty ambitious kid," he said.

When he arrived out here, "I jumped on Craigslist and the first ad I saw was for Ardica under fuel cells. I did a lot of research on the company," he said. "I definitely realized there were challenges. But I always looked past the challenges and jumped right in. I came to Ardica when they were kind of in a bind, which is normal around here."

That's when he was assigned the job of rebuilding the board of the

Technology Connector as we chased our little Holy Grail of connecting to everything. Of course, Kyle wasn't merely focusing on that product, nor was he the only one. Adam Rodriguez, in fact, was in charge of the entire design. Kyle, meanwhile, evolved into working on the fuel cell side, and once he was even an emergency fill-in for Tibor on a road show to Mississippi. "We used to have a contract where we worked with these guys in Mississippi, Ultralife," recalled Kyle. In fact, Ultralife was working with us to develop the hybrid fuel cell system for the military, with the goal of lightening a soldier's load. "Tibor was going on vacation," said Kyle. "And it was typical for how these guys [Ultralife] operated that they would call the day before and say we need a sample and we need you here as well. I got a call from Dick on Sunday. .We're going to Mississippi next week. I hadn't really worked on the fuel cell controller code. So Tibor did a brain dump."

"We threw it all in a case, wires everywhere…and we got through airport security," he said. "We got down there, me and Dick and Kei [design engineer Kei Yamamoto]. Kei was there to be knowledgeable about the fuel cell, Dick was there to work the politics and I was there to demonstrate the fuel cell controller. We got down there and one of the sensors broke and part of the code we originally wrote wasn't working. So I stayed up all night working on code modification." After all that, Kyle met the folks from Ultralife and found out that "These guys were really difficult to work with. They wanted you to do things that weren't physically possible to regulate hydrogen."

It was corporate BS, and Kyle was smart to recognize it as such. But he also quickly recognized something else. "The stuff I'm learning here, you can't learn anywhere else."

When he was interviewed for the book back in September 2009, Kyle loved talking about how the fuel delivery system that the company had designed was a way to regulate the pressure of hydrogen flowing through a fuel cell. "When you pull power through a fuel cell, it's converting hydrogen on demand," he explained. "This conversion actually reduces the pressure...we actually regulate the pressure." It was the science and the thrill of discovery that drove him. Kyle explained with clear admiration that our Chief Technical Officer, Tibor Fabian, came up with the idea of a circuit that monitors the voltage of every cell in a fuel cell array and then regulates it with the use of a short circuit.

In addition, Kyle talked knowledgeably of our pursuit of working with alane, the rocket fuel made from aluminum. "It's the best way to store hydrogen on Earth that we know of," he said. "The clever and simplistic way we are getting the hydrogen out is excellent...we're coming up with procedures and methods." Again, explained Kyle, "We had a big break-through. It's Tibor. He usually actually does it." The problem, as Kyle and others have explained, was that "Russia is the only place that knows how to produce it." Tibor had to translate various Russian papers to learn more. The problem was that there's not a lot of alane being produced anywhere.

Like everything we did, alane was *almost ready.* Big Silicon was *almost ready* to buy us. That's because the F-43 development was in the same place but, as Kyle explained, "the last 10% of development takes 90% of the time." The Technology Connector was *almost ready,* and so were most of Dick's fundraising efforts. And now we were faced with the obvious fact that we had placed a product on the market that was just as almost ready as everything else. Because of safety issues, it wasn't ready.

The sad part was that the Moshi really was ready, and the heated coat would have been too if we had done better quality control and training of our engineers. Any sane business model says to expect glitches in a first product. Still, the safety factor had dictated a recall.

There was the predictable inclination to cover tracks by our Captain Queeg while he also tried to isolate the problem. "Dick Martin thinks this is not a big deal," said Greg. "He thinks we will not see that many returns."

The fallout with our customers was swift. On February 10th, Mountain Hardwear filed a report about the burned jackets with the Consumer Product Safety Commission. Mountain Hardwear also ordered an ab-solute recall. Not a recall-and-replace, a money-back recall. And so we were promising to refund money, about $200,000 by our initial estimates. But we had no money. And we were not making a big deal out of the announcement. "We plan on doing what the CPSC (Consumer Product Safety Commission) forces us to announce. Beyond that, we're not saying anything," said Miriam.

44

THE OSTRICH STRATEGY was the opposite of my philosophy.
In fact, I knew that a recall could actually enhance the reputation of a company, and in a very public way separated the bull
shitters from the honest companies. I'd seen it. I knew it both intellectually
and viscerally. At The North Face when I ran the company we had two
separate recalls, one for tent poles that were breaking, and one for Gore-
Tex products that were delaminating. We quickly made the recall upon
noticing the problem, honestly communicated the problem, and immediately offered to make it right to the consumer through a cash payment
or a product replacement. The customers were happy. Many wrote that
it proved the value of our warranty at a time when the customers were
becoming skeptical of such offers. They also mentioned that to them
it showed our company's commitment to quality and straightforward
company dealings. Internally we knew it was a wakeup call to make our
next products better—all the time. And, not to be underestimated, it put
us directly in touch with our consumers. The clear question that was
waking me up at night was, would Dick handle it this way and would
Dick learn from a recall?

As a result of the recall, Mountain Hardwear cancelled their big order for 2010. Sitka did the same. They reluctantly explained they just
didn't have adequate time to test and prove the safety of a new, improved

product. Our pending deals with Hugo Boss and L.L. Bean were in jeopardy, and James Palmer of Legend said he was having doubts about us.

The prospective sale of Ardica to Big Silicon had gone quiet or had gone on the back burner, the military money had dried up, and Dick was on the road. Or he was Palo Alto with our consultant, Dave Epstein, dreaming and scheming up ways to raise money and keep Ardica afloat. In fact, as soon as Dave was hired, Dick began courting him. And Dave, knowing who signed the paychecks, seemed to only talk to Dick and no one else. I only met with Dave once and when I did he asked about Dick's management I was honest about Dick's shortcomings and Dave responded, "Well then why are you still here?" He didn't search for ways to fix things. And while this was going on, Dick had only been in the office for three days out of the entire prior two months. He said he was "raising money." While our turmoil was ongoing, he and the Board had essentially ignored my letter dealing with my departure.

Epstein was also "never in the office," said Miriam. Even though he was hired by the Board to help the company and work for the Board, he seemed to be working from other places and communicating only with Dick. In fact, Dick had started calling him a "personal consultant." And now that my departure was imminent, Miriam added, "there's not as much tension. There's not as many meetings. It's not as in-your-face as it was before."

It couldn't continue the way it was going and so I had forced the issue and we were at a new strange place. The tension was lessened but the excitement was gone. Instead, there was open talk of splitting the company. But even that was not achievable under the current circumstances of complicated investment structure, high debt, technology that was not ready, and an ongoing recall for a faulty product. Nevertheless, change was necessary. Since Dick wouldn't go, I had to.

On February 9th, I talked to James at Legend and told him of the recall, the cancelled order from Mountain Hardwear, and my planned departure. James was one of the biggest believers in the upside of the Moshi and the apparel market, but his only comment was, "This all makes me really concerned about my investment."

On February 11th, Dick finally responded to my letter of my planned departure with one of his own: "The terms look fine generally," he wrote. That being said, he wanted me to agree to not hire any Ardica employees—including all of those I had personally brought into Ardica. We clearly had more to discuss.

As it turned out, much to Dick's surprise I think, it wasn't completely up to Dick to decide about my departure. In fact, my offer to resign seemed to have provoked action from James and Fritz. They asked for a meeting.

On February 15th, I met them to discuss my departure. Fritz, who had been essentially backing Dick on whatever Dick said, was led towards reality by James, who suggested that my departure would make it very difficult to raise money, and that the sales and marketing team would likely follow me out the door. James further made it clear to Fritz that Dick was not the kind of experienced and proven business leader who inspired money to come in the door. And he told Fritz that he was concerned Dick wasn't being upfront with him. Specifically, when Dick and James met in James's office, James had asked how everything was between me and Dick. Dick had responded, "Everything's fine." It was later that James learned that I had already offered my resignation, and that Dick mentioned nothing about it to him. "This isn't good," said James to Fritz.

"No," responded Fritz. "This isn't good."

45

"Hap's hated in the company by a lot of people," said Shawn. It was sad, but I was perceptive enough to see reality even if the reality was tarnished by dishonesty and back room meetings. I knew that Dick, also, was hated by a lot of people in the company. It didn't make it any better. Dick talked to Dan and Tibor, who talked to the other engineers. They knew what he told them, but what he didn't revealed a lot. Promises kept getting made and then not fulfilled, so it seemed odd that the smartest guys in the room didn't see it.

"I don't know that they don't see it," said Miriam. "I just think they want to align themselves with the most powerful person, Dick...and I tend to believe that Dick has guaranteed them some sort of payment."

Maybe.

I know that at one point Dick pushed hard for Dan to get 900,000 new Ardica options (equal to about 20% of the option pool). Dan was already the highest paid employee in the company and giving him all those additional shares and 20% of the option pool when there were over 20 other employees who should be receiving shares and options just didn't make sense. And, it didn't seem fair. It also didn't happen, at least in part because the existing option program only had 40,000 authorized but unissued shares remaining.

I also know that when Tibor's options were going to result in him being taxed because he didn't file the proper papers in a timely fashion, Dick agreed to have the company cover the cost of Tibor's tax liability. Tibor had another problem. To qualify for favorable tax treatment when one receives options, they need to register those options with the tax authorities. Not doing so can result in a much higher tax rate. Tibor had failed to notify the authorities and, as such, was going to have a higher tax rate.

The bottom line on all of this is that in a professionally run company these sorts of decisions are made at the Board level by compensation committees who consider all of the employees in the company. Not by fiat, by one individual for his favored employees, even if that individual is the CEO.

But as Shawn said, "There's always going to be Dan and Tibor."

For months, Dick was meeting every night with the engineers when he was in town. Taking them to dinners and meeting into the wee hours always lobbying. Trying to convince them that he was is a great business leader despite his absence of a business background. Selling his belief that success can happen overnight with no planning. Lobbying for solely focusing on building a better fuel cell mousetrap that he would magically monetize into a great value via a sale of the company to some Silicon Valley company starving for patents and ideas.

With all of this and the recall and the lack of a deal to sell the company, everyone at Ardica somehow pushed forward. Miriam said that Dan "actually likes the challenge." And although no one in sales and marketing wanted to deal with a recall, we would be up for that challenge as well if there was clarity of purpose and transparency. Shawn understood. So did Rich, and Greg, and Miriam, and a few others. "There were several paths to the future," said Miriam, "but we've always been aware of the fact that we don't have any money." But Miriam perceptively pointed out that the lack of money was related to our lack of strategy. "If no one knows where the hell they're going…it's a disaster."

While the chairs got rearranged on the deck of the Titanic, I tried to find a way forward. My departure clearly made sense. But in the interest of the employees, shareholders and customers, Dick had to go as well.

In my February 15th meeting with James and Fritz, I proposed that we appoint Maynard Holliday as our Chief Operating Officer. Maynard, who had been quietly professional while operating in the midst of our management feud, was the person who originally brought Big Silicon to us. He had been working, like most of us, under impossible conditions. Maynard's title was Fuel Cell System Production Manager, which was a tough job to do when we remained in the prototype stage. Nevertheless, he tirelessly researched the best ways to pursue large-scale production of our two different kinds of fuel. Specifically, he had been researching the best places to place a plant to convert wind, solar, and hydro-power.

In my opinion, Maynard was the perfect person to take over operations of Ardica in the short term. He could even be a long-term solution. He knew the company, and he had a great educational background. Plus, he was wise to the ways of business. He also was not a lightning rod, which was what I had become. Maynard was respected by both the engineers and the sales and marketing team.

Maynard Holliday, who was 49, grew up in New York City and graduated from Scarsdale High School in Westchester before heading on to Carnegie Mellon University, where he received a Bachelor of Science degree in mechanical engineering and met Fritz Prinz. He was tall, about 6'2" and shaved his head bald. He was the only African-American in the company, which was not necessarily any more relevant than the fact that Adam was the only employee from Minnesota. It was, however, an obvious fact.

When Maynard graduated from Carnegie Mellon, Ronald Reagan was president and the United States was involved in a large defense buildup. Maynard was recruited to work at the Lawrence Livermore National Laboratory, a government defense laboratory about 50 miles east of San Francisco where he worked on experiments to increase nuclear yield. Maynard, steady and ambitious, also went to Stanford and acquired a Master of Science degree in mechanical engineering, robotics, and international security. "I wanted to over-qualify myself for future assignments," he said.

One of his professors at Stanford was the future Secretary of State, Condoleezza Rice. "She was sharp as a tack," he recalled. He graduated from Stanford in 1988 and he was still working at Lawrence Livermore when "peace broke out," he said, speaking of the end of the Cold War. While at Lawrence Livermore, he studied advanced robotics and when the Nunn-Lugar Cooperative Threat Reduction Program passed Congress in 1991, the United States began working cautiously with the former Soviet Union on reducing the nuclear threat. Maynard, as a representative of the government, was sent overseas.

"I went to the Ukraine, Kiev. It was like the Russian Silicon Valley where all the guidance and control for all the ballistic missiles were. They had very good engineers," recalled Maynard. "But we had been adversaries. They used to tease us and say, 'We've looked in your windows. We know where you live.'"

In time, because of the same cooperative government program, another project came to Maynard's attention. It had been a half a decade since the 1986 Chernobyl nuclear accident in what is now Ukraine. Although, after the initial radiation leak, the Russians had encased the building, there was no way of knowing what state the building was in. And there was no way of going in there; it was simply too contaminated.

The only way in was with a robot. Maynard, as an investigator from the Lawrence Livermore Laboratory and the Energy Department, led the design team that worked with Carnegie Mellon and William "Red" Whittaker to build the Pioneer Robot that went into the damaged facilities Chernobyl and brought back crucial data. He dealt with complex international relations and problems that made Ardica's issues seem like child's play. He was directly involved in solving a dangerous problem and getting things done. He even saw how the Soviets kept part of the reactor still working. They built a new city outside of the contamination zone, and brought workers in by train every day. Unlike most of our young engineers, he had spent time outside of academia.

In the late 1990s, Maynard continued his quest to learn and experience more. He applied to be an astronaut. He was among the few chosen to be interviewed. He was then brought back to be interviewed a second time, but not ultimately selected. He had discovered, though, that he was now a robotics specialist and he worked for a few robotics startups, but he discovered "nobody makes much money in robotics. The only killer application was surgical robotics."

In time, he developed an expertise in project management and he found his way to Intuitive Surgical, the company that made the DaVinci surgical system. Maynard managed the migration of the visuals for that robotic surgical system from standard definition to high definition. It involved a lot of sourcing and evaluating of technology.

In 2007, he found his way to Speck Design in Palo Alto. He became a project director, which involved "having the right tools and having the discipline…sometimes you've got to be the bad guy, and you've got to have the backing of management. But I can't be these guys' peers. They have to report to me."

Maynard got it. He understood how to get things done and how to be a good manager and the discipline and scheduling and assigning of responsibility that was involved in business. He understood, as he said, the concept of "tasks, resources, and delivery dates." And he understood Ardica. After all, he was the one who had researched Ardica's fuel cell research and then recommended us to Big Silicon. He learned about our corporate background when he researched the birth of the company and the difficulties between the founders. "It was a little sketchy," he recalled. "I understood they had been through some chaos. And I understood that Fritz brought Dick in to right the ship."

And Maynard understood what he had seen during his time in the company. I am sure that he was the one who could actually right the ship.

He knew the problems and the history, and he still remembered the big goal. In fact, it was June when he was interviewed for this book, and he said that the goal was to "site and build a plant in a year." The plant was going to be for our manufacture of fuel canisters at a place that would transmit clean energy into our fuel, either sodium borohydride or alane. That was then.

But in late February, Maynard was working hard to find an alternative partner in case our relationship with Big Silicon failed. He helped us start talking to a battery company about developing a miniaturized fuel cell system. To me they seemed like a more natural fit than Big Silicon, but at that point I believed it would have been easy to rationalize anything. In any case, Maynard had made contact and continued to work diligently, yet without resources. He understood all aspects of what we were doing.

46

I THOUGHT MAKING Maynard COO was the best option, and James Palmer of Legend wrote the Board to agree. In a letter to the Board on February 19th, James wrote a letter scolding the Board for how we handled some of our fundraising efforts. "Transparency and conservative estimates going forward will help manage the process much better and make sure everyone is on the same page," he wrote. He included a number of suggestions including, "Help Dick by delegating greater responsibilities to a COO. We discussed having Maynard assume this role, as he is respected by both the fuel cell and Moshi teams. He already managed manufacturing contacts and could coordinate activities and priorities for the fuel cell and Moshi teams. This would free Dick to focus on much broader strategic issues or fuel cell initiatives."

At the end of February as my exit from the company arrived, I again brought up the idea of Maynard taking over as COO again to Fritz. Despite all of Maynard's education, experience, and knowledge, Fritz voiced a different opinion to me. "Maynard's not as smart as the guys at Ardica, so I don't see how he can be COO," said Fritz. I believe he was referring to Dan, Tibor, and Dick. That seemed to me as if Fritz was speaking with an academic bias. I didn't know how ivied-hall IQs stacked up, but I knew that Maynard had business IQ, integrity, knowledge of business processes, street smarts, and peer respect. This was what Ardica needed, a competent manager.

Fritz had a different idea. He simply asked me to stick around for an extra week, until the money came in. What money? The money Dick was raising? It seemed Fritz had realized, with the nudging of Legend, that my actual business background was valuable. James also continued to ask me to stick around. I didn't know, but yet I knew. I was conflicted. I felt obligations to the employees, to the investors, and to Legend, but I knew neither Fritz nor Dick would listen to me or make the changes I recommended. It was time for a change—for Ardica and for me.

The Board finally had a meeting on February 27th. Dick Martin, Tom Covington, Dave Epstein (our new consultant), and myself were there in person. Tobin Fischer and Fritz Prinz both attended by phone. Near the end of the meeting, Tobin and Fritz said they had to leave, but I interjected: "I don't want to leave this meeting without the Board taking up the letter I sent in." That was my letter of departure from the daily operations of Ardica.

I had intended to leave the Board too, but I had heard from Legend and from Board members that they preferred I stay on the Board to provide counseling, and that my name would help with fundraising. So, with my lawyer, I wrote my revised letter of departure reflecting that.

Tobin said he only had a minute or two to discuss it. And Dick Martin said he hadn't had time to discuss my departure letter with our law firm. In his monotone, he tried to push the issue away. But I insisted and finally they agreed to have me recuse myself while they discussed it. Ten minutes later, they invited me back in and Dick said, "We can't decide right now but we will get back to you in a few days or a few weeks."

I wish I could say I was flabbergasted. But I wasn't surprised. This, after all, was standard operating procedure at Ardica. Push all issues down the road. But I was, nevertheless, astonished that they would push *this* down the road. I became heated at this point and said, "If you don't get it done by Sunday, I'll leave completely." I had been discussing my departure with Board members separately for more than a month. It didn't need to take months for them to work out the details. I knew it, and they knew it.

In reality, everything was a promise kicked down the road. We had discussed doing something about financial governance, inadequate management, and having actual Board meetings for seven months. Always, there had been promises that these things would be dealt with "very shortly." But nothing ever happened and the crisis worsened. Now I forced the issue. Or so I thought. But although our Board had ignored the crisis for months, there was a new dynamic to the meeting: Dave Epstein.

Epstein came in theoretically as an advisor to the Board but, in reality, he served as personal business advisor to Dick. He was a frenetic guy, maybe 5'6" with dark curly hair, a dark mustache, horn-rimmed glasses, and a narrow feline face. He always seemed too busy, ready to move to the next thing even when he was talking to you. Epstein had an agenda— Dick's agenda. He made it clear that he didn't trust Legend, who had saved the company. Legend had requested numerous meetings with him, which he repeatedly avoided, until they finally met with them for a mere 15 minutes. And now he was commenting on my status. "Why are you around?" he asked me.

The question should have been asked of him.

Instead, Dick asked the Board to vote to approve the financials that he, Dave, and Jim Retzlaff had put together. Dave and Dick both said the forecasts look fine to them. I strongly dissented. I pointed out there were many questionable numbers and I went through my laundry list of flaws I found in the submitted financials. I pointed out that although the Board and management are supposed to see financials before they are submitted to investors, this had not happened and these clearly inaccurate figures had been given to prospective investors. No one other than I had any questions on the numbers. The collective silence in looking at this dog's breakfast of sloppy financial statements screamed to me that we needed a new, competent Board and, more than ever, I needed to get out. As usual, the meeting ended without resolution of anything.

There was one precious moment afterward. As Dick and I were alone he said to me, "You know, you are really good at those numbers so it would help us to have you around to work on them."

HAIL MARY INCORPERATED
March 2010

47

THE FINANCIAL PROJECTIONS, which were being sent to potential investors, included income from a contract with a battery company to develop our fuel cell system. It was to start on April 1st and would yield $100,000 a month in income to Ardica. Maybe, but in reality our first meeting with the battery company had not yet been held and was actually set for March 25th with no guarantee of, if or when, a deal might happen. Still, for no logical reason, those numbers were solidly embedded in the projections.

I had been asked by the Board, and practically begged by Fritz, to stick around as a Board member, helping with the financial statements and projections. I was given past financials and projections that were flawed to the point of laughable. I was not amused. I suggested that the Board and specifically our advisor, Dave Epstein, needed to look much closer at what was going out to investors. I had a number of questions, including the real status of the discussions with the battery company.

I was particularly upset with our CFO, Jim Retzlaff. He was a good guy but in terms of generating financials, it wasn't happening. I had, in fact, been upset with Jim for a while because he had had months to develop the financials and they were still not close to ready for Legend to proceed forward with an institutional round of fundraising.

"Dick threw up roadblocks and I was part of that, not providing the information that Legend wanted," said Jim. "He wanted to get his own funds." When Jim was asked by me or by Legend to provide financials, he recalled, "Dick would basically say, 'It really isn't important. Don't worry about it. We're not going down that road anyway.'"

All along, I had been fighting to get the financials straight. It turned out the CEO was not interested and the CFO was going along with the CEO's plan. Meanwhile, they'd now come to the Board meeting and presented highly flawed documents, expecting no questions. Dick then pushed for the financials to be quickly approved. I raised numerous questions. Jim promised to get back to me with answers.

Jim and Dick had both been out of the office a lot. Often they met in coffee shops in the neighborhood near the office. Legend never received the information they requested to move forward. Dick's plan to drag his heels on producing complete financial statements was stalling Legend. I was not involved except that I had a fiduciary duty to oversee what was going out. And I pointed out that we now had an advisor, Dave Epstein, who was hired by the Board to help with the financials. If he was truly as skilled as his resume suggested, he should have been able to see what I saw, that the financials were blatantly, unequivocally flawed.

But the pirate who had taken over our ship seemed to wear an eye patch over both eyes. Yet, even blindly, he managed to pillage. Dave Epstein's bill went up. And up. "I don't know what the hell we got for the $50,000 we now owe him," said Jim.

"Apparently the Board hired him to be a consultant to the Board," said Jim of Dave. "The reality is he is a consultant to Dick. They spent hours and hours together. I don't know what the hell they were doing. The idea was that Epstein was going to help the Board and Dick navigate the situation. I'd then spend hours and days putting together a five-year plan, which in itself is hard—it's such a nebulous thing. But I'd put together these detailed forecasts and I'd work on things for days and then Dick and Dave would change them."

On what basis they changed them or for what purpose, or why they didn't add up, I didn't know. But they were a mess. When I later found out that Jim had only generated part of the financials we had seen and that some of his work had been "tweaked" by Dick and Dave Epstein, I realized that I didn't know where the blame should be placed. But there was plenty to go around.

"They'd say, 'we need to work on the forecast,'" said Jim about Dick and Dave.

As for the new numbers that were sent out to prospective investors, Jim said, "They're rosy. I don't know how realistic or unrealistic they are."

The time-consuming tedious process of putting the forecast together was one in which, said Jim, "if you make one mistake, it fucks up the whole thing."

In addition to Jim's work going through the filter of Dave and Dick, Jim found I was also waiting to review his work. "Hap is a very thorough guy," said Jim. "He'd come up with four pages of written comments." The problem, said Jim, is "now we're getting a lot of cooks in the kitchen and I'm the one trying to keep the pan from boiling over."

"Some of Hap's comments were helpful to me," said Jim, "but it's incredibly frustrating for me and not sustainable."

I agreed completely.

"It's a shame," said Jim. "I'll probably get fired for this stuff." Worse, though, was the fact that because he produced only part of the work, he was not accountable. He was encouraged to be not accountable. It went beyond Jim. The company itself was trying its best to be not accountable. Thus, the skewed numbers in the financial statements. I was trying to find transparency but it was really difficult when secrecy was the standard set by the CEO.

On March 2nd, I spent four hours on the phone with Dave trying to make sense of what I was shown. Though it was frustrating, Dick claimed to be on the verge of raising $625,000 (the same $625,000 he was promising in December) in a couple of days, so it made sense to get our books in order to show these prospective investors. Fritz, Dick, and the

Board asked for help and I answered the call. I owed it to the employees, the stockholders, and myself. It could still be fixed, I told myself. I am an eternal optimist.

A week after Dick had said the $625,000 was just about here, the money remained "just about here." To give it more credence, this time he put the statement in writing. It did sound definitive. It also sounded familiar.

By the second week of March, two more Board meetings had gone by and the details around my departure from the company were still tabled to deal with more urgent matters—the recall and financials. It was true, we urgently needed at least $200,000 to pay for the recall. But my request seemed to me to also be vital. My departure needed to be finalized and the gaps caused by my departure needed to be filled. But, as was the history of Ardica, the urgent was getting in the way of the vital. Of course, the biggest red flag of all was that the financials that we were going to use to raise money were still a mess.

At 8 pm on March 9th, I asked for a copy of the revised financials based on my input so I could further review the adjustments. I sent my request to Dick Martin, Jim Retzlaff, Dave Epstein, and to James Palmer at Legend. One hour later, Epstein wrote me asking why James was included among the recipients of the discussion of financials. "I'd like James to be given finished product, not interim works in progress," wrote Dave.

I was taken aback by Dave's comment. The next morning, I responded that James was a critical partner in Ardica (because of his investment and his ability to raise funds). I pointed out that James along with Fritz and the Board were the ones who had asked that I help with getting the financials corrected and in shape to show new, prospective investors who were eager to see the financials.

I wasn't surprised to get the next missive from Dave a few hours later. We were in a pissing contest.

Dave wrote, "Copying James on internal work, or informing him of things that are not approved by the CEO or the Board is at best bad form, could jeopardize the company and at worst violates confidentiality."

Even if you threw out the fact that Legend had a contract via the bridge loan that said they had a right to be an observer to the Board and that James had to be consulted on all major financial transactions, the reality was that James was the one presently saving the company and needed to be cultivated. He also had the rights to the IP and had shown that he really did want to help Ardica. I was sure he needed to be integrally involved. But my guess was that Dick, and therefore Dave, still somehow thought that Dick could raise enough money to buy James out. So they were trying to work behind his back and give James little or no information.

One other thing: There was only $46.00 in the bank.

Given this sobering financial fact, and the fact that Fritz and others had told Dave that he was wrong to try to exclude James from communication, Dave wrote the Board on March 12th: "I have heard so many things about yesterday's email traffic as a top off of unhealthy, unproductive, self serving, destructive comments that are such a distraction that I think I'm not helping this cause. We should talk about my role, if you'd like me to play any moving forward."

Dave hadn't yet been paid and there was a paltry $46 in our bank account. It could be a coincidence but he appeared to be mailing in his performance by his obvious lack of attention to the details in the financials. When it appeared to him that he may not get paid, he looked prepared to leave. Fine with me.

I was also moving on, but there continued to be push back. Fritz didn't like leaving terms and so we had no agreement. Instead, the urgent beckoned.

It was the middle of March and Ardica had missed another payday.

48

"**I** VOLUNTEERED $30,000 TO MEET PAYROLL" [the one for the end of February], said Jim Retzlaff. "It's not the first time I've lent the company money to cover payroll. I've done it three times. I am privy to the financial situation. I know how disruptive it is to miss a payroll. The first time was last summer. But earlier in the company we had receivables from the Army and from Big Silicon. Those were just payments that did not come in before payroll so I helped out. This time was different. There was not a customer that already owed us money. I am basically going on a promise from people," said Jim. Now another payroll was due and Jim had not been paid back for the last one.

Next up, the landlord's demands. Jim described the landlord Greg as "an ass when he's owed money," and added that the landlord and his wife drive matching Maseratis.

The landlord stopped in the offices looking for Dick or Jim. Neither was there but I was, so he came to me wearing a scowl and a don't-screw-with-me demeanor. He handed me his note intended for Dick, a three- day eviction notice for Ardica. "Get Dick to call me," said the landlord. "He totally ignores me."

Then there was Shawn. Shawn, who was prone to emotional interpretations, wrote me on March 18th, "Dick is out of the office and unreachable. The postage meter won't work because we have no money to buy postage.

Our FedEx account is frozen so we can't even send the labels out to the people who are sending in jackets on the recall. We have no money or way of paying people for the jackets they are sending in and the biggest retailer will be owed $68,000 (they want full retail for jackets in their possession). Seems like rent is not yet paid, but Dick set up a meeting with the landlord for next Friday to buy us time, but where will we get money for Friday? Does Dick think he can just shine the landlord on Friday?—the eviction notice says tonight is the last night, but MAYBE he will hold off until Friday—but what happens then?"

While all this was going on, we were trying to hire an electronics sales-man to sell the Moshi to electronics stores. This would be a way around the heater problems we've had. There were no problems with the Moshi, only the jacket wiring portion of the power system. So, we could sell that part of the system without worrying about the overheating problem. We had that inventory in the warehouse ready to go. But, the problem was that after the January CES show where we signed a contract to engage the salesman, we never paid him his engagement fee. So he didn't start. We had agreed to pay the salesman $1,500 a month for 6 months to underwrite his education of his 10 salesmen and get them on the road. However, we never had the money to pay him and we couldn't get him samples because the shipping warehouse was holding all our inventory hostage and wouldn't ship until they were paid the $30,000 that was long past due to them. Why, when it seemed to be our best and perhaps only short-term remedy for sales and cash flow, didn't we scramble to find cash for this? Why indeed.

And, on the home front apparently not everyone was paid on Tuesday—only those who squawked the loudest and "legitimately" needed to be paid got paid, as Dick put it.

Later that day, Shawn summed it up this way: "I have nothing to do… It baffles me…Everybody's down. Nobody's stoked anymore."

Shawn told me that he saw the CFO, Jim, sitting at his desk with both hands on his cheeks and his hair askew as if he'd been running his hands repeatedly through it. He was talking, muttering to himself, "We're fucked, we're fucked." Shawn said he tried to talk him down from the ledge but Jim said, "I hope Dick knows what he's doing or we're doomed and I'm personally doomed."

All Shawn could say to Jim was, "Dick doesn't know what he's doing. He never has. Let's hope he finds that acorn in a pile of manure."

I saw Dick briefly and he was very oblique about money. He said, "The money is in the bank." I asked "How much?" and he suddenly spun away saying he had to place an urgent call. The $625,000 that he claimed he had lined up at Christmas and again claimed was lined up in March was, it seemed, delayed again. But not to worry, said Dick, he "has a handshake on it."

When I asked Dick about the landlord, he said he had a meeting scheduled to "get everything squared away." I wondered if it meant he was just talking his way past another bill. I had started taking my computer and important papers home at night just in case there was a padlock on the door some morning.

I finally received Dick, Dave, and Jim's revised financials, after asking for them in front of the full Board and using the Board's authority and leverage. What I got was not a pretty sight. For instance, there was an assumption that sales would go from $800 thousand to $14 million in four years (about 400% a year) but expenses would only go up by 10% a year. In 30 years of business, I'd never anything like that happen. Expenses grow in concert with sales. Expenses hopefully grow slower, but there is never a disparity like that. And in 25 pages of financials with at least 100 items on each page, the recall was buried under one vague reference to "heater repair," not "recall." And those numbers totaled $100,000, not our initial calculation of $200,000. It was not exactly accurate or full disclosure. Like everything with Ardica, it was worrisome. When I again received no response to my questions, I had to ask Fritz to direct Dick and Dave and Jim to work with me and get me answers.

The wheels were coming off. I got no answers. Dick continued to think he was about to raise enough money to buy out Legend. "The biggest problem," said Jim, "is that Dick's friends make promises to him and for some reason they have not come through. He's so stoic it's just amazing to me. I don't know how he does it. It's got to be eating him from the inside out. It's got to be crushing his soul. The company is in a downward death spiral."

And yet...

We still, somehow, had a cheerleader at Big Silicon, the product design engineer who had championed our technology from the beginning. Although Big Silicon had stopped supporting us financially, the design engineer still liked our technology and had led us to a well-known battery company. Big Silicon did a lot of business with the battery company. Going to an energy company to develop our power system was a natural fit, but it went against Dick's professed vision of "turning Big Silicon into an energy company." Still, it seemed to be our best last chance and Dick jumped on board.

Coincidentally, Maynard had also contacted the battery company a few days before the Big Silicon design engineer suggested it, because Maynard suspected that we might need an alternative partner. The dialogue with the battery company was to become a live conversation on March 25th. Dick, of course, had already gotten it into his mind that this was a done deal with the battery company and accordingly budgeted $100,000 a month in payments from them starting on April 1st. Six days from their initial meeting to signing a contract and getting payments of $100,000 a month to us? That would be amazing. My fingers were crossed and the battery company made a lot of sense as a partner. But I had doubts that they would act that fast.

Miriam saw people coming in and hoped this meant a solution. She still thought there was enough continued belief in our technology to strike up a new deal. "We would be the fuel cell power source, exactly what we were going to be for (Big Silicon)," she said. The battery company "would be the manufacturer and we would provide the fuel...imagine some sort of refill program, like a toner situation."

She thought a deal with the battery company had a good chance of happening. Big Silicon "never agreed to put the F-43 into their product line. [The battery company] already makes things that are portable power. Plus they said the sheer intelligence of our system is far superior to anything else they've seen," said Miriam. Since she hadn't personally talked to the battery company, it seemed she was parroting what she had been told by Dan or Tibor or, more likely, Dick. According to Miriam, Big Silicon still remained interested in the system as well, but she added, "We're still working with (them) but we're not being paid."

Dick now believed that the battery company would save the day. He was using this belief as one way of holding off paying employees, and delaying the landlord's rent payment, and stiff-arming the vendors about the recall, etc. We were in a deep hole of etc. But maybe we could get the deal that Dick believed we would. Maybe he would raise the money he said he would, and maybe the landlord would be patient, and maybe the employees would hold their cool, but I heard ticking.

Dick still claimed to have investors lined up. So on March 21st at a Board meeting he asked the Board to approve a negotiation with a potential investor, who, as a condition of putting in his money, had demanded that Legend convert their loans to equity. And Dick further requested approval of the issuance of additional shares to another investor friend of his from the B round who claimed he was due these because the company hadn't done as well as planned, nor had it closed the deal with Big Silicon that Dick had described to him. This was the first any of the Board had heard of such a deal with this B round investor. These were major issues so, much to Dick's dismay, instead of voting on them we agreed to get legal advice.

No money came in.

One could sense further employee disgruntlement, so two days later Dick, outwardly a bit frazzled and apparently desperate, asked Legend for some money despite the fact that nothing had changed. Legend said no, unambiguously. Undaunted and obviously trying to put pressure on Legend, Dick sent a responding email to James, with a copy to Fritz, saying, "James, we are counting on you to put in another $300,000."

James fired back in a letter to Dick and Fritz:

You can't put this on us. It is unprofessional and just wrong.

We have continued to try to help the company and you and management have just not listened or ignored our suggestions.

We went from 1 million to 1.2 million to 1.5 million to 1.7 million all the while making suggestions and requests that were just ignored.

Case in point # 1

(Big Silicon) will buy us so we don't need to focus on the real issues:

- *You would not listen to any other way Case in point # 2*
- *Inability to get the core team to have a true clear vision for the company*
- *You didn't get this done until you were in trouble Case in point #3*
- *Not hiring the right person to help the company - Epstein is not right*
- *You need to admit that you need more help than he can provide Case in point # 4*
- *Not putting the right internal controls in place to produce up to date and current financials.*
- *5 months to get the financials...come on?*

I could go on but I think you get the picture. My proposal is as follows: Fire Epstein. Hire Scheinrock. Listen.

James, like myself, Shawn, and Jim, thought Dave Epstein didn't bring any value and was, frankly, not helpful. "He was a ghost," recalled Rich. "He was never really in the office."

Dave was hired by the Board but immediately jumped into Dick's pocket because, I guess, he thought Dick was the one who would pay the bills. He then started attacking Legend and me. He wasn't making himself very popular. In fact, one of the employees started calling him that "slimy little shit." Based on how he acted, I must say I concurred with that assessment.

Shawn said, "Epstein was a fucking loser, that's all I know. Epstein was a creep. He was out to bury Hap. He'd do whatever Dick told him to do."

Back when we first thought about hiring a consultant, James had recommended we hire Jeff Scheinrock, but we opted for Dave Epstein because he charged only by the day and because the Board had been told by Dick that we were about to be purchased. Well, Dave provided a big bill and no results. Plus, on numerous occasions, he parroted Dick's logic that the Legend guys were the bad guys. This galled James. It really galled me. And, of course, Big Silicon had not bought us.

On the night that James wrote to Fritz, I also wrote and suggested Dave must be removed in favor of Scheinrock. I knew how much we needed Legend, and I also knew that Dave wasn't looking closely at the financials. He certainly wasn't bringing any other value.

But Fritz remained resistant. He responded that Dave had established a good relationship with a potential investor and, as he expounded, "terminating him would jeopardize this link. The company is close to bankruptcy and we cannot afford risking that potential. Once we are through this we may rethink everything."

49

MARCH 25TH, 2010 was another morning without a padlock on the door. That had to be considered a positive. The battery company was coming in that day and Dick was expecting to seal the deal with them to support our expenses to the tune of $100,000 a month. It was a delusional expectation considering this was the first face-to-face meeting.

A lot was riding on the meeting. No employee had been paid for ten days and another payday was fast approaching. The recall was a daily throb in the company. Mostly, Rich Walwood and Miriam dealt with it, but the truth was they couldn't effectively deal with anything without money to pay for it. The engineers couldn't buy material to work with. The previous night, Dick had met with the insurance people and decided to cancel the employee health insurance. He could have laid off one person and saved the same amount of money, but instead he cancelled insurance for everyone. The anger was palpable.

But when six people (four from the battery company and two lower-level people from Big Silicon) showed up, Dick proudly showed them around the place. Dan Braithwaite, Tibor Fabian, and Dave Epstein were in the meeting. All the rest of the team, including myself, were told to stay out. Dick later reported, in an email distributed company-wide, that "The meeting went well today and we will meet again tomorrow ... to complete the way we will work with them. [The battery company] said they wanted agreements in place in two weeks, so we'll be working to make that happen."

I was beginning to recognize the melody. Same song, different radio station. Was this accurate information or was it simply being sent out to appease the unpaid? I was forced to wonder.

That night, I had an hour-long conversation with James, who wanted to assure me he was not a bad guy despite refusing to get Dick another $300,000. "If we are to raise any more money, we are going to need a lot more ownership," he said. "I hope you understand this is just business." I assured him that I understood what business was all about. James wanted to help but he felt constrained by Dick and Dave's maneuverings. When I told James that Dave was in the meeting with the battery company, his comment was, "What the fuck is he doing in that meeting?"

The day after Dick, and Dan, and Tibor were courting the battery company, a number of other employees were at lunch having a very different discussion. They had just found out the insurance was cancelled, and other items had recently come to light as well, including the fact that Big Silicon and the Army had quit funding the fuel cell project.

Miriam recalled the scene this way: "Kyle freaked out at lunch. [Kyle] thought that Dan and Dick lied to him. He was frustrated. It started when myself, Kyle, Adam, and Kai were having lunch and bitching about Ardica. Kyle was talking about how he should sue Ardica and then Eric and Shawn joined the conversation. You know Shawn, he provokes you more. Kyle started to raise his voice saying Shawn lied to our partners and didn't tell the truth about the recall. Shawn said, 'What do you mean I didn't tell the truth? I told the truth.' And then Shawn looked at Kyle and said, 'Dude, why are you shaking?' And then Kyle threw his sandwich and yelled 'Fuck you! Fuck you all!'"

So Kyle resigned.

Kyle was stressing. He had moved from Florida, gotten married, given 120% and then had learned that the project he was working on had not been funded since November. No one had had the courtesy to tell him. He felt disrespected. His accusation against Shawn showed he saw a conspiracy around every corner, and it was hard to blame him. He had been kept in the dark about things. It wasn't fair to accuse Shawn because Shawn is 100% honest and, while Kyle wasn't aware of it, Dick also kept Shawn in the dark regarding this and a lot of other things. Kyle's frustration was understandable. He was just the first to crack in such a public way. With no paychecks on top of everything else, everyone felt the pressure. And then the insurance was apparently cancelled without any advance warning, making the pressure even worse. When pushed by employees to explain this, Dick blamed the decision all on Jim.

Meanwhile, Dick still claimed his two new investors were on the verge of bringing in big money. Friday evening, March 26th, we had a telephone Board meeting. Dave Epstein was in the call. We covered the topic of no money for payroll. Dick said that management had met and suggested cutting people. He said one of the people planned to be cut was Kyle. I then had to tell the Board that Kyle actually quit earlier that day and was upset about management lying to him. Tobin Fisher, acting as director, asked which story was the truth. The stories seem dramatically different, he said. It seemed Dick was in constant spin mode and he needed a truth meter at all times.

Dick then brought up his proposed way of dealing with payday going forward: he would "furlough" employees, meaning they would take an involuntary unpaid leave of absence. The positive of this approach was that, unlike a layoff in which employees must, by law, be paid, Ardica would not be legally forced to pay the employee anything, at least for a while. I suggested we get legal advice and then added that since Kyle had actually quit, by law we had to pay Kyle all of the wages owed him within 72 hours. And we would have to do the same for everyone who chose to leave the company. Dick seemed surprised by this fact.

Dave then suggested that everything we knew and everything we said in the Board meeting should not be shared with anyone in the company and we should keep it to ourselves until we knew our direction. I openly disagreed. I pointed out that all the team at Ardica was in a crisis and we were all in it together. To keep the team together, I thought it was essential to be transparent and not appear to be secretive or duplicitous. I said we needed to quit treating employees like mushrooms—in the dark and covered with manure. Dave responded by saying that I have a bias. Yeah, a bias towards transparency and honesty. I bit my tongue.

Next Dick described the funding with one of the proposed investors as "a Mexican standoff because of Legend." Dave expounded, saying the investor "refuses to talk to Legend because they are being so heavy handed. The investor will only invest after Legend has given up all their collateral for their loans and made themselves secondary to the new investors." I explained this seemed both impractical and imprudent from Legend's point of view, and therefore there was no reason for us to expect them to do it. I explained that James Palmer from Legend seemed to me to be very reasonable and had offered to talk to the new investor to explain his position and try and work things out. I recommended this course. Dick was resistant to this idea.

Dick and Dave had so far kept Legend and the new potential investor totally apart and weren't allowing any dialogue. From my perspective, with no contact between Legend and the prospective new investor, there would be only one reason for the new investor to think Legend was being heavy handed, because they were told so by Dave and Dick.

I explained that, given the urgency of getting cash into Ardica, there was no logic for keeping the two parties apart any longer. Unless, I told myself, the prospective investor was not actually serious.

That night, James wrote to the Board to ask about the Board meeting and to make some specific points: "We are at a very crucial stage right now and we have no time to waste…If you have decided to let Epstein speak with the investors IT WAS A MISTAKE. Simply because I believe he has a negative image of Legend and that will most certainly come through in conversations and will only serve to hurt those discussions.

But the most important reason is simply he has nothing to gain or lose at this point. Simply put, he has NO SKIN IN THE GAME."

When Dick replied back, he gave information about the Board meeting and then proceeded to summarize Dave's role…"Dave has been focused on the C round players to get them on board."

It was as if Dick occupied a parallel universe in which, as he had told me just a day earlier, "things are going very well on the C round. We've got all the lead people lined up and things are moving ahead nicely." That was his universe. In the other real one, the one the Ardica team and I were living in, we couldn't pay anyone.

And in the real universe, James's letter concluded that the Board needed to fire Dave Epstein and hire Jeff Scheinrock before Legend would consider raising any more money. "We at Legend feel there is a huge upside potential in Ardica and are willing to work hard to make it a big success. We do not want this company to file for bankruptcy. However, we do have a fiduciary responsibility to our current investors. I do not think it's too late."

James asked for a meeting with Dick, Fritz, me, and our lawyer. The meeting was set for Monday, March 29th at 11 am. James said he was going to push to get Dave Epstein fired, Jeff Scheinrock hired, and for Dick to step aside as CEO. James had one request of me: that I shouldn't be too emotional or aggressive because Dick was "stressed enough as it is."

50

DESPITE TRYING MY BEST to be level-headed, at the meeting I ended up blowing it. We agreed that there was a need for a new CEO. Dick mumbled his assent but then said, "but since there is only me and Epstein available and Legend has stated they don't want Epstein, I guess it is me."

I couldn't accept that. We were where we were because of poor management and the CEO had to accept the responsibility for that. I made it clear to the Board that, in my view, if we raised $4 million but stayed with the same CEO, namely Dick, that we would surely and quickly just piss it all away. I reminded the Board of the old adage: "The definition of insanity is doing the same thing over and over again and expecting a different result."

Dick suggested that I bring some of my friends, like the one from Utah, in for investment. I lost it and said, "I can't do that because you are totally dishonest and lied to him."

Dick said he had only told my friend that "we are close to closing with (Big Silicon)," which, he continued, "we were, but it didn't happen."

I argued back, "That isn't what you told him, what you told him was that we had a $50 million offer from (Big Silicon) but were holding out for $100 million, which was a total lie."

Dick responded, "He must not have understood me."

I retorted, "He definitely understood you. I asked him a couple of times to clarify the point and he did. He is the straightest shooting guy I know and, frankly, you harmed my relationship with him by having him wonder why I would try to bring him into a company where the CEO was outright lying."

The lawyer told me I was being too blunt and later said, "You need to not be so aggressive." I told him that Dick didn't understand anything that wasn't blunt. He had to hear me lay it out in front of the other Board members so that everyone with fiduciary responsibility knew the facts, and so that Dick didn't think that he was getting away with his dishonesty, much of which, up until that point, only he and I knew about. I agreed that I could have and probably should have been more politic, but exclaimed, "I am really terribly, terribly concerned about the survival of the company and about the fact we are insolvent. We must have action ASAP!"

In fact, we finally took action. We agreed to hire Jeff Scheinrock as our advisor and give him the authority to develop a go-forward financial plan, what some bankers would call a "work out plan." We also agreed that Dick would vacate his role as CEO and focus solely on fuel cell development as well as assist in fundraising.

I later talked by phone with James. He asked, "why aren't you happy when, in essence, we got what you wanted?" I explained that when Dick said that he was going to be CEO because Epstein wasn't, I was totally fed up and believed it could be a death knell for the company. James's response was, "you know I was never going to let that happen."

But the reality was, when we left the meeting, Dick remained as CEO. The agreement reached was that he was CEO "until we found a suitable replacement." But, knowing Dick, he saw that as an opportunity to hang on.

So my concerns remained because, even though Dick assented, I knew in my heart of hearts that this was just his way of saying *I don't agree but have no other choice so I'll go along until I undermine any other candidates and then find a way to shoehorn my way back into the top role.*

That night, I talked to James about all things Ardica. Recognizing the gravity of the situation, James was taking time away from his family's Passover dinner to talk to me about the future of the company. He told me a call with one of Dick's potential investors, who owns a wind farm in West Texas, went well. Except that Dave Epstein was on the call and, according to James, Dave made him so angry "that the bile is still in my mouth." He said that Dave bad-mouthed Legend on the call to the potential investor and had openly said that Legend was strong-arming everyone. James said that following the meeting he called Fritz and told Fritz that if Dave was still involved in the Ardica deal, Legend was out.

Perception is such a funny thing, especially when it came to Dick Martin's perception of events. The next day, I asked Dick about the conflict between Dave and James, and Dick said, "It's just a style thing. Dave is doing really good work with the investors." That same morning, Dick sent out a letter to employees reiterating what he had said in the phone meeting. He said he was working on bringing in money to meet payday (now the second payday overdue), and he would have an update later in the day. The update never came. Neither did the money.

51

WITH TWO PAYDAYS NOW MISSED, health insurance about to be cancelled, and a second advisor coming in to help, Tom Covington suggested it was time for the Board to meet with employees and open up dialogue. This was probably a good idea since tensions were high. Tom, who everyone still recognized as one of the guiding founders, had been resistant to the switch from Dave Epstein to Jeff Scheinrock. But once it was made, he felt the employees needed to be brought into the light.

Dick Martin then scheduled the meeting for 6 pm on April 1st. Yes, we were April's fools. Coincidentally, I had a dinner scheduled at that exact time with someone from Facebook. The dinner had been scheduled for a month. Dick knew it was scheduled, and he scheduled the meeting with employees at the same time, despite my dinner—or perhaps because of it. He said it was because "it was the only time Fritz could make it."

I had to cancel my dinner because things were boiling over and I didn't trust Dick to be accurate or honest with the employees if I was not there. A list of talking points sent out by Dick showed that he planned to discuss lessons learned and the way ahead in what appeared to be broad strokes, but he did not plan to address when employees were going to be paid or how any changes were going to actually help. Miriam Dower proved prophetic when she wrote to me, "I'm going to take a wild guess and say his outline will be laughable."

That day before the meeting, former marketing director Greg Nevolo sent out a create-your-own-animation project from a free website, Xtranormal.com, that allowed him to create a minute-and-a-half cartoon called "Paycheck," in which an employee asks a boss named Dick, "Where is my paycheck?"

Cartoon Dick: "*Uh, um, paycheck? Instead of paying you, I think it would be best if you work for free.*"

Cartoon Employee: "*Seriously, where is my paycheck?*"

Dick: "*What? You don't want to work for free?*"

Employee: "*Seriously, Dick. How much longer do you think we will believe your lies? You never had the money. You are never getting any money and you should shut the fuck up. Tell us all the truth and come clean.*"

Dick: "*I've run companies before. I know what I am doing. I've got secret deals in the works with my invisible friends. They are listening right now. If you tell anyone, I will have to kill you. That's how I operate. I know kung fu.*"

Employee: "*Up yours, you old delusional fool. Where the fuck is my money and my health insurance?*"

Greg Nevolo was a former employee by this time, but his cartoon quickly found its way into email inboxes across Ardica. This was a reference point for the people coming to meet the Board.

Meanwhile, I didn't tell the Board in advance that my dinner was cancelled. I just showed up. Of the Board, only Tobin Fisher was not at the meeting. He had a crisis of his own, with the computer server crashing in his own business.

"Tom and Fritz, to me, looked pretty worn out by the whole thing," recalls Miriam.

It was a bizarre setting. All of the employees and the Board crowded into the Ardica conference room. There were too many people to sit at the table, so everyone sat in chairs pushed to the edge of the room along three walls, the two long side walls and the back wall. Only the front whiteboard wall, for writing, was vacant. Dick then pulled his chair to the seat at the head of the long rectangular table in front of the white wall. Just as in the meeting with James Palmer and the attorney, Dick dressed up, wearing his sport coat over his black shirt, and his best pair of unironed chinos. He was the only one seated at the table.

Fritz opened with a nice speech and said that it was time for a new, albeit interim, CEO. Tom followed and reiterated the point.

Then Dick started talking about how hard he was trying to raise money. He droned on and on in his signature monotone way. Most people sat quietly and listened. And listened. At one point, Dick said everyone would be paid shortly, "maybe even tomorrow because Jeff Scheinrock will be bringing in money." It almost seemed that Dick felt if he stopped talking he would lose control of the situation. And at a few points, Fritz asked if there were questions.

"Who do I report to? And what roles will Dick and Hap have?"

Tom answered first: "That will be for the new CEO, Jeff Scheinrock, to decide when he is here next week.

Dick piped in, "It will be the same, I will be the one making decisions."

And then I pointed out that our goal was to have one person as a central decision maker and that Scheinrock would be interim CEO until we found a new CEO, which could take six months. I said I would be a Board member advising on marketing and finance, and that Dick would focus on government projects and the F-43.

More questions came, the meeting dragged on, and Dick droned on, but there was finally starting to be some transparency. It had been a long time coming.

"Who is going to decide which bills are paid, and in what order?"

I answered that would be Scheinrock's role, with input from the management team.

"Would we entertain an offer from the battery company?

Fritz answered, "We probably haven't impressed them enough yet." Tom added, "Absolutely, but we haven't heard anything."

And Maynard Holliday, who had contact with the battery company, said, "Things are moving fairly fast so you never know."

"Are we going to be evicted?"

Dick answered in his not-so-specific way, "I've taken care of that."

The meeting lasted for 2-1/2 hours as Dick talked as much as possible to avoid facing any questions. There were a couple of startling points to me. Dan Braithwaite, at one point, made a heartfelt statement: "We focused too much on (Big Silicon) and I take responsibility for that," he said. "We ignored the potential of the jackets or the Moshi." The other startling thing was that a couple of engineers said in the meeting that they had never heard before that there had been negotiations to buy us. Transparency is a learned skill.

When the meeting ended and the employees walked out of the room, Dick asked the Board to stay. He wanted us to discuss the interim CEO comments we had made. He said he never heard this in the discussion the day before with James and the Board. He said he was surprised "when Hap brought this up in the meeting." Of course, I brought it up *after* it was raised by both Fritz and Tom, but selective memory can be helpful for those who need it. Sigh.

Dick's posturing didn't matter. Fritz, Tom, and I all held our ground and Tom insisted "we have to have a major change to get the employees fired up again." Fritz concurred and pointed out that we'd already agreed a new CEO was necessary, so the interim CEO move was on the path to that.

Dick kept babbling about how he had "never heard any of this," and then he tried to convince us again that there was no need for an interim CEO. His eyes stared straight out and he gripped the edge of the table with a Zen-like focus. Despite his obvious inner turmoil, he remained calm. It was like watching him physically strain to think and realize he finally couldn't get out of the mess he'd created, but he was still trying to figure out how to do it anyway.

52

"A LOT OF THINGS HAVE CHANGED in the past couple of days," said CFO Jim Retzlaff. Jim, like the rest of us, was hoping the promised structural changes would lead to improvements and an infusion of money because "it's horrible. It's terrible," he said. "There is no money."

It was April 3rd, the day before the actual Easter of 2010 and Jim was still waiting for an infusion of cash. Only then, unlike last June when Jim first used Easter as a metaphor for fundraising, he needed cash infused into his own bank account. The $30,000 he loaned the company for a couple of days more than a month previously had not yet been paid back and Jim said, "I can't sleep at night."

Insomnia had become the default state for the entire company. For all of us it was personal, financial, and extremely troubling. Jim was in up to his eyeballs. "I'm a little bit…just beat down," said Jim. "I have a lot of anger at the company for sinking into the state it's in. And anger at myself for loaning this money to the company."

"Jim is a train wreck," observed Rich. "The guy's gonna have a breakdown. I feel bad for him. He personally invested a lot of money. He got drunk on Dick's Kool-Aid."

Shawn's favorite statement in recent weeks was, "Dude, we can't even buy stamps," while Rich and Miriam spent most of their days trying to soothe angry customers and retailers looking for their recall checks.

"The recall is pretty much what we expected," said Miriam. "It costs $300,000." (Actually, we expected the cost to be $200,000, but who was counting when you weren't paying any of it anyway?) "I do the backend of the recall," she said. "I handle all the interaction with the consumers." Rich deals with retailers. "Rich is pretty fed up," she added. In both cases, with consumers and with retailers, the answer was the same: *we will pay you soon.* And the returned merchandise was piling up.

Mountain Hardwear and Mountain Hardwear's biggest customer wanted full retail even though it was for products still in their inventory because, they explained, they had run a lot of ads, put it on their website, and undertaken costly promotions. There was some debate whether to reimburse them the full retail of the Moshi power system and the jackets that used them, but I believed if we wanted to do the honorable thing and preserve those relationships for the future we had no choice. Dick agreed.

The story of Ardica, according to Miriam, was "the mosaic of still no money. Hopefully maybe Tuesday or Wednesday we will have money is what they tell me. Part of me believes it. They are bringing in an interim CEO."

"Legend's point of view," said Jim, "is let's get the right person in running the show and I don't think they think that Dick is that."

A lot of hope was riding on Jeff Scheinrock, who was supposed to take over as the interim CEO. Hope and a good dose of realistic fear. "Most people know we have no money because we are not getting paid," said Miriam in an understatement. "There are rumors of layoffs and trying to cut half the company to save money…I feel like the new CEO is going to clean house and shed weight…do everything a normal company would do."

With no money and a payroll of $90,000 every two weeks, there was lot of weight to shed. Of course, even if jobs were cut, it didn't really matter without dealing seriously with the past-due debt. The shit and the fan were courting each other.

"It's pretty much over," said Shawn. "They are playing a game of chicken."

53

ON APRIL 5TH, Dick Martin sent out an email to all employees stating that effective April 1st "we are reducing all employees to minimum wage while we continue to bring in more near-term funding. We expect, however, to pay the regular salaries but we must have the funds before we can commit to that."

Just prior to Dick sending out his email announcing the retroactive move to minimum wage, he showed it to me and I strongly urged against it. When he had previously brought up the idea in a Board meeting, the Board was against it. He made the move on his own.

According to Shawn, Dan went ballistic over this move. Rich responded in writing, with an email to Dick that also went out to every employee:

"Dick – This email is vague, misleading, and confusing! What does "bringing in funds" mean precisely? Do you have an exact date when you will remit payroll?…Will salaries actually be cut to minimum wage or will that wage serve as a partial payment against contracted salaries until such time as Ardica can return to full salary payments? Do you have a timeline or plan for expense reimbursements? I would greatly appreciate some clarification."

But clarification had never been one of Dick's strong points.

So the next day, after the letter had been sent out and even Dan was visibly angry, Dick sent another letter to all employees stating: "The Board was operating with incomplete information when the decision was made to go to minimum wage. I hereby rescind the decision...we will proceed with normal pay days and continue to work hard to bring in funding by Ardica and Legend."

Wow. The Board had nothing to do with it. Talk about disingenuous.

Jeff Scheinrock, the proposed interim CEO, was not involved in the decision to go to minimum wage or to rescind the decision. He actually had his initial talk with employees without even knowing the note announcing minimum wage had gone out. Who was running things? Somehow, it seemed that Dick Martin was still in charge. He even sent a note around saying, "I'm still in charge."

Scheinrock then said, "I don't need to be CEO, I'm really just a paid advisor." Maybe. Or maybe he was also saying, I've now seen Ardica up close and don't want my fingerprints on it.

Dick apparently convinced James Palmer that there was no reason to have Jeff as acting CEO when "he won't be here daily anyway." This from a guy who has not been at the office daily for more than three months. Yet somehow his shell game continued. He kept assuring everyone that the $3.5 million he was raising was "almost here." $625,000? $3.5 million. Whatever. It became like a bad jingle you couldn't get out of your head... *have no fear, the money's almost here.*

He tried to get me involved...again. He asked me to call a previous investor I tangentially knew from Stanford to see if the investor would put $100,000 into the Legend bridge loan. I told Dick I would put the investor in touch with James. Dick became defensive about involving James and said, "Maybe you should just talk to him."

Meanwhile, Jeff had done some preliminary work and estimated the company needed $800,000 just to get through the next two months. As Jim said, "the biggest expense we have is payroll. We have a lot of people on the payroll for a company that doesn't produce anything."

It had been an issue for a long time. Dick had placed blame on the sales and marketing budget. Jim once said, "Shawn's an idiot when it comes to keeping a handle on expenses." But the truth was that the cost that was driving the company downward was the high payroll on the engineering side. And at this point, said Jim, "we're not working on a lot."

Dick had casually proposed to the Board that he might lay off eight employees. Jeff was again surprised to find that out from employees, not directly from Dick.

The previous night, at the insistence of James Palmer, five of us had dinner at La Mar, a trendy San Francisco waterfront restaurant, with Jeff Scheinrock; Jeff's assistant, Craig Finster; Shawn; Palmer; and myself. There were five of us there. Dick didn't like that this meeting had been set up at all, and did everything he could to keep Scheinrock away from me. He even set up a meeting between Jeff and Fritz in Palo Alto, a 30-minute drive each way, for exactly the same time. But James told Dick that Jeff's meeting with me was more important because it was the only time the two of us had available to see each other. James knew that Scheinrock was focused on operational improvements and that I had valuable information to share with him.

I was blunt. I told the people at the dinner that I thought the inevitable conclusion was that James should foreclose on the assets and start a new company and leave Dick with the old investors and debt.

James said, "That just isn't me." And then he asked Jeff to do his study quickly and give everyone the various alternatives as fast as possible.

Scheinrock, who was very bottom-line oriented, understood. He was also blunt. Having seen our books, he wanted a guarantee he would get paid even if it came from James's personal bank account. James said that Jeff would get paid but before James brought in any more bridge loan money, he wanted Dick to bring some in. James added that he was glad to have Dick's investors join the bridge round. After saying that, he assured Jeff that Jeff would get paid. Jeff then talked about what he'd seen in briefly looking at Ardica. His initial impression was, "I've seen worse."

So we had that going for us.

54

"**D**ICK HAS WEEKLY UPDATES that are a lot of hot air," said Rich. "He wants you to listen to his bullshit and you'll keep punching the clock."

Rich said he couldn't continue much longer without pay, and he was not interested in Dick's offer of an unpaid leave. And he knew, "Even if they pull this off, heads are going to roll. They probably have to fire half the people in here—just walk through and say 'you, you, you, you, you.'"

But with Greg and me out the door, I doubted that Rich would be someone they would want to go. That would only leave Shawn on the sales and marketing side. On the other hand, there seemed to be nothing to sell.

Of course, any talk of getting rid of people was complicated by law because of the unpaid wages Ardica owed. If we fired someone, Ardica had to pay those wages immediately. And we didn't have any money. It was a bad situation, one that could force the company into bankruptcy. So, Dick was trying to sell employees on the idea of working for free.

Dick sold hope and always had a new plan. "He's tried Plan B," said Jim. "Plan B being different people." And now he was pursuing new different people, old investors for new money, and new potential investors. Anyone. And now he updated everyone about his "progress."

The meetings, intended to soothe the employees into believing, instead reinforced the idea that there was not much to believe in. "What is the strategic plan?" asked Miriam. "We don't have that figured out yet."

The one thing that was very figured out was that Legend Merchant Bank had taken much more control. "These Legend guys are our only hope," said Rich. "Nobody else would touch this thing with a ten-foot pole."

Legend, understanding with complete certainty all of our flaws, still saw the potential in Ardica. Having Jeff Scheinrock around to double-check things buoyed their confidence. Scheinrock knew what to do. He was an expert at these sorts of "work out" situations. His assistant, Craig Finster, showed up on the first day and announced to Jim, "we are going to become your next best friend."

As a baseline, James Palmer from Legend asked Jeff to check on Dick's version of reality. For instance, Dick and Jeff did a conference call in early April to the supplier that made the faulty heaters to discuss a reimbursement. Afterward, Jeff told James that the supplier had no inclination to help on the recall, and furthermore didn't have the means. James then asked Dick about the call and Dick said, "I think that was a pretty good call, seems it went well to me."

Despite all evidence of odd dealing by Dick, his most adamant supporters remained the "brains of the company," Dan and Tibor. "They're just dumb kids," said Shawn. "I tell them every day that Dick's an idiot."

And Rich said, "Dan and Tibor think it's all going to work out. They're so deeply invested, they have to believe."

Jim believed that finances and the emotional investment were driving both Dan and Tibor. He cited their "unusual amount of founder's stock" and said, "They definitely have a vested interest in having the company succeed one way or another." And for the longest time, there was only one way, the F-43 project and Big Silicon. Dan believed that a deal with the battery company, or even Big Silicon was still possible. Dan became much more involved in the recall and the Moshi side of the business. Dan and Tibor somehow continued to believe in Dick's leadership.

Legend's patience, however, seemed to have run out while Dick, who was "still in charge," was doing everything he could to keep control.

In the middle of April, I traveled to Boston for a meeting. While I was gone Dick scheduled another employee meeting in the conference room.

When I asked him what he was going to talk about specifically, he wrote that he was going to express concern for the welfare of the employees and offer a 15% bonus when funding came in. He said he would give an update on progress with the battery company, and tell people that he was bringing in investors into the Legend bridge loan.

I was 3,000 miles away but it still sounded crazy to me. Dick was unilaterally offering a 15% bonus to employees who are already three paychecks behind? Was it 15% of one month salary? Was it 15% of annual wage? What was it? Was it some arbitrary number that Dick thought was big enough to appease the unpaid. I asked all these questions and more. I asked what was the status with the landlord?

Dick wrote back: "I'll answer in more detail tonight but things are positive."

His skill at avoiding questions rivaled that of a boxer avoiding a jab.

While I was traveling, Tobin Fisher called me and said that he met with Dick, and Dick said that two new investors were asking everyone except Dick to resign from the Board as a precondition for them making an investment. Tobin was extremely upset after the meeting with Dick, and the next day he fired off an email that was more than just a jab. It was left hook followed by an uppercut.

In five seething paragraphs followed by a final paragraph that said he would remain willing to consider any written proposal including one asking him to resign, Tobin made it clear that he didn't trust Dick at all:

During your time at Ardica you have obstructed the effective operation of the board in multiple ways, including not meeting legal requirements for the frequency of Board meetings (despite our strenuous objections), not providing financial statements as required by law (despite our strenuous objections again, and having a full time CFO), and repeatedly presenting the board with incomplete, inaccurate, and misleading information, including your repeated claims that you were certain a major investment was coming "next week" for two years that have never materialized.

Tobin's letter to Dick went on like this for three more brutal paragraphs accusing Dick of taking action that "hardly seems in the best interest of the Board." He said that Dick previously used "false pretenses" to try to get him to resign, and began summarizing by stating "your timing seems to encourage the Board to act out of fear and in your best interests instead of in the company's best interests."

He finished by saying he would do whatever was in the best interest of the company.

Dick responded like Sugar Ray Robinson in his prime: "Thanks for your last paragraph which was needed to move ahead with our investors."

On April 15th, I requested a Board meeting to deal with our serious issues, including the request for resignations. Dick had also asked me to resign from the Board, as he said he needed my resignation in order to get in the new investors. Before I did, I wanted to hear the recommendation from Jeff Scheinrock. Four days later, only Tobin had responded, so I again requested a Board meeting, stating "We have major problems we cannot and should not duck in the company." Finally I heard from Tom Covington, who had been traveling, and Fritz, who had had a death in his family. We worked on trying to schedule a meeting soon.

I was getting increasingly strident questions from employees about potentially cancelled insurance and their lack of pay. The insurance issue was particularly troubling for a couple employees who were afraid that due to past illnesses, called "pre-existing conditions" by the insurance industry, that they would not be able to get continuing insurance coverage if Ardica had its insurance terminated. Meanwhile, Maynard Holliday had announced he was looking for another job and would only stop in periodically. He had a daughter in college and a son on the verge of going to college and he could not afford to live on Dick's dreams. In fact, the office was becoming a ghost town. One of the few people who showed up every day, oddly enough, was Jim. Maybe he just wanted to assure himself the padlock hadn't been put on his investment and loan quite yet.

Eric Folsom had threatened to go to the State with a complaint of unpaid wages. This could shut Ardica down. "You have dealt with this situation very poorly and I'm giving you the ability to make this right," wrote Eric. "At this point I can't wait any longer so I must do what I need to take care of myself."

Meanwhile, it was seemingly increasingly difficult to get any financing for Ardica, and it seemed that Legend could, at any moment, just shut us down.

And while responses from Board members ostensibly trying to schedule a Board meeting had trickled in, Dick had not responded at all. He apparently continued to delude himself that if he ignored something, it would just go away.

For almost two weeks, there was little movement on any front at Ardica. Shawn, trying to do whatever he could to save Ardica, had Sitka ready to go for a redesigned Moshi system for 2011. All we had to do was give them samples by June. But Dan, as the person who had taken charge of all engineering and manufacturing, said that he didn't think the product would be perfect by then so he told Shawn, "I'd like to make it happen for them but I don't think it's in the cards."

As Jim pointed out, "Shawn went out and did his job. He did his thing and sold." Now he twiddled his thumbs with nothing to sell.

The Board meeting I was pushing for remained unscheduled. Dick continued working with his investor friends to bring in some money to catch up to the past-due payroll, and leaning on James to put some more money in as well. A couple of names, familiar from before, surfaced again. They were previous investors who seemed interested in protecting their previous investment. That's the best I could figure out of their motivations. Dick said he had now brought them in and James was letting them into the bridge round without fees. At least that's the theory. The gears were finally moving. Or maybe not.

On April 27th, James wrote the Board:

"I am at a loss as to why the board cannot find the time to meet asap given the current status of the company…Clearly, the potential new investors are coming to the same conclusion as everyone else which is [that] the current management structure does not work…period."

He then suggested that, "in order to ease concerns going forward and provide some comfort," an interim Board be appointed consisting of Dick and two new investors. Further, James suggested that Fritz, Tom, Tobin, and I become Board Observers. He also suggested that Jeff Scheinrock be designated a Board Observer and special advisor to the Board, empowered to make decisions.

I immediately agreed that this was a good idea. But first I asked that the Board finally address the details remaining after my departure from Ardica, all of which had been submitted more than two months earlier. I was particularly interested in the part where the Board formally acknowledged the company owed me $125,000 from 2008 and 2009 plus more than $15,000 of unreimbursed expenses.

Fritz answered in a typical Ardica pass-the-buck way: "We need to leave this to the new Board members to decide."

This was bullshit.

In a letter, I told Fritz exactly that: "All I can say is this comment is nothing short of unmitigated b.s.!" I explained that I simply wanted him to acknowledge obligations that happened while he was Chairman of the Board and the money owed me. "I've been doing everything I can to make this company survive despite the misguided efforts of some who have been managing the company—using my money, my contacts, and my credibility to keep Ardica afloat in business. What I seem to be getting in return is total disrespect, total ignoring of standard business protocol, and an effort by some to block every Board meeting I've have requested during the last two weeks."

Fritz's one sentence answer to everything I stated and asked was: "Even in times of distress, choosing profanities in communication does not solve anything."

It sure the hell didn't. Dammit!

That afternoon I gave my Board resignation to James and Jeff Scheinrock without qualifications. Then I had a nice talk with Jeff about the company and his most telling comment was, "Dick is really a package isn't he? I can't get one straight answer from him."

Meanwhile, I planted a seed with James and Jeff: Along with Shawn, I would be interested in acquiring the Moshi division for the right price, perhaps with the $140,000 of past due wages and unreimbursed expenses that I was owed by Ardica plus the $30,000 in wages and expenses that Shawn was owed. James and Jeff responded that the right price was more like $500,000, plus giving Ardica 50% ownership in the new entity. They agreed that Shawn would be the right person to run it, and I could guide him from the Board of the new company. We had not yet reached the right price, but we were talking.

"Hap looked like he was about to cry today," Shawn recalled about seeing me right afterward.

It was extremely emotional for me. I believe in failing forward, not failing. But this was over.

A business manager's role, I believe, is to protect the interests of all the stakeholders— investors, employees, customers, and vendors. Most of us at Ardica felt the same way, and we, for a while, had been on a roll. But failure and self-interest of leadership derailed all the hard work. Logically, I knew I had done everything possible to change things. But emotionally, I was still searching. What could have been? What could I have done? What could anyone have done after all the bad decisions were made?

55

"**G**OOD NEWS!" was the opening of an email from Jim about the company's plan to save the employee's health insurance. In fact, "save" wasn't totally accurate. What it actually meant was Ardica was going to continue the policy but shift a significant portion of the company's cash obligation back on the employees.

Shawn found out his portion of this "good news" meant he would *only* have to pay $900 additional a month.

"What the fuck!? What the fuck!?" were the first words out of Shawn's mouth when the employees met with Dick to discuss the plan. Shawn described the scene to me this way: "I then screamed at Dick and told him to quit hiding behind his desk like a fucking little coward and start acting like a leader." Shawn recounted that Dick tried to deflect the blame from himself by claiming he hadn't heard anything about the insurance change, that the decision was all Jim's. Shawn called him "a fucking little liar." Shawn said Dick sat silently while Dan and Miriam looked on.

Dick "looks like a wreck," said Shawn. "He's in so deep, he'll do anything to get out."

And Rich observed, "he's got to be pulling his fingernails out."

On April 28th, Miriam Dower resigned and demanded the money she was owed within 72 hours, as legally required. When she talked to me about Ardica, she cussed out Dick in ways that would make a sailor proud.

Two days later, on the final day of April, Eric Folsom resigned and demanded the money he was owed. Also within 72 hours, as required by law.

That same day, April 30th, Dick actually got enough money from one of the two prospective investors to pay the March 31st payroll. He was then only two payrolls behind.

ADRICA'S ASHES
May 2010

56

On the first six days of May, the Board of Directors of Ardica formally accepted the resignations of four of its five members, including everyone but Dick, while two more employees resigned and demanded back pay within 72 hours. I officially became a Board Observer.

Two new people joined the Board while the advisor, Jeff Scheinrock, worked in conjunction with James Palmer of Legend Merchant Bank to save Ardica, and save James's investment.

"There's not a hell of a lot going on," said Jim Retzlaff after the resignations. As CFO, he should know. He continued. "I can't do my job. There's no money. Everything's come to a standstill. I play defense. I don't know what I do. It's weird. Let me tell you that."

The latest employees to leave were Maynard Holliday and Rich Walwood. "Everybody on my team left me here to deal with the bullshit," said Rich on his last day. "I'm taking phone calls from hundreds of irate customers looking for their checks. There are dozens of irate retailers, lots of pissed off people and we're doing nothing." On his final day, Rich showed up to help with the transition and look for his final check. A check he didn't get.

When Miriam Dower left the previous week, Rich found he was dealing with the recall issues on his own and still not being paid. He was dealing with ever-increasing anger from customers and retailers. So Rich was also moving on, and hoping to force full payment of his past-due money, two paychecks plus a lot of unreimbursed expenses.

"Dick is here just pulling his hair out," said Rich. "He's probably trying to figure out how he's going to pay me today."

For a week now, it had been the running theme. Someone quit because they finally realized they couldn't live without a paycheck or no guarantee of when they would get a paycheck. Then Dick would scramble to find a way to pay that person everything owed before they filed a complaint with the State of California. Rinse and repeat. "The only way to get paid," said Shawn, "is to threaten to sue."

Within 30 days, Greg, Kyle, Miriam, Eric, Rich, and Maynard had resigned. Clearly, the lack of pay combined with pure frustration drove them to finally leave.

"When I left," said Miriam, "they hadn't paid anyone that had returned the product. It was heinous. That's obnoxious. It's just not a fun environment. You're not getting paid and you're telling people that their money will come soon when you know there is no money." Finally, she had enough and had to leave, demanding her money. She didn't want to leave. No one who left wanted to leave. No one.

"I didn't really want to leave the company," said Eric Folsom. Though he was barred by Dick from being interviewed for this book for the last few months he was at Ardica, as an ex-employee he felt free to talk. "I actually enjoyed working there, even with all the stress," he said. "But in order to take care of myself, I had to leave."

Like Miriam and everyone else, Eric found the money issues had worn him out. The personal money woes of no paycheck and uncertainty around health insurance were obvious. There were also professional money issues that affected his work. "I was lied to all the time," he said. "Money was coming in at certain times, and then I'd tell the vendors it was coming in." But the money didn't come in.

It was tiring covering for the company, and it was becoming clear that the only way to force a paycheck was to quit. I had explained to the Board that this could happen, and when Dick saw it start to happen, he moved quickly with an alternate plan to furlough employees. He had managed to get money for Eric and Miriam, but he was struggling to find enough to pay Rich and Maynard and he knew the floodgates of other employees quitting could open soon. I told him so. Jeff Scheinrock told him so. James Palmer told him as well.

While I had seen Dick trying to spin the resignations in a positive light, Jeff was now around to see through the haze and come to his own conclusions. In fact, Jeff tried his best to get Rich to stay at Ardica even while agreeing that a furlough for others was the best option.

"It's pretty apparent that Scheinrock is now the guy calling the shots," said Rich. "He seems like a real shrewd guy, an easygoing kind of guy... He said all the employees will get paid but he can't say when. It could be six to eight weeks. I can't last that long. Plus the fact that I'm stuck doing the shit that I don't want to do, the shit that makes my life miserable. I told him the issues run too far and deep here. The lack of management. The confusion. The fact that we're in the position we're in."

"I definitely feel like I took a leap of faith," Rich said of his time at Ardica. "It was a positive experience working with Hap and Shawn and Greg. We made some good things happen and we developed some solid relationships. It's a bummer we left some of those relationships hanging."

Rich said he told Jeff that if the company ever turned around, he would be happy to come back. "It's not in my nature to quit and walk away from something I've invested this much time in," said Rich. "But I need the money. My mom's sick with cancer. Fuck it, I'm going to spend some time to go see my mom."

57

"**D**ICK, YOU ARE A LIAR!"

On May 5th, Jeff Scheinrock held a meeting with Dick, James Palmer, Dan Braithwaite, and Tibor Fabian, and said in the meeting at least twice, "Dick, you are a liar." Jeff filled me in on details the next day. Dick had apparently told Jeff that one of his sure investors was immediately going to invest $100,000 when the four of us stepped off the Board and when the prospective investor was put on the Board. Well, four of us—Fritz, Tom, Tobin, and myself—stepped off the Board and he was put on the Board, but he did not invest the $100,000.

I talked to Jeff at 7 am on May 6th, and he said he thought Dick seemed frazzled. He challenged Dick on his logic of offering a 15% bonus. He said that Dick had no answer for why he offered a bonus when the company had no money and, in fact, was unable to pay even base salaries.

The bottom line from Jeff was that he was recommending the company cut off every unnecessary expense. He agreed with the recommendation of furloughing several employees. By furloughing, the hope was to avoid having to pay accrued pay, including vacation pay, that would have to be paid immediately if employees quit, were fired, or were laid off. The company acted fast.

"They furloughed everyone working on the Moshi side," said Miriam a few days after she left Ardica.

"The best way to say it is the Moshi has been furloughed," said Jim. "It's not exactly dead but it's not exactly being worked on. But there is a real possibility it will live on."

Rich disagreed. "The Moshi is going to die. All the apples are in the fuel cell basket," he said.

But James Palmer of Legend firmly believed in the Moshi and didn't want it to die. So he was encouraging Shawn and me to make a bid to buy the Moshi side of the business and develop it separately, while he looked for investors interested in the fuel cell side.

James, a bit agitated, told me he felt like we all walked away from him and left him holding the bag. I explained I was being marginalized, my reputation was being blemished, and I had better things to do with my life. There were companies that actually wanted my contribution.

James was a good guy and we got along well, but it was clear from his statements that we had wildly different ideas on what the Moshi side of the business was worth. James didn't own the business, but since, as part of the bridge loan, he had the rights to all assets, any deal Ardica decided it wanted required his final approval. So his idea of the value was crucial to any deal actually getting done. Despite all the problems, I remained very interested in the Moshi business. Shawn and I had discussed exactly this: the two of us getting away from Dick, acquiring the Moshi, and taking advantage of all the groundwork we had already done.

I would be an investor and Board member, and Shawn would run the company. We reiterated the form of an offer that would be mostly composed of the debt already owed to us. I was not sure if James would accept it, but it was what we thought was a fair offer. Shawn and I had agreed that a new company could not afford any uncapped recall exposure. This was a big expense that could continue to grow. It could make more work than a new company could handle and more risk than a new company would want to take on. James and Jeff were adamant that the new buyer would have to accept that responsibility. So, the recall exposure became a point of contention.

Lots of gears were moving at once. On May 10th, an Ardica draft investor letter and convertible loan term sheet was put together to eventually go to existing investors asking for more money to help the company survive. Of course, it wasn't put in exactly those words. The letter began, "We have had a truly amazing 18 months." But it went on to state, "As is the case with any young high tech company, we have had to operate continually in a cash-strapped state." It stated the shareholder rights offering, in which the company expected to raise $3 million to $4 million, would be completed in 30 to 45 days. Although the draft letter was written by Dick as CEO, the impetus and concept of the rights offering seemed to be coming from Legend working in concert with Jeff Scheinrock. They seemed to be forcing a put-up-or-go-away moment for existing shareholders, something they were calling "pay to play." Fortunately, later in June when the actual letter was sent, some of the hyperbole was left out.

On May 11th, I received a letter from Dick informing me that I had been put on furlough. The letter was dated May 6th. I was glad to get it, but given the fact that I had already left the company, it seemed the furlough was unnecessary. But maybe he thought this was a clever way of avoiding an acknowledgment of the money I was owed and the confirmation of my appointment to the Advisory Board to ensure my stock options were still valid. Although this exchange between me and Dick was typically convoluted and complicated, it was easier than most anything else we had done in the last six months. By the time of this letter, much had already played out and half the company had either quit or also been furloughed. Those furloughed were Shawn, Martin Corpos, Sergio Galvan, and Kei Yamamoto, essentially everyone working on the Moshi system. Everyone except Adam Rodriguez.

"I knew that half of the company was going to be gone regardless," said Miriam. The purging had to happen: it was obvious to Jeff Scheinrock as well as to the employees. Those who quit got out with cash in hand, while those put on furlough were promised they'd be paid sometime, and maybe rehired sometime. The purging couldn't have been unexpected, but not everyone put on furlough expected it to happen to them.

On May 12th, Jeff Scheinrock held a phone Board meeting in order to update the new Board members on the situation. Dick Martin and the two new Board members were on the line. Since they were all the members of the Board, they constituted a quorum and we could consider that an official Ardica Board meeting. Tom Covington, Tobin Fisher, James Palmer, and I were on the call as observers. Fritz couldn't make it because of a conflict in his schedule.

Jeff explained that Ardica did not have enough money to run the two businesses, the Moshi and the fuel cell. If money came in from the battery company and/or the government for more army work, Jeff said the company should focus on fuel cells and sell off the Moshi or just shelve it. But, he said, if the battery company and the government didn't come through, Ardica should focus on the Moshi and shelve the fuel cell.

He then explained that the company was in dire straits. Employees were owed $290,000. Rent had not been paid and the company had been given another three-day eviction notice from the landlord. James then said he would go to the landlord personally to ask the landlord to give Ardica more time.

When Jeff outlined the true financial situation of the company, it seemed as if one of his key objectives was to try to get the two new Board members to put money into Legend's bridge round. One pointed out that he had already put in some money. His money, in fact, had paid one payroll. The other expressed surprise at the situation. He indicated that he was hearing about those problems for the first time. Prior to this Board meeting, his information on Ardica had seemingly all come from Dick.

58

"LACK OF MONEY STARTS to bring out the true sides of how people feel," said Eric Folsom. Of course, it's one thing if the company has no money to pay vendors. When the company can't afford to pay anyone, that takes it to another level.

"Everybody in the company is sitting around looking for jobs," said Shawn. "There's nothing to do. There's no money."

Rich noted, "People come and go as they please. I don't know what the hell anybody does at their desk. There's never a day when everyone's here. Yesterday, there was like four people here."

The joy of early Ardica had faded into the act of treading water and listening to angry customers who were looking for recall checks. With Rich, Miriam, and Eric out the door, the administrative duties formerly covered by those three left a gaping hole that had to be covered by the engineers. "Shawn has already punched out," said Rich on his last day. "He has no specific tasks."

"In a way, I'm envious of Rich," said Jim. "He said 'Screw it, I'm done. I'm out of here. I don't want to deal with this shit.'"

And Rich expressed sympathy for Jim. "Jim's about to jump out the window. He's a guy that's been suckered by Dick into investing a bunch of personal money."

There was no specific work left, it seemed, except to deal with the angry customers looking for their recall checks. Rich said, "I sat Dan down and said, 'Next week, I'm out of here. Get your team ready to tackle some tasks they never expected to do.'"

Miriam also went to Dan and passed on her duties.

"Dan's going down with the ship," said Rich. "This is Dan's baby." And the employees knew it.

Eric observed, "There's more rallying to Dan than Dick. That's where the loyalty is."

Jim said, "Dan is really the emotional leader of the company. He's definitely a company leader. He's gotten involved in the recall…To me, he feels like a business owner. He owns the business. He's willing and able to take on any of the problems that come up. I have a sense that he's not an employee, but an owner. He's willing to do anything like an owner. As an owner, you'd clean the toilets if you had to. His is not just participation in the recall. It's full ownership of it and ensuring that it gets done."

On the other hand, Jim pointed out that Dan was "just so Pollyanna. I don't know if he grasps how serious our situation is. The landlord could lock us out."

While it seemed to me that Dan was incredibly inexperienced in business and his blind, unflagging support for Dick was the reason the Board didn't remove Dick in a timely fashion, he was one of the most admirable people I had ever met. I wish I could have reached him, gotten him to understand business. My inability to reach Dan was perhaps my biggest personal Ardica failure. Dan really was the soul of the company, and was full of passion but somehow he had blinders on and I couldn't get him to look at the big picture. I tried, but I admittedly failed.

Dan is one of the smarter people I know, a brilliant technologist who always seemed on the verge of a major fuel cell breakthrough. Perhaps he'd already made a big breakthrough because he remained remarkably confident, even at that late date, that Big Silicon and/or the battery company would soon turn on a hose of money to douse Ardica's flameout before it consumed everything.

"Dan truly believes in the technology," said Jim. "I've heard him talk about it. He knows it's good."

And Dan continued to tell people in the company that a potential deal with the battery company (previously it had been Big Silicon, just like with Dick) was imminent. And Shawn noted, "Dan controls the whole company."

And while the remaining employees, the engineers, rallied to Dan, Dan stuck by Dick. "He has a less rosy view of Dick," said Miriam, "but he still understands…Dick has been managing the whole relationship with (Big Silicon) and [the battery company]."

"It's the same shit I've been hearing forever," said Miriam. "If we're such an awesome company, why didn't they just buy us on the spot?"

Like all of us, Miriam veered between that cynical attitude and the dreamy *they act interested* fog about Big Silicon and the battery company that still permeated parts of Ardica. "It's impossible to know to what degree it's real," she noted.

In a moment of frustration, Shawn called Ardica's belief in the viability of Big Silicon and the battery company "a big Ponzi scheme." As good money chased bad with the promise of a huge payoff, the analogy was, at the very least, interesting.

But with Jeff Scheinrock and James Palmer of Legend working hard to cut costs and raise money, the fuel cell development and partnering in a submissive role to a bigger company and name was apparently the all-in strategy. If they could get the big name to go all in, Jeff and James might be able to pull it off. Dick tried and tried, resulting in a resounding thud and in many employees questioning his logic of sequentially pursuing one company at a time without creating any competitive tension.

Yet through it all, those two huge companies continued to talk with us. It was the oddest part of the Ardica death spiral. Originally, the product was going to launch in 2010. Then, the goal got moved to 2011. "There is a lot of potential," said Miriam. "But I think the end of 2011 is a dream date for a product launch."

However the intellectual property, developed mostly by Dan and Tibor, clearly interested Big Silicon and the battery company. The IP was controlled by Legend through their UCC-1 filing. Clearly, Legend understood business and through their lobbying had finally gotten someone installed to guide the company in a professional way. That was Jeff Scheinrock. Maybe the company could be saved.

"I don't think Palmer and Scheinrock want to see this company go belly up," said Rich. After the void of Dick and the absence of our last consultant, Dave Epstein, Jeff is "a guy I have faith in," said Rich. "He's a CFO/CEO type."

Jeff Scheinrock was a tall, fit guy with an almost shaved-bald head and a white beard. "When he first walked in the door...he had the most calming demeanor," said Jim. "He talks very controlled. He commands a room when he walks in. He knows the right thing to say. He puts everybody at ease."

Finally, there was someone running Ardica in a systematic and logical way. Jeff was the operational guru Ardica had needed all along. He was a true CFO and a skilled COO. He understood finance, cash flow, corporate governance, and how to deal with irate creditors. He was decisive and practical, not a dreamer or a schemer or an ostrich who stuck his head in the financial sand. He even spouted the obvious, like, "you can't spend money you don't have." Unlike with Dick, Jeff believed in instituting constraints on the existing situation rather than relying on dreams of the pot of gold at the end of the rainbow.

"He's very straightforward," said Jim. "There's no bullshit. No nonsense. He knows it's a fucked up situation but it's kind of his business. He's a turnaround guy. He's used to it. He's not emotionally involved...He's taking control. He's involved himself talking to [the battery company], and talking to the landlord."

Dick, meanwhile, continued with the title of CEO. It was more than a ceremonial role, but less than he was doing before. He continued to try to spin things as better than they were while working within the confines, almost always, of one-on-one conversations.

"If I were Dick," said Jim, "I'd want to go fall on a sword and be done with it. He looks harried—sallow face, sunken eyes. People are fed up. I'm a good employee and I respect my boss and all that but I'm done with it. I'm just so fed up there."

Dick had heard Jim's venom. "My attitude has changed," said Jim. "I've basically become hostile towards Dick. I can't sleep. I told Dick that I need my money back. My attitude is not going to change until you repay me. Dick's response was typical Dick…'I'll repay you. I won't let bad things happen.'"

The last conversation Miriam had with Dick was by telephone and it was "the most awkward conversation I've ever had with him," she said. "He was just really weird. The things he said, I thought this is really uncomfortable and weird. I can't even make sense of it. He started by thanking me for everything I've done and then it deteriorated." Miriam declined to elaborate.

59

THE ENTREPRENEURIAL LESSON of the story of Ardica, according to Shawn, is "don't trust an engineer."

Miriam simplified the story further to: "How not to be a leader."

Rich called the lesson, "The story of mismanagement and egos gone awry. It's Dick's ego and the arrogance of all these engineers. None of these kids have any experience delivering anything."

Jim recalled a recent phone meeting with the owner of one of the companies we owe money. "The owner of that company is so pissed off at us," said Jim. "At one point, he said, 'you have the worst case of Stanforditis I've ever seen in my life.'" On the call were Jim, Jeff Scheinrock, Dan Braithwaite, and Tibor Fabian. "I'm thinking, that's true," said Jim. "Tibor thought it was kind of funny. Scheinrock chuckled. Dan wasn't quite sure how to take it. We only owe the guy $27,000."

Stanforditis. Now that's hilarious. As a Stanford graduate who had just spent a couple of years working with a bunch of engineers I once called Stanford geniuses, I had to applaud the succinct description of our disease. We really did think that we knew more than we actually knew.

Trying to make sense of it, I spoke to someone who I had met during my travels, Bill Aulet, managing director of the MIT Entrepreneurship Center at the Sloan School of Management at the Massachusetts Institute of Technology. Bill and I were both featured speakers at a business conference at Mississippi State University in October 2009, and we hit it off immediately. He was bright, easy to talk to, a huge sports fan, and ingrained with a great deal of common sense.

Bill had an "equation" he used in his speech that struck me for its clarity:

Innovation = Invention + Commercialization

This simple equation crystallized my thinking about the central business problems at Ardica, the focus solely on invention. The engineers had contempt for anything beyond making a better product. But I thought, after meeting Bill, that he would be a great resource who might offer guidance. He had built and sold three highly successful businesses. He was a lecturer at a top-flight school, MIT, so the engineers would respect him. Bill Aulet, I suggested, could come out and visit Ardica and educate the engineers on entrepreneurism and maybe give more credibility to the case I had been making. But Dick rejected that idea. The engineers were "too busy," said Dick.

What a shame, and what an opportunity missed. Aulet offered some fascinating insights that I believe, if taken to heart by the right people at Ardica, could have changed the fate of the company. Aulet had an erasable white board on his office wall at MIT that he often used to illustrate his thoughts. But he had one permanent sign in his office:

Keep The Main Thing The Main Thing Words to live by.

"Almost all startups have more than one path to success," said Aulet. "The surest path to failure is to try to pursue too many. You have to pick what to pursue and you have to de-select the other ones. You have to figure out the one thing you do well and do that better than anybody else in the world. Then you get to succeed, and you get to move on to the next thing."

"When you start out with a company in the early stage...the founders, whether they know it or not, have DNA. That DNA becomes the culture of the company. But then they pass on the DNA to the next person, you have a situation that is problematic. Where is the beating heart of this company?"

And if the switch happens before there are even products for sale, as Aulet said, "the baby can't even walk yet."

The most important thing in a new technology company, said Aulet, is not technology. "The technology is easy. The marketing is harder," he said. But he added, "It all comes down to the people. It's about getting people aligned on the same page." So when the original culture is taken over by new management, as was the case with Ardica, getting everyone working passionately towards a common goal is even more crucial.

"A startup, especially a Silicon Valley startup, has a life cycle," said Aulet. "But when it drags on and on, you lose your momentum. You get company fatigue. The original employees can't keep sprinting...Until you actually sell something, you still have technology risk, market risk and execution risk; risk to the third power."

A startup in its sixth year, as was Ardica, "is definitely into the fatigue," he suggested.

Hearing of the split between Dick and myself and between the engineering department and sales and marketing, Aulet pointed out that getting the alignment of all of the people towards a common goal was the crucial element in an entrepreneurial venture. Writing on his board, Aulet said that the three most important elements of a high tech company's success were:

1. An aligned great team
2. A great market
3. Focus

"What's not there," he pointed out, "is technology."

If everyone in the company is thinking, "If I do one thing 100%. If I wake up in the morning thinking about it and go to bed thinking about it, it's a recipe for success," said Aulet.

A recipe for disaster, said Aulet, was the structure of Ardica, specifically my role as an employee of the company as well as a member of the Board of Directors, theoretically overseeing Dick as CEO. "That's like I'm going to grade my boss's homework," pointed out Aulet. "Overseeing the person who's technically your boss. Structurally, that's likely to fail."

"A Board of Directors has three possibilities," said Aulet. "It can be a negative force of confusion and trouble. It can be a neutral Board, giving no value. Or it can be a positive Board. But Boards should not be operational. A Board has an oversight role—nose in, hands out."

Aulet, who has built high-tech companies and sold them, said he was not a big believer in fuel cells. He called them "the energy equivalent of the Segway." The Segway, introduced in 2001 as a hyped new wave in personal transportation, had evolved into a niche product for quirky urban dwellers. "Fuel cells are not a hot investment area," said Aulet. Perhaps that had been proven true by the lack of buyers for Ardica.

As for relying on government funding, Aulet pointed out that, "Government-funded companies rarely achieve exponential growth."

Months earlier, the question was posed to those in the company: "Do you build what you can sell, or do you sell what you can build?"

Aulet said, "The answer very clearly is you build what the customer wants."

60

"IT COMES DOWN TO ONE PERSON AND HIS STYLE," said Miriam, talking about Dick. "Two years ago, I remember thinking, we've got to do something about this guy. He doesn't seem to have what it takes to get us to where we want to go. To have some jackass run everyone into the dirt. So many things at so many points could have been different."

"The strategy meeting could have been the point," said Shawn. "We had the world in our hands. But different synergies came into it...We were trying to become one voice. *This is our plan.*"

"The engineers felt disconnected from us," said Miriam. "It felt like two sides fighting for what they wanted versus working towards a common goal."

Eric Folsom, unlike most people in the company, said, "I bear some responsibility for some of the things that happened."

Eric's responsibility, it seemed to me, was that he tried to do too much— outsourcing, supply chain management, some quality control, purchasing, getting regulatory certification, and on and on. He tried to "do it all" while saving money. In one case there was a piece of critical information he passed on to another employee and then didn't follow up on it. He didn't have time. Somewhere in the midst of too few people with too much to do, steps were missed. Still, the biggest problem was our structure and our priorities. As Eric told me, "In the summer of 2009,

I saw the potential for quality problems coming and I told Dick that someone needed to be hands-on in the factory to ensure quality. I was glad to do it. But Dick turned me down, saying we didn't have the money."

"For quite some time, we had an engineering mindset," said Eric. "An engineering mindset is, item number one, they never finish the process. And item number two is they don't regularly realize they don't finish the process…Dan was busy on the F-43 project. The Moshi project disappeared from his mind."

It wasn't until after the safety issues surfaced, said Eric, that Dan became involved again with the Moshi. Most of the issues, said Eric, came down to leadership. "They definitely need to get Dick out of the role of CEO," he said.

The money issues affected every day at work, said Eric. "Dick decided he wanted to take on all the fundraising, and that's exactly why the company is in the shape it's in."

But I always reminded myself, Ardica was not just a company. The company, as all companies—and as this book illustrates—was full of real people with real stories. Many lessons had been learned through this. Some, I tried to teach to those in the company. Others, we all learned by hard experience.

By the end of May, Jim had still not been paid back the $30,000 he had loaned the company. "I'm a little bit fatalistic," he lamented. "I've accepted that there's a good chance I'm not going to get the money back."

On the bright side, he said, "The doors are still open and the lights are still on." Legend had loaned the company some more money. According to Jim, "It's easier to work through these problems rather than foreclose." Still, the company remained two paydays behind.

But the always lurking optimism of a deal with a big Silicon Valley company had emerged again, this time with the battery company, while Big Silicon, according to Dick, kept a close eye on it. "We've signed a contract for two months for show and tell. We'll show them our secret sauce and they'll think about it in terms of how to commercialize it," said Jim.

There's that word. Commercialize it. Fascinating.

"The idea now would be to introduce it at the Consumer Electronics Show that happens in February 2011, " says Jim. "We don't have signed contracts for big money," he added.

Meanwhile, it appeared the Moshi business was up for sale. Jim said Shawn and I had expressed the most interest. I wondered if we were also the only ones who understood the opportunity. We continued to talk.

And Jim said he had a meeting scheduled to sit down with Rich and Maynard and the State of California to iron out the legal issues with them. Both had been paid, according to Jim. If so, I wondered why the state was pursuing it. It was another Ardica conundrum.

The rights offering was finally going out to existing investors, but very late. The sluggishly developed document, originally targeted for the first week of May, was looking as if it wouldn't go out until the middle of June. Prepared by the company—I suspected by James Palmer of Legend and Jeff Scheinrock, and probably delayed because of their heavy reliance on Dick—the offering would determine the fate of the company, said Jim. "They're going to go to current investors and say if you don't put more cash in the company, it's going to go bankrupt. However, if you invest, we have a plan…It's a cliffhanger. The final chapter isn't written."

There were two open seats on the Board of Directors, available to any large investor who wanted to sit on the Board, said Jim.

The recall refunds had still not been paid. Many people who were owed money were still calling, very angry, and threatening action.

Jim said he learned never to loan a company money and never get friends and family to invest in a company he worked for. "I'm going to feel shitty about that."

According to Eric Folsom, he learned that "Every time I go in looking for a job from now on, I'm always going to ask for the financial records of the company." He said he will never again go into an interview with a company with "the assumption they know what they're doing."

61

T HE STORY OF ARDICA is a story of what could have been.

"It was amazing," said Shawn. "I was having the time of my life. We were ready to take on the world and be the best and greatest company."

But in one year, hockey-stick growth potential that everyone talked about 12 months earlier became, as Shawn described his final day at Ardica before he was furloughed, "like a military war zone. It's obliterated. There's nobody there."

It was vexing and sad. An obliterated dream, with real lives suffering as a result. A company is not just a bunch of shares of stock and the executives who make decisions. It's also the employees and the customers and the suppliers and yes, the stockholders, who after all, are real people who stood to really lose.

I thought back to the last year and as I reflected on everything, I thought of Dick proclaiming, "I allow people to fail. If there's an environment of, 'Oh my God, something went wrong now I'm in trouble,' that's not good. I like to move into problem solving. You're not in trouble for screwing up. You're only in trouble if you don't tell me about it."

In other words, if you screw up, don't keep it a secret. You can fail, but fail forward.

When I initially heard the words from Dick, I loved the philosophy.

And I agreed with it. But I didn't realize that those were words that only applied to others and that what Dick really most cared about was, in fact, keeping secrets.

And that was on me. I liked to pride myself in recognizing motivated people, but in the case of Dick and the key managers of Ardica, I didn't realize that the real motivator wasn't to build a business. The key motivators were all personal.

Without a strategy and alignment, it eventually backfired. Power and personal gain were motivators rather than alignment. Cliques formed. Sides were taken. I played a part. I know that it was my insistence on sticking to the rules of corporate governance that rubbed Dick wrong, but I also know that I was undermined by too many secretive conversations that led to distrust.

So what about me? What could *I* have done differently?

Maybe I should have left when the strategy meeting didn't materialize as I had hoped. That clearly was a sign that open and inclusive wasn't going to be Dick Martin's style. And I know that failing to plan is planning to fail. I have always believed that planning is cornerstone of any business. So why didn't I just walk out the door right then? Well, I wanted to make the situation right. I believed I could make things right and fix the culture.

It's simplistic of me to just blame Dick. It's maybe even a little disingenuous. If creating a plan and fixing the culture was important, I should have done more. Maybe it was my hubris. Maybe I shouldn't have believed so much in my own ability to convince those involved that we really did need a plan. I thought I was getting somewhere. But it was now clear that it was a stillborn idea.

As I look back, the question that crops up again and again is should we have even attempted the product and brand launch with no certainty of money coming in? Part of me says I knew that without such a launch with retailers the brand and Moshi product would never materialize. But since Dick was adamant that he had millions of dollars of investment lined up, the remarkably low investment we were making to launch could be easily absorbed. Moreover, in my heart of hearts I was certain that having a commercial product in the market was a key to actually concluding a successful fundraising.

However, the more prudent part of me says, no matter how important the goals, we should just never have spent money until it was in our hands—not Dick, not the engineers, and not me. And, rather than just bull-headedly going forward with my plan to build a branded commercial division, one that actually sold products, that launch point was the time to have a "come to Jesus" meeting with Dick regarding the status of his original commitment to selling products and building a brand. Demanding to receive concrete evidence of the promised equity financing.

In retrospect, if the answer was negative to either question, I should have immediately stopped what I was doing and just walked out of the company. Because, for good or ill, it was Dick's company to run. But, for myriad reasons I didn't force that meeting.

Brilliant individuals working towards a common long-term goal can easily be derailed, especially in Silicon Valley where quick wealth is god. I learned that concepts like brand building and strategy are sometimes too abstract. I also learned that after 30 years in business, there is lot more to learn.

62

ONTHS EARLIER, on the morning of Dan's birthday, the product design engineer from Big Silicon with whom we'd been working called Ardica to inform us that THE top management of Big Silicon would be visiting Ardica to see a live demonstration of our fuel cell. He never used names, because that is the company's secretive way. But Dan thought he knew who was coming.

This was it! The world renowned CEO of Big Silicon was visiting Ardica.

When Dan went to our demonstration prototype fuel cell, which had been functioning perfectly, he found it did not work properly. Dan couldn't believe it. He was frantic. He ran around yelling at everyone, "This is the biggest day in our history!" He demanded help. He also demanded to be left alone to fix the unknown problem.

When the time of the "appointment" arrived, the famous CEO did not appear. Instead, the Ardica employees brought in a birthday cake for Dan. In fact, Tibor and the other engineers had purposely sabotaged the fuel cell to pull a prank on Dan. They even recruited the Big Silicon's design engineer, who was in on the joke. But no one from Big Silicon was at the party.

EPILOGUE

So what happened?

Well, years later Ardica is still almost there, only in a different format. And "there," to the company, now means something completely different. They have forsaken the idea of being an overnight success, and settled in for the long haul.

Ardica is now smarter, wiser, smaller, and more experienced. The company has eliminated the problems that plagued it during the year of this book. For one, they eliminated me. And that's probably a good thing.

They have decided on and embraced one culture rather than two—a culture around R&D and engineering.

They have refocused the individuals on what they do best and they have slimmed down the team considerably to a like-minded group of inventors and engineers. Although the joint venture work they were doing with a battery manufacturer has ended, the quest to develop a miniaturized fuel cell continues.

The core team at Ardica remains incredibly resilient.

The arc of Ardica, the company and its team, seems to be following the rocky but rebounding path so familiar to Silicon Valley startups. In Silicon Valley it's not how many times you are knocked down, but rather how many times you get back up. And, it is a place of eternal optimism where the culture is one that actually embraces and values failure.

Ardica has survived by consolidation and by re-inventing itself— focusing on one product, the fuel cell, and focusing solely on R&D. This R&D effort has been supported by short-term commercial partnerships, a few more government grants, and a few more rounds of financing. Like many R&D firms in Silicon Valley, they cobbled it together.

The new financing rounds have predictably not been cheap. Rather they have been ones described as "pay to play" in which you have to invest to cover your prior investment or face being heavily diluted.

The great news is that the great patentable Ardica ideas are still alive, and there continues to be government and commercial interest. Some old investors, and some new investors, are optimistic that commercial success is just around the corner. Being almost there remains as alluring as ever.

Some of the same team has stayed on board at Ardica and gelled in the new, streamlined environment—people like Tibor Fabian, Dan Braithwaite, and Jim Retzlaff. Dick Martin is back in an environment that fits him, securing government contracts. Jeff Scheinrock continues to offer his experienced leadership.

How far will they go and how much of a business success will there be? And who will make a profit from the company? That is still a question. It is the standard question with all restarts in Silicon Valley.

In the eyes of the culture of Silicon Valley, this is just Ardica 2.0 and the sky is the limit.

Like many other Silicon Valley companies that go through the turmoil and near shuttering of the company, many key people have moved on, taking the knowledge they gained at Ardica with them and adding it to their resume that shows they had real life experience in the fast-growing and constantly changing Silicon Valley environment. And, as is often the case, they are highly valuable.

Martin Corpos joined Apple and is thriving as a new Product Development Manager, and Adam Rodgriguez is now a key player in Product Development at Google.

Maynard Halliday has taken the prestigious job as Special Assistant to the Under Secretary of Defense.

Eric Folsom set up his own engineering, compliance, and quality control company called YourSource, helping U.S. companies manufacturing in China.

Greg Nevolo, Rich Walwood, Kyle Hagin, and Shawn Biega continued to be bitten by the entrepreneurial bug and have started their own companies in the sports product world. Greg's company, PWRD does marketing and advertising for fast growing sports brands. Rich owns his own San Diego surf shop called Mission. Shawn has his own sports consulting company helping brands launch globally, while on the side developing products and plans for his own health and wellness company. Kyle is designing, building, and starting to market his unique 22nd- century bicycles.

I've lost touch with some of the others but presume they are flourishing, after all it is Silicon Valley and through the arduous year at Ardica they have learned a lot and made themselves a lot more valuable.

I've moved on too. I'm advising a number of new companies with disruptive technologies that are facing the dilemma of deciding "do you make what you sell or sell what you make?" And ones that are trying to reconcile the age-old engineer–sales conflict into rapidly growing, highly successful companies.

In other words, I'm doing it all over again. I've almost got it figured out.

ACKNOWLEDGMENTS

FROM HAP & BRIAN

Thank you to all who cooperated with this book, even if only for a little while. Thanks also to those energizing people in Silicon Valley who keep bouncing back and creating newer and better ideas and then products—the stuff from which the American dream is built and rebuilt. Thanks especially to Bill Aulet for your insight.

FROM HAP

To all the Klopps and Richmonds who never fail in their support for whatever I do and for my intrepid band of vocal supporters in this endeavor, led by Shawn Biega. Thanks especially to James Palmer and Hector Chao for your unflagging support.

FROM BRIAN

Thanks to Hap, the most inspirational person I've ever known. Thanks to my brothers, Gary & Dave—you are my heroes. To Denim, Derek, Kayli and Marissa, thank you always. Thanks most of all to Laura for believing in me.

ABOUT THE AUTHORS

HAP KLOPP is the founder of the iconic brand, The North Face, a Stanford graduate, and a serial entrepreneur.

Hap consults around the globe, and lectures on the topic of entrepreneurship—particularly entrepreneurship as it is found in Silicon Valley. He is the author of two previous books on business, including the acclaimed leadership book, Conquering The North Face: An Adventure in Leadership.

Hap, who holds an AB and MBA from Stanford University, founded The North Face where he served as its President and CEO for 20 years. He runs an international consulting firm, HK Consulting, with offices in the U.S. and Japan.

He has lectured at the business schools of Stanford, University of California, MIT, Carnegie Mellon, University of San Francisco, and a number of international universities. He has been profiled on national television and in such publications as *BusinessWeek*, *Forbes*, *The Wall Street Journal*, and *Inc. Magazine*.

In addition to mentoring entrepreneurs, Hap is presently the Executive Chairman of Obscura Digital, a San Francisco based digital communication company, and serves on numerous Boards of Directors.

BRIAN TARCY is a journalist and the co-founder of CapeCodWave.com, an online magazine featuring long-form journalism. He started Cape Cod Wave in May 2013.

Brian is the author or co-author of more than a dozen books, including several he collaborated on with professional athletes such as Cam Neely, Joe Theismann, and Tom Glavine. In addition, he has written books with business leaders, CEOs, consultants, and medical professionals.

As a journalist, he has written for the *Boston Globe, Boston Magazine, Boston Business Magazine, The Cape Cod Times* and several others. He is especially fond of character-driven business journalism.

Brian has a degree in Radio/TV news from Ohio University.

Made in the USA
San Bernardino, CA
16 August 2018